D1506301

The Book of SEX LISTS

compiled by
ALBERT B. GERBER

LYLE STUART INC.   Secaucus, N.J.

Books by Albert B. Gerber

BASHFUL BILLIONAIRE
THE JOY OF DIETING
THE LAWYER (a novel)
THE LIFE OF ADOLF HITLER
SEX, PORNOGRAPHY AND JUSTICE

First edition

Queries regarding rights and permissions
should be addressed to: Lyle Stuart Inc.,
120 Enterprise Ave., Secaucus, N.J. 07094.

Published by Lyle Stuart Inc.
Published simultaneously in Canada by
Musson Book Company
A division of General Publishing Co. Limited
Don Mills, Ontario

Manufactured in the United States of America

Library of Congress Cataloging in Publication Data
Main entry under title:

The book of sex lists.

   1. Sex–Miscellanea. I. Gerber, Albert Benjamin,
1913-
HQ64.B57   306.7   81-16600
ISBN 0-8184-0320-9   AACR2

This book is dedicated to the many individuals and organizations that provided lists for this book.

Special mention must be made of the contribution of my wife, Rhona, who probably worked harder and gathered more lists than I did.

My thanks too to Frank Freudberg, our brilliant young research assistant. My daughter, Lynne Gerber Saionz, prepared all the legal lists. The staff of the Association for Research, Inc., did a tremendous amount of the carefully detailed checking.

And finally, to publisher Lyle Stuart, who gave me the assignment and who gathered as many lists as I did (but refused to be co-compiler), browbeat many of his friends into contributing lists, and gave up two cherished visits to his beloved Jamaican estate and to Las Vegas in order to complete the book on schedule.

ALBERT B. GERBER

Philadelphia
September, 1981

Contents

Lead to Sex Problems and Disturbances...4 Ways Women Respond to Male Sexual Failure...6 Ways People React When Presented With a Woman's Frigidity Problem...

12. Sex as Something to Sing About 97

2 Sexy Operas...3 Operas in Which the Music Alone Conveys Sexuality...12 Sexiest Metropolitan Opera Sopranos...Mitch Miller's 8 Popular Songs to Play While Enjoying Sex...A 6-Pack of Sex-Packed Songs...Nat Hentoff's 12 Albums to Make Love By...Wolfman Jack's 12 Famous Songs With Dirty Lyrics...Wolfman Jack's 12 Sexiest Popular Songs...12 Suggestive Double-Entendre Songs...3 Obscene Song Lyrics...4 Famous Homosexual Songwriters...

13. Literary Light on the Subject 106

9 Great Writers of Sex Letters...7 Literary Works About Lesbians...20 Novels, Plays and Films in Which the Central Character Was a Prostitute...3 Respectable Movies That Broke Sex Taboos...The Real Names of the Authors of 2 Best Selling Sex Books...9 Popular Books with Double-Entendre Titles...10 Books Objected to by Censorship Groups...10 Best-Selling Sex Books...Greg Nash's 6 Sexiest Comic-Book Heroes...12 Famous People who Wrote Secret Pornography...The Best Parts of 9 Novels...Michael Perkins' 10 Favorite Erotic Novels...11 Classics of Hardcore Pornography...

14. Sex and the Courts 122

20 Landmark Obscenity Cases...25 States Where Any Sexual Act Between Consenting Adults Is Legal...States with Highest and Lowest Rape Rates...10 Cities Where You Have Your Best Chance to be Raped...12 Important Sexual-Freedom Decision Handed Down by the U.S. Supreme Court...The High Cost of Defence in 4 Pornography Trials...

15. Where to Find It 132

9 Swingers Clubs in New York City...4 Unusual Correspondence Clubs...7 Ways a Woman Can Meet a Man...10 College Campuses That Have Reputations for Wild Undergraduate Sex...25 Apartments in New York City Where Men Can Buy Sex With Women...10 Hot Gay Spots Throughout the World...4 Sexy Things to Do While in Las Vegas...10 Foreign Nude Recreation Opportunities...12 Places for S&M Sex...12 Girls Who Will Talk Sexy on the Telephone...37 Abbreviations Used in Sex Ads...2 Sensuous Islands...

Get An Obscene Phone Call...5 Reasons Given To Justify Massage Parlors...14 Rules for the Care of the Female Breast...6 Exercises for the Female Breast...18 Women Who Demonstrated That "Weaker Sex" is Nonsense...

Introduction

One morning several months ago, Lyle Stuart telephoned me, and his first terse and laconic words were, "Al, I want you to do a book for me." (Lyle has no patience for small talk.)

Involuntarily I replied, "I am doing a book for you. Remember? It's called *Gold* and it's all about that popular shiny stuff."

"Put that one aside," Lyle said. "It'll keep. This one won't keep. Its time is now."

"So what is 'this one'?"

"An anthology that we'll call *The Book of Sex Lists*. It should be informative, entertaining and fun."

Few people ever say "no" to Lyle Stuart. He has that perennial winner instinct.

I considered the idea. I pondered it. I circled around it. I examined it from every angle.

Certainly, I knew what a book was. I'd written many. I'd also read all or part of an estimated 100,000 volumes.

I also knew what sex was. I have three adult children and I taught them, each and every one, about sex. For the past decade I've been administrative director of a national association of lawyers (The First Amendment Lawyers' Association), whose members specialize in the legal defense of individuals and groups charged with selling or exhibiting explicit sex material.

Some years ago I even wrote a book titled *Sex, Pornography and Justice*.

The word "list" was interesting. What is a list?

I found it not that easy to define. Try it. You'll discover that, as with words like "time" and "space," it's a concept you know well but can't define.

11

I opened my old reliable *Noah Webster's New International Dictionary*, second edition unabridged, 1934. Fascinating. The meaning that my projected book involved was number seven in Webster's. Altogether there are thirteen different meanings for "list."

In the volume you hold in your hands we use the meaning "a roll or catalogue, as of names or items; a register, inventory, or classified record or memorandum, as a *list* of books, voters or real estate, a tax or price list...."

I used the free association ploy on friends: "When I say 'list' what word comes to mind?"

Response included:
shopping
laundry
active
retired
voting
enter
race
number
long
short

–and there you have your first list!

The wildest reply I received was "Friedrich." The reference was to Friedrich List (1789–1846).

By now I recognized that a book of sex lists could be flexible, lively, interesting and educational. And, it seems to me, it was going to be fun to compile and fun to read.

I also learned that a list could comprise one item or many. For example, "How many items are on the shopping list today?"

Answer: "Only one."

On the other hand, my Webster lists more than five hundred thousand words!

My next step was to plan procedures. There were two ways to go. Research and armchair cerebration. I decided to use both.

My associates and I went through every book catalogued under "sex" and allied subjects in the Library of Congress, the New York Public Library and the Libraries of the University of Pennsylvania. The number of books on the subject astonished me.

Of course, there's sex in almost every topic, from Anthropology to Zoology. And all the subjects in between—religion, history, biology, medicine, law, you name it. The fact is that there are few subjects that do not have a sexual aspect of some sort.

This means that there are drawers full of reference cards under the various headings relating to sex. Fortunately there's lots of duplication, but still we had to examine a vast number of books. We made one interesting discovery (not in any list): U.S. Congressmen are themselves very interested in sex. Scores of sex books are charged out each month to our legislators.

In addition to books, we went through a decade of popular and learned periodicals. A veritable treasure trove of list material developed.

Next came the volumes of doctoral dissertations at the universities in the United States and Europe. We did not neglect the Index to *The New York Times*.

Finally, I pressed into service friends and relatives, not only to make lists but to suggest other lists. Some are acknowledged; others requested anonymity.

I quickly discovered that lists have a life of their own. They grow by some form of mitosis. It works this way: You get a book on the strange sexual customs of the Ancient Jews and you make a list. This obviously suggests doing the same for the Muslims.

Fine, but the staff then says, "There are other major religions in the world with their own unique customs: Hindus, Buddhists, Christians, Confucians, Taoists, and many others."

It became a matter of picking and choosing. We set up tests. The list had to be either humorous, informative, helpful, some combination thereof, or just plain interesting. Dozens of completed lists were rejected under this standard. For example, the sex practices and customs of Christians are so well known that such a list does not meet any of the criteria.

In short, that was the way it was throughout the compiling. A list of synonyms for "penis" brings one to "vagina" to "breast" to ... but we had to have a cut-off point and we always went back to the criteria.

My most recent discovery was that it is apparently impossible to turn off the flow of lists. They keep coming in by mail, phone, and personal delivery.

Some of the lists are the result of days of work. For example, most people don't know that there are tests for sex in its varied aspects. Tests for sex personality. Tests to measure knowledge of sex. All kinds of tests to measure every aspect of sex that is measurable or examinable. It was our intention to include a list of sex tests. But some of the most important tests, ordered by mail months ago, are just arriving.

So now we're collecting more lists and filing them away. Obviously there must be a *Book of Sex Lists #2*. And if you'd like to contribute—if you have a good sex list or an idea for a sex list—please share it with us.

Write to:

The Al Gerber Book of Sex Lists
Lyle Stuart Inc.
120 Enterprise Avenue
Secaucus, N.J. 07094

Now read the cream of the crop already harvested. And have fun!

The Book of SEX LISTS

1

Starting with basics…

8 Reasons Why People Have Sex

You may wonder why people need reasons. However there was a survey made and these are the results.

1. They love each other.
2. They want to have children.
3. They feel randy at the time.
4. They want to find out more about each other.
5. They need reassurance about their own attractiveness.
6. They want to please the other person.
7. They enjoy each other's company.
8. They can't think of anything more interesting to do.

> —Part of the evidence submitted by the Sex Is Fun Society and reported in the *Report of the Committee on the Operation of the [British] Sexual Containment Act* (1978)

The 6 Human Outlets for Sex

The Institute for Sex Research, founded by Dr. Alfred Kinsey at Bloomington, Indiana, found that there are six basic sexual outlets for men and women. These are:

1. Dreams (both sleeping fantasies and those experienced while awake)
2. Masturbation (self-pleasuring)
3. Petting (includes all heterosexual acts, such as mouth to genitals, tongue to anus, etc.)
4. Coitus (penetration of the vagina by the penis)
5. Homosexual acts (all actions between members of the same sex)
6. Zoophilia (all acts with creatures not human)

13 Euphemisms and Circumlocutions Couples Employ to Ask About Sex

Despite all our modern sexual enlightenment, heterosexual couples still have problems communicating in matters of sex. Even the simplest of sex questions, "Would you like to have sexual intercourse tonight?" is, in an overwhelming number of couples, asked by using euphemisms.

Here is a list of the most frequently used expressions or circumlocutions to convey the thought.

1. "Are you in the mood?"
2. "Shall we do it tonight?"
3. "Want to make love?"
4. "Feel like making 'bang-bang'?"
5. "Is Oscar (Herman, George, Junior, Peter, Baby-Maker, Ding-A-Ling, Penie, Spritzer, Joy Stick, etc.) looking for action tonight?"
6. "Is Jennie (Vagie, the Love Box, the Love Nest, my Furburger, etc.) receiving tonight?"
7. "Are we going all the way tonight?"

8. "Can I get my ashes hauled?"
9. "Are we in business tonight?"
10. "How do you feel about some exercise (acrobatics, bed jogging, athletics, track and field, golf, horizontal work, etc.) this rainy Sunday afternoon?"
11. "Want to hide the salami?"
12. "How would you like to jelly-roll (jazz around, jing-jang, jive, knock off a piece, etc.)?"
13. "How about a little pom-pom (poontang, push-push, push-pull)?"

For an interesting discussion, see Sanders and Robinson, "Talking & Not Talking About Sex: Male and Female Vocabularies," No. 2, p. 22 (1970), *Journal of Communication*

The Best (and Worst) Sex News of All

"The test was positive. I'm pregnant!"

The Worst (and Best) Sex News of All

"The test was negative. I'm not pregnant!"

2 Circumstances Under Which A Man Won't Have Sex

1. He can't get it up.
2. He's dead.

13 Excuses Offered By Wives
to Avoid Action in Bed

1. I've got a headache.
2. I'm too tired.
3. I have to get up early in the morning.
4. It hurts right now.
5. I forgot to take the pill.
6. My temperature says it's not right for tonight.
7. We did it last night.
8. We just did it the night before last.
9. You haven't been very nice to me.
10. I'm about to fall off the roof (have my menstrual period).
11. I don't want to.
12. I'm not in the mood.
13. I can't be bothered (when really mad).

2

Let's talk about celebrities

23 Comments About Sex Made by Famous People

1. I was balling in cars up until the age of thirty before I knew what a bed was. It was wonderful. You never knew what was going to happen. It could be on a kitchen floor, whatever. It was this type of spontaneity you once could enjoy.

   —Telly Savalas

2. A girl who says, "Pass me the fuckin' salt," "pass me the fuckin' salad," "pass me the fuckin' wine," and then says, "Let's go fuck"—by that time, who wants to?

   —Burt Reynolds

3. Europeans used to say Americans were puritanical. Then they discovered that we were not puritanical. So now they say that we are obsessed with sex.

   —Mary McCarthy

4. I can't imagine anybody growing up who hasn't had the desire to see her own cunt.

   —Erica Jong

Burt Reynolds

5. It is very hard to photograph the penis without it looking kind of depressing in three dimensions.

—Gore Vidal

6. Clinical jargon and polite evasions aside, in proper language there is no word for the act of love. "He fornicated her" is ungrammatical, and so is "She wanted him to coit her" or "I'd like to copulate you," to say nothing of "Please sexual intercourse me, darling."

—Ray Russell

7. I understand that more people are living together before they get married and testing their marriage. I think this is an individual decision. I don't think it's a necessary part of getting married. I don't think you have to have this testing period. I think you can be sure.

—Julie Nixon Eisenhower

8. I think astrology is a parlor game. It's a way of passing some small talk before you fuck. You've got to say *something* before you fuck, and that's it—"What's *your* sign?"

—Lee Grant

9. "To take a lover"—isn't that as ridiculous a phrase as "the farmer takes a wife"?

—Cloris Leachman

10. Ain't nobody gonna believe a woman gonna go all her life and say, "I ain't never had a man," and is happy. And a priest saying he'd never touch a woman—that's against nature, too. What's he gonna do at night? Call upon the hand of the Lord?

—Muhammad Ali (on nuns and priests)

11. I believe that exhibitionists are repressing feelings of shame.

—Brigitte Bardot

12. People were always having love affairs with their poodles and putting tiny flowers in strange places.

—Alice Roosevelt Longworth (at age 90, reflecting on the sexual mores of her own day)

13. For brief affairs, Europeans are best: sexual, jealous, and extremely manly. But for protracted liaisons, an American has to be better: less overprotective and sexist and more giving and fun-loving.

—Glenda Jackson

14. Women, you know, are not just things that sit on stumps waiting for people to come along and fuck them. They're very active in that. They think about it a lot. They think about it because they are women.

—George Peppard

15. A whore practicing fellatio looks up and says, "Are you a Communist?"—that's what the modern world is all about, in a way.

—Norman Mailer

16. As far as I'm concerned, this type of sexual solo holds no appeal, as I am so wary of electricity I won't even sleep under an electric blanket and I'm apprehensive of being electrocuted every time I screw in a light bulb, so I'm certainly not going to

fool around trying to screw myself and maybe blow a fuse as well.

—Helen Lawrenson (on electric vibrators)

17. Most of my male friends are gay, and that seems perfectly natural to me. I mean, who wouldn't like cock?

—Valerie Perrine

18. My impression is that impotence is increasing these days despite (or is it because of?) the unrestrained freedom on all sides.

—Rollo May

19. We have such an appetite for sexuality as to be surprising. Not since the early Romans when, after they'd eaten, gorged, and debauched all the boys—the girls already having been debauched—and tickled the backs of their throats with a scarlet feather in order to start all over again, has one seen such carryings-on.

—Janet Flanner ("Genet")

20. It used to be that you had to go to a whorehouse and pay money to watch a lesbian performance. Nowadays, you just stay home and invite your friends over.

—Helen Lawrenson

21. My reaction to porn films is as follows: After the first ten minutes, I want to go home and screw. After the first twenty minutes, I never want to screw again as long as I live.

—Erica Jong

22. My neighbors don't pay any more attention to me than to any other 54-year-old lady wandering around the supermarket looking for a bargain.

—Christine Jorgensen (transsexual pioneer)

23. Sex is a form of temporary insanity.

—Martin Greif

—Compiled by Martin Greif especially for The Book of Sex Lists

Elizabeth Taylor's 7 Husbands

1. Nicky Hilton
2. Michael Wilding
3. Mike Todd
4. Eddie Fisher
5. Richard Burton
6. Richard Burton
7. John Warner

Richard Burton

Artie Shaw's 7 Wives

A man of many talents, Artie Shaw was #1 in the days of the big bands. Handsome and (surprisingly) shy, he attracted some of the most beautiful women of his time. His list of "other women loved" includes Judy Garland and Bette Grable among scores of other famous ladies, including Joan Crawford. (He married Lana Turner on their first date.)

A brilliant thinker and chock-full of candor, Shaw walked away from swing bands, pop entertainment and millions of dollars in order to write and to live as he pleased. These are the ladies he wed. For those who don't know, #3 is the daughter of famed composer Jerome Kern and #5 authored the best-selling novel *Forever Amber*.

Although they haven't had a face-to-face in several years, he remains married to Evelyn Keyes.

1. Margaret Allen
2. Lana Turner
3. Elizabeth Kern
4. Ava Gardner
5. Kathleen Winsor
6. Doris Dowling
7. Evelyn Keyes

Evelyn Keyes' List of 8
Sexy Men, Past and Present

Evelyn Keyes was a film star for Columbia Pictures. She acted in more than thirty films, including *Gone with the Wind* and *The Jolson Story.*

Her romantic life was more exciting than her movies. She was married several times, once to John Huston. She lived with Mike Todd. She is married to Artie Shaw.

She described the men in her life in her autobiography, *Scarlett O'Hara's Younger Sister,* which has become a model for kiss-and-tell tales of Hollywood, though none of the imitators has matched it in wit, perception, and fine writing.

1. Artie Shaw (if he would promise not to say anything)
2. Pablo Picasso (as is/was)
3. Isaac Asimov (if he would shave off those absurd sideburns)
4. Lyle Stuart (if he lost a couple of pounds)
5. Gore Vidal (if he were straight)
6. Benjamin Franklin (if we had met in France)
7. Isaac Stern (if we could work the violin in, too)
8. Gloria Steinem (if she were a man)

Warren Beatty's Wives

Artie Shaw (see previous list) once explained that he wed so often because in his time, "you married them." In the case of Ava Gardner, with whom he was living, MGM gave him the alternative of getting married or breaking up.

Today's mores are somewhat more relaxed. Film actor Warren Beatty is the Artie Shaw of his day in that he has been linked sexually with many of the beautiful women in Hollywood.

Here is a list of the women he has married.

0.

Evelyn Keyes

23 Famous People and Their Description of the First Time They Had Sex

1. *Maya Angelou*, writer and poet
   Raped by mother's live-in boyfriend at age 7.

2. *Art Buchwald*, humorist
   Seduced by chambermaid while working in resort hotel at age 15.

3. *Dyan Cannon*, actress
   On the afghan in the living room with a member of the temple choir, where she also sang, at age 17.

4. *Al Capp*, cartoonist
   Got it off with father's 21-year-old secretary at age 17.

5. *Bernard Cornfield*, entrepreneur
   At age 18, in the cabin of a Liberty ship in port at Bremerhaven with a German schoolgirl picked up on the street.

6. *Joseph Cotten*, actor
   At age 8 in a backyard tent with a 19-year old light colored girl.

7. *Bob Guccione*, publisher of *Penthouse* magazine
   At age 15, with a girl, 16, in the back seat of her car after trying for two hours to get it up.

8. *Clifford Irving*, writer
   At age 13 or 14, homosexual experience with a friend in his apartment. At age 15 went to a whore who serviced bowling alley customers in the bathroom of a rooming house while sitting on a toilet seat.

9. *Erica Jong*, writer and poet
   At age 17, with a Columbia sophomore in his off-campus apartment.

10. *Sally Kellerman*, actress
    At age 21, with an older man at his house.

11. *Jack Lemmon*, actor
    At 18 or 19 in a Harvard Square parking lot in a convertible car with a stick shift and his feet stuck through a rip in the canvas roof.

12. *John Lennon*, entertainer
    At age 12, a strange man did it with his hand.

13. *Liberace*, entertainer
    Raped at age 13 by a nightclub blues singer on the front seat of a car parked on a dirt road.

14. *Loretta Lynn*, country music singer
    Married at age 13, with no prior sex education, her first experience was very frightening. Pregnant by age 14.

15. *Yoko Ono*, entertainer
    At age 9, a doctor serviced her while treating her for an illness.

16. *Victoria Principal*, TV actress (one of the stars of "Dallas")
    Age almost 18, in the front seat of a car parked on a deserted road.

17. *Debbie Reynolds*, entertainer
Virgin until marriage at age 23 to Eddie Fisher.

18. *Bobby Riggs*, tennis player
At age 7, while visiting on ranch, with an 8-year-old girl in the hayloft; next, at 17, he went fourteen times in one night, keeping track with pencil marks on a piece of paper.

19. *Joan Rivers*, comedienne
At age 20, visiting a sick friend, in a minute and a half.

20. *Artie Shaw*, bandleader and writer
Met a girl in a dance hall, drove her into the woods, took the back seat out of the car, then took her.

21. *Rudy Vallee*, singer and comedian
First time at age 6, in the icehouse near the beaver pond behind the school with a few friends and one girl.

22. *Irving Wallace*, writer
About age 18, on the Mexican border with a prostitute.

23. *Mae West*, entertainer
At age 13, with her music teacher on the stairway of the vestibule of her house, with her parents upstairs, while wearing her fur coat.

> —For the full stories on some of these, see *The First Time*, by Karl Fleming and Anne Taylor Fleming

The 11 Wives of Tommy Manville

Tommy Manville was the much-married eccentric heir to an asbestos fortune. Night clubs were his nursery, and his marital playmates sometimes stayed with him for less than twenty-four hours after they pronounced the vows. He'd meet them anywhere. One was a reporter who interviewed him on behalf of the *Hobo News*. With few exceptions, they all left with a chunk of the Manville inheritance cake.

1. Florence Huber
2. Lois Arleen McCoin
3. Avonne Taylor
4. Marcelle Edwards
5. Bonita Edwards (no relation to Marcelle)
6. Wilhelmina "Billy" Connelly Boze
7. Macie Marie "Sunny" Aimsworth
8. Georgina Campbell
9. Anita Roddy-Eden
10. Pat Gaston
11. Christina Erdlen

Charles Hamilton's 20 Greatest Lovers and the Value of Their Autographs

Charles Hamilton is the world's foremost authority on autographs and has written many books on the subject of philography (autograph collecting). His most recent is *Great Forgers and Famous Fakes*, a study of the manuscript forgers of America and how they duped the experts.

1. *Pope Alexander VI*, religious leader.
He loved orgies with scores of naked girls. $1800

2. *Brigitte Bardot*, actress.
She boasted publicly of more than 5,000 lovers. $20

3. *Giovanni Casanova*, librarian and swordsman.
He seduced thousands of women, usually two at a time. $1800

4. *Catherine the Great*, Russian empress.
She is said to have satisfied the entire imperial guard. $800

5. *Gabriele d'Annunzio*, poet.
   Even his hexameters bounce up and down. $75

6. *Marquis de Sade*, author and pervert.
   He invented bizarre ways to do it. $1100

7. *Madame Du Barry*, courtesan.
   She delighted a king and hundreds of jacks. $800

8. *Isadora Duncan*, dancer.
   She even greeted delivery boys in the buff. $300

9. *Errol Flynn*, actor.
   He died of exhaustion at 50, with the body of a man of 75. $325

10. *Benjamin Franklin*, statesman.
    He had a mistress on every street in Paris. $3000

11. *John Garfield*, actor.
    He also died in action. $100

12. *Allen Ginsberg*, poet.
His selectively scissored pubic hairs are sought as love charms. $30

13. *Mata Hari*, exotic dancer and spy.
She picked up military secrets between the sheets. $1500

14. *Jean Harlow*, actress.
She also was a "blonde bombshell" in bed. $550

15. *Frank Harris*, author.
Either he belongs in this list or he was an unconscionable liar.
$75

16. *Marilyn Monroe*, actress.
She flaunted her talents in high circles. $425

17. *Lola Montez*, actress and singer.
Suitors fought duels for the favors of a single night. $850

18. *Nelson A. Rockefeller*, statesman.
He died in action. $20

19. *Frank Sinatra*, singer.
He kept a list of his conquests until he ran out of paper. $30

20. *Mae West*, actress.
Thousands of lusty men accepted her famous invitation. $35
—Exclusive for *The Book of Sex Lists*

Barbara Hutton's 7 Husbands

"Babs" as she was called by the press, was a "poor little rich girl"—a Woolworth heiress. This five-and-dime princess craved affection and was an easy seduction for anyone who would hold her hand, gaze into her eyes and ask her to lead him to the nearest bedroom. From time to time she married the men in her life, and these are the seven bridegrooms:

1. Prince Alexis Mdivani
2. Count Court Haugwitz Reventlow

32

3. Cary Grant
4. Prince Igor Troubetzkoy
5. Porfirio Rubirosa
6. Baron Gottfried Von Cramm
7. Prince Doan Vinh Na Champacak

People Magazine's 10 Sexiest Elegible Bachelors

1. Mikhail Baryshnikov (ballet dancer and director)
2. Harrison Schmitt (astronaut who walked on the moon and now a member of the United States Senate)
3. O.J. Simpson (football player, actor and TV commercial spokesman)
4. Vitas Gerulaitis (tennis player)
5. Prince Andrew (second son of Great Britain's Queen Elizabeth II and Prince Philip)
6. Jim Hoge (Chicago *Sun-Times* editor-in-chief)
7. James Caan (movie star)
8. Andy Gibb (singer)
9. Erik Estrada (movie and TV actor)
10. Phillippe Niarchos (billionaire shipowner)

8 Great Photographers of Nudes

Here is a selection of the most skillful and imaginative photographers of nude men and women during the past century.

1. André de Dienes
2. Robert Farber
3. Marilyn Hillman
4. Ed Lange
5. Man Ray
6. Edward Steichen
7. Alfred Stieglitz
8. Edward Weston

Richard Lamparski's "Whatever Became of the 10 Most Asked-About Show Business Sex Symbols?"

(Richard Lamparski is the author of seven books titled *Whatever Became of . . . ?* in which he details what celebrities of the past are doing today.)

1. *Irish McCalla,* star of TV's *Sheena, Queen of the Jungle,* is divorced and the mother of two grown sons. She is a successful commercial artist and lives in Malibu, California.

2. *Gardner McKay,* star of TV's *Adventures in Paradise,* is single and lives in Beverly Hills with an assortment of animals. He reviews plays and movies for a Los Angeles newspaper and has written several plays of his own for both television and the stage.

3. *Richard Beymer,* whose acting credits include the films *West Side Story* and *The Diary of Anne Frank,* is single and living in Hollywood. He is both a filmmaker and an instructor in Transcendental Meditation.

4. *James Fox,* star of *The Servant* and *Performance,* is now a fundamentalist minister in northern England.

5. *Lili St. Cyr* ("The Ecdysiast") is divorced for the seventh time and lives alone in Hollywood. She is currently working on her autobiography with Matthew Tombers.

6. *Ty Hardin,* star of TV's *Bronco* and the movie *The Chapman Report,* is living in Prescott, Arizona, where he videotapes his evangelical television program, which is syndicated around the United States.

7. *Tom Rettig,* star of TV's *Lassie,* is divorced and the father of two grown sons. He works for an insurance firm in Los Angeles.

8. *Louise Brooks,* star of silent film classics *Pandora's Box* and *Diary of a Lost Girl,* is single, in very poor health, and living by herself in Rochester, New York.

9. *Christopher Jones,* star of the films *Wild in the Streets* and *Ryan's Daughter,* is single and living in Hollywood with a woman and their young son.

10. *Debra Paget*, movie star of the fifties, is the mother of one son
    by a multimillionaire nephew of Chiang Kai-Shek. She lives in
    Houston, Texas.

—Exclusive for The Book of Sex Lists.

The 10 Sexiest Soap Operas

Probably no person knows and has viewed more soap operas
than Paul Denis. A former Broadway gossip columnist, Denis was
the natural person to become founding editor of *Daytime TV*
magazine, which immediately became the most widely circulated
magazine for TV soap opera fans.

These are his selections as the sexiest soap operas:

1. *The Young and the Restless.* The first soap opera to offer so
   many young and beautiful bodies in sensual situations. The
   male actors, particularly, display magnificent chests as the
   girls swoon with delight.
2. *General Hospital.* The Luke-Laura rape (or was it seduction?)
   caused this soap to float right to the top of the Nielsen ratings.
   Plenty of nurses and doctors here, and they always seem to
   have plenty of time for hanky panky.
3. *The Guiding Light.* On the air, radio and TV, for forty-five
   years. This one has caught up on adultery, rape, and scenes of
   passion both in and out of bedrooms.
4. *One Life to Live.* The life they live is mostly between the
   sheets, and Texas big shots now overwhelm the yielding
   females. Lots of threats, blackmail, vindictiveness, and s-e-x.
5. *Days of Our Lives.* Always emotional, these people always lust
   happily for each other and bed down quickly, in and out of
   marriage.
6. *As the World Turns.* Once a traditional antiseptic place, this
   world now turns on heavy passion, love, and hate. The nurses
   and the doctors are very busy in all departments, and among
   their hobbies is married rape.

7. *All My Children.* Sharing a joint or two and downing vodka stingers seem to be persuaders to quick sex, as these people charm their way through mystery, violence, passion and love.
8. *Ryan's Hope.* The Irish do it too. At least when they are not too busy at the bars or the political powerhouses. Lots of ambition for power and money, but first they lie down in bed and talk it over.
9. *Texas.* Murder, drugs, money, power, and Southern accents all mix dramatically as the rich mess with the lower classes on and off the mattresses. Lots of puffing and passion.
10. *Another World.* The rich tangle with criminals. Result? Double crossings, murders, illegitimate babies, seductions, rapes and sometimes (on rare occasions) even normal love. Villains are most charming.

—Exclusive for The Book of Sex Lists

5 Presidents of the United States With the Greatest Sex Appeal

1. John Adams
2. Warren Harding
3. John Fitzgerald Kennedy
4. Franklin Delano Roosevelt
5. Theodore Roosevelt

—Prepared by Consensus, Inc.

3 Presidents of the United States with the Least Sex Appeal

1. Calvin Coolidge
2. Herbert Hoover
3. Richard M. Nixon

President Calvin Coolid

12 of the World's Most Desirable Men

Man Watchers is a nationwide group of hundreds of women, with headquarters in San Diego, California.

In the spring of 1981, they picked the men they considered "the 12 most desirable guys in the world."

Here they are, in alphabetical order.

1. *Prince Albert of Monaco*—The son of Princess Grace and Prince Rainier of Monaco, and brother to Princesses Caroline and Stephanie.

2. *Prince Andrew of England*—The younger, but apparently more dashing, brother of Charles.

3. *Burt Bacharach*—Songwriter and composer also known for his good looks and sensitivity.

4. *Governor Jerry Brown*—The enigmatic governor of California appeals to many women, including famous rock singer Linda Ronstadt.

5. *Harrison Ford*—Very much the Hollywood heartthrob, especially since his starring role in the successful film *Raiders of the Lost Ark*.

6. *Senator Edward Kennedy*—Politically and socially prestigious, Ted has a long history of romantic entanglements.

7. *Burt Reynolds*—This superstar is not only handsome and a top box office draw but is intelligent and has as much admiration for the ladies as they have for him.

8. *Tom Selleck*—The star of TV's *Magnum P.I.* has merely to flash a smile and the ladies wilt.

9. *Grant Tinker*—New chairman of NBC and once part of the Mary Tyler Moore team demonstrates how power has great sex appeal.

10. *John Travolta*—Is it his eyes, mouth, youth or talent that turns women on?

11. *Pierre Trudeau*—The prime minister of Canada combines his own good looks with power to make it to this list.

12. *Ted Turner*—A man who dares to be different and who has the capacity to throw himself completely into whatever his interests may be, whether competing aboard a sailing vessel or establishing the Cable News Network.

3

—And now to the infamous...

---

12 Famous Madams

"Madam" is a polite term of address to a woman. It was once used only for women of obvious social status. Eventually, when preceded by the article "a," it came to designate the woman who ran a brothel.

1. *Alice Thomas* operated in Boston from 1670 to 1672. She was convicted of "whoredom"—one of the first such convictions in the U.S.A. She was whipped on the streets of Boston before being jailed.

2. *Madam Gourdon,* rue des Deux Portes, Paris (circa 1715), had a secret passage from a merchant's shop so priests and women could slip into her quarters for their needs without embarrassment. In addition to a collection of pornographic material to stimulate the sexual desires of her patrons, she featured amulets, aphrodisiacs and salves. She also boasted a chamber of horrors for those whose preferences were sadistic or masochistic.

3. *Madam Paris* operated from 1740 through 1752 from the rue de Bagneaux. She is believed to have originated the practice of having her girls sit or stand in a central waiting room. They wore clothing that was slight and seductive. In the later years she moved her establishment to Hotel du Roule in the Faubourg Saint-Honoré.

4. *Madam Montigny* operated in Paris. In 1852 she made history when she posted a price list for each of her fifty girls.

5. *Mary Jeffries* established a series of specialty houses in London around 1880. These catered to individual preferences. For example, one of her houses featured very young girls. Another featured flogging. Many members of the British royal family were among her customers—and this allowed her to operate without police interference for ten years.

6. *Nell Kimball* operated a successful house in San Francisco from 1898 to 1901. She had a glamour of her own and at one time was engaged to Paul Dreiser, brother of the novelist Theodore Dreiser. She is believed to be the model for Sister Carrie in the Dreiser novel of the same name.

7. *The Everleigh Sisters*, Ada and Minna, founded the notorious Everleigh Club around 1900 in Chicago. They were very proper, almost prudish ladies. The posted price for a session with one of the women of the establishment was $50—relatively high for that period. The decor was lavish, and barbers and masseurs were on the premises on call for customers. To enter, one had to be a special guest or a stranger with a letter of introduction. The police closed the place in 1911. It is believed that the expression "get laid" originated from men saying "I'm going to get Everleighed."

8. *Mammy Pleasant (Mary Ellen Smith)* was a black lady who owned large amounts of real estate along San Francisco's Barbary Coast around the turn of the nineteenth century. Her thirty-room mansion on Octavia Street was known as "the house of mystery." It was destroyed in 1906 by a fire, believed deliberately set by "reformers."

9. *Polly Adler* named her autobiography *A House Is Not a Home* and took pride in the fact that many of the "greats" of show business in New York in the late twenties were her regular patrons at 880 Park Avenue. A souvenir of a visit to Polly's place was a matchbook with nothing on it but a parrot (Polly) and a phone number.

10. *Madam Sherry (Ruth Barnes)* ran the famed Moorish Castle, Rancho Lido, in Miami for twenty-five years. In her autobiography, *Pleasure Was My Business*, she describes (and names) many of her famous guests, who ranged from public enemies and politicians ("the same thing," she said) to gamblers and judges, police chiefs and con men, pimps, hoodlums, and royalty.

Dade County officials were so embarrassed by her revelations of bribes that her book was banned there until the ban was overturned by the United States Supreme Court.

The book also precipitated a libel suit by Fuad Farouk, former King of Egypt. Publisher Lyle Stuart obtained a court order forcing Farouk to appear at the American Embassy in Rome. For seven days Farouk had to testify as to his personal sexual proclivities and experiences. It was the first time in history that a member of royalty had to testify under oath. Stuart won the suit when Farouk dropped dead a few weeks later.

11. *Beverly Davis.* In the 1940s her biography, titled *Call House Madam* and written by Serge J. Wolsey, sold several hundred thousand copies. Though tame by today's standards, it was shocking by the mores prevailing thirty-five years ago. After a protracted legal battle, it was banned.

12. *Delfina, Eva and Maria Gonzalez.* These three Mexican sisters gave the profession of madam a bad name. In a ranch near Leon, Mexico, they murdered at least thirty-five women (some reports said the total was more than a hundred) who had been attracted to the ranch by the promise of jobs as maids with upper-class families. They were raped and transported to a training brothel in San Francisco del Rincon, a farm area. Girls who didn't follow orders or who protested were beaten and tortured. The torture most feared was the *cama real* (royal bed), a narrow board on which girls were placed and wrapped in barbed wire so that even the slightest movement caused cuts. In 1964 the sisters were convicted and sentenced to forty years in pr:son, the maximum penalty allowed under Mexican law.

3 Famous Male Madams

1. *Charles Luciano* ("Charley Lucky") was a notorious gangland figure. District Attorney Thomas E. Dewey jailed Luciano for his involvement with prostitution—probably the only racket in

which he was not involved. Dewey's success in this case helped elect him Governor of New York State. He then ran twice as the Republican candidate for President. President Franklin Roosevelt defeated him, winning a fourth term. Then Dewey ran against Harry Truman. The *Chicago Tribune* headlined DEWEY BEATS TRUMAN, but it was wrong. Again Dewey was beaten at the polls.

Luciano, in the meantime, was approached in his prison cell by the military. He is alleged to have been helpful to the Allied forces when Sicily was invaded by sending word that certain mob-connected Sicilians were to cooperate with the Americans. For this his sentence was commuted to deportation. He lived out the balance of his life in Italy.

2. *Eugenio ("Gino") and Carmelo Messina* were the infamous *souteneurs* who during World War II and the years immediately afterward introduced organized prostitution onto the streets of London. Gino insisted that his girls follow a ten minute rule—they couldn't spend more than ten minutes with a client. He had his girls travel in threes so that two could report on the third. If a girl spent even a minute or two extra, she would be slapped and beaten.

Marthe Watts, who earned more than $250,000 for the Messinas before being discarded when she became ill, wrote in her memoir *The Men in My Life,* that she suspected the ten-minute rule reflected Gino's inferiority complex. He didn't want any of his girls to enjoy sex with any man but himself. He didn't permit them to go to movies or even to read movie magazines in which male films stars were pictured.

3. *Joe Conforte,* who once worked as a clerk at a fruit stand on Ninth Avenue in New York City, developed what may be the most prosperous house of prostitution in American whorehouse history. The Mustang Ranch in Sparks, Nevada (just outside of Reno), is legal because in Nevada prostitution is allowed by local option.

Conforte made sure Sparks stayed in the positive option column by moving the families of his women to Sparks so that on election day his people constituted the majority of the voting citizenry.

The Mustang has been the subject of books and films, among them Conforte's biography, *The Girls of Nevada.*

To get to the Mustang, a customer must drive through the desert, guided by arrows painted on large rocks.

A large fence blocks entry until the customer rings the bell. He is admitted when someone at a one-way mirror presses a buzzer that opens the gate. This buzzer also serves to alert some thirty to forty women on duty, who stand in a semicircle when the customer walks into the room.

Joe Conforte

The women are permitted to do nothing more provocative than smile and say their names. This, to limit the competitiveness. Prices are reasonable; pimps are not allowed on the premises; the girls are required to get constant medical checkups.

The Mustang women, some of whom are university students, married women, etc., have access to a huge kitchen with every conceivable type of food. They pay fifty percent of their earnings for room and board.

When Joe Conforte ran the place, accounts were settled in cash each midnight, at which time all records of earnings were destroyed. The women earned as much as $1,000 a week. Since it was all in cash, few of the Mustang ladies declared their income.

Conforte himself was convicted of evading $5 million in income taxes. He thought he'd sold the place for big dollars but at the last minute the buyers pulled out because of the notoriety he'd received during his trial and conviction. Although he had an appeal pending, he decided not to spend any time in jail. He managed to flee the country. He got to South America and, more recently, to a country elsewhere in the world that doesn't have an extradition treaty with the United States.

Conforte put the Mustang Ranch into the hands of his estranged wife, Sally. While the girls of the Mustang were very loyal to Joe, they don't seem to care much for Sally, who, in turn, makes very little effort to get along with them. Because of this, the Mustang is said to be in trouble.

4

We hear more about the problems of sex than the pleasures.
Here are some of the most common ones and some sound advice about solutions.

The 7 Most Frequent Sex Problems
Brought to Sex Therapists by Men

1. *Coital aninsertia* (inability to insert penis into vagina of partner)
2. *Penile anesthesia* (lack of feeling in the male sex organ)
3. *Anorgasmia* (inability to achieve orgasm; either delayed ejaculation or none at all)
4. *Erectile impotence* (inability to have an erection)
5. *Premature ejaculation* (having orgasm before partner desires it)
6. *Coital pain* (discomfort upon penetration of vagina by penis)
7. *Erotic apathy* (little interest in sex)

—From *Love and Lovesickness,* by Dr. John Money of The Johns Hopkins Medical Institutions

4 of the Most Frequent Problems
Submitted to a Former *Playgirl* Advisor

1. Imbalance: "He/she doesn't want to have sex as much as I do" or "always wants sex more than I do."
2. Jealousy: Either party is too possessive of the other.
3. Lack of orgasm for the woman. (Some, asked what it felt like, did not know.)
4. Unrequited love: "How can I get him?"

—Prepared by Jackie Davison especially for The Book of Sex Lists

The 7 Most Frequent Sex Problems
Brought to Sex Therapists by Women

The most common sex problem of American adults today is a lack of sexual desire. This is manifested in many ways. Dr. John Money, in his book *Love and Lovesickness*, refers to the problem as *hypophilia*.

Incidentally, few patients complain of excess sexiness.

1. *Coital aninsertia* (the inability to be penetrated by a penis)

2. *Vulval anesthesia* (lack of feeling in the female sex organ)

3. *Anorgasmia* (Some women come to orgasm only during solo masturbation. Others require clitoral stimulation. Others come only during intercourse or oral contact. There is a wide variety in female sexual response. Anorgasmia is the inability to come to orgasm under *any* condition.)

4. *Persistent vaginal dryness* (Failure to lubricate or to maintain lubrication. Some women solve this problem with the use of an aid such as KY jelly. Others learn to assert themselves and demand longer foreplay.)

5. *Vaginismus* (A condition in which the muscles of the female sex organ contract too quickly. This causes the premature onset

of what sexologists call the "postorgasmic refractory period" and effectively excludes the penis.)

6. *Dyspareunia* (Difficult or painful coitus, regardless of cause)

7. *Erotic apathy* (The lack of interest in sex. This is the most common complaint of both women and men.)

Dr. Albert Ellis's List of 21 Irrational Beliefs That Lead to Sex Problems and Disturbances

According to Rational-Emotive Therapy (RET), people upset themselves emotionally mainly by devoutly accepting and creating three absolutist, musturbatory beliefs. When they are sexually troubled or neurotic, they disturb themselves by at least 21 derivatives of their three basic irrational musts.

Here is Dr. Albert Ellis's list of 21 of their main sexual irrationalities:

Musturbatory Idea 1 (leading to feelings of ego anxiety, depression, inadequacy, and worthlessness): I must perform well and win great approval for any performances from all the significant people in my life, else I am an RNGP (rotten no-good person)!

1. I must be loved thoroughly and be lusted after all the time by everyone I find sexually attractive. Otherwise I am a real shit.

2. I must be completely competent, adequate, and outstanding in bed—the goddamned greatest sex partner since Cleopatra or Antony (not to mention Heliogabalus or Sappho)!

3. I must give myself a global rating as a human, be holier than thou in all important sexual respects, and only consider myself worthwhile when I am as horny as Gargantua and as orgasmic as Lassie.

4. If I am anxious or depressed about sex—as, of course, I must not be—I am a total turd. I can't stand my sexual *mishegoss!*

46

5. I must follow normal sex conventions and rules and must never flout them and thereby have a hell of a harmless ball!

Musturbatory Idea 2 (leading to feelings of hostility, resentment, rage, and homicidalness): Others must treat me considerately and kindly, in precisely the way I want them to. If not, they are damnable people, thoroughly deserving of horrible punishment!

6. Others must serve me sexually and do exactly what I want when I want it. If they don't, then they are putrid, unsexy bitches and bastards!

7. Others must read my mind and *know* what I want sexually, without my having to tell them. If not, unfuck them!

8. Others must follow the right sex rules and customs—those I subscribe to—else they are (unlike me!) thoroughly stupid, incompetent, and worthless!

9. Others must achieve their full sexual potential (as I, of course, do). Otherwise, they have no right to live, love, copulate!

Musturbatory Idea No. 3 (leading to discomfort, anxiety, self-pity, and depression): The conditions of my life should ensure that I get all my important needs fully and freely fulfilled. Otherwise, I might as well kill myself!

10. Conditions must be arranged so that all my sex desires—and avoidances!—are easily, quickly, and completely fullfilled. No shit!

11. Things must go the way I like them to go sexually, for my entire life is an awful, terrible, and horrible pain in the ass when they don't.

12. Life must not have any sex hassles or dangers, and if it does I must continually obsess about them and desperately try to control them. They are so painful that I must additionally terrify myself about them!

13. When sex problems exist, I must hide my head (and genitals) in the sand and cleverly avoid facing them. That will fix them!

14. I must not have to work for sex pleasure. It should come spontaneously and easily, damn it!

47

15. If changing some obnoxious or handicapping element in my sex life is hard, that difficulty must not exist! It is *too* hard to do anything about it and it *shouldn't* be as bad as it indubitably is!

16. There must be an absolutely perfect solution to all my and my partner's sex problems. Else I can't bear it, and I have to perpetually whine and scream!

17. Fairness and justice in all sex areas must exist—particularly for me! Otherwise, life is unethical and unbearable!

18. People and external events cause my sexual unhappiness and make me helpless. I have no control over my feelings or reactions, poor victim, I!

19. My sex life must continue forever. I must not die impotent or inorgasmic—or ever die at all!

20. The universe must provide me with some magical guarantees that sex will always be perfectly enjoyable. Else I won't play in this ball (and tit) game!

21. The discomfort of my sex problems and anxieties must not exist. Woe is me—I can't stand it!

> —Prepared by Dr. Albert Ellis especially for *The Book of Sex Lists*

4 Ways Women React to Male Sexual Failure

1. 50% will be comforting and consoling.
2. 23% will get angry or hurt.
3. 16% get into a frank discussion of the matter.
4. 11% ask for noncoital stimulation from the male.

> —Source: *Bottom Line Newsletter*

6 Ways People React When Presented With a Woman's Frigidity Problem

The problem was presented to a group of people as follows: "We have a case of a woman who has never had an orgasm during sexual intercourse although she has accomplished orgasm by other methods. Why do you think this is?"

The responses were:

1. There is something wrong with her sexually—22%
2. She is not receiving enough stimulus to her clitoris—21%
3. She should be satisfied with what she's already getting—21%
4. She is just too up-tight—16%
5. She doesn't care for her partner enough—13%
6. She is just not sexy—7%

—Dana Wilcox and Ruth Hager,
"Towards Realistic Expectations for
Orgasmic Response in Women," *Journal
of Sex Research*, vol. 16, no. 2, May 1980.

5

*Sometimes, before you have sex,
you have to ask for it or at least talk about it.
Here is some of the language of sex....*

147 Synonyms for the Penis

1. Almond Rock
2. Banana
3. Bar
4. Bean
5. Bent Stick
6. Big Brother
7. Blind Jack
8. Blind Bob
9. Bone
10. Bowsprit
11. Box Opener
12. Butcher Knife
13. Canasta
14. Candy Bar
15. Charlie
16. Cheese Cutter
17. Chopper
18. Cock
19. Cookie
20. Dark Meat
21. Dead Meat
22. Dick
23. Dingus
24. Dink
25. Dirty Barrel
26. Dong
27. Dork
28. Fancy Work
29. Gadget
30. Giggle Stick
31. Giggling Pin
32. Golden Rivet
33. Goober
34. Green Thumb

35. Groceries
36. Gun
37. Hammer
38. Hidden Treasure
39. Hand-Made
40. Hand-Reared
41. He
42. Honey Stick
43. Hot Dog
44. Impudence
45. Jack-in-the-Box
46. Jang
47. Jerking Iron
48. Jing-Jang
49. Jock
50. Johnny
51. Johnson
52. Joint
53. Joy Knob
54. Joy Stick
55. Knob
56. Linga
57. Lingam
58. Little Brother
59. Lollipop
60. Long John
61. Lower Deck
62. Matrimonial Peacemaker
63. Meat
64. Meat Whistle
65. Meat with Two Vegetables
66. Membrum Virile
67. Mickey
68. Middle Leg
69. Mortar and Pestle
70. Muscle
71. Mutton Dagger
72. Old Blind
73. Old Thing
74. One-Eyed Monster
75. Organ

76. Pax Wax
77. Pecker
78. Pencil
79. Peter
80. Phallus
81. Piccolo
82. Pintle
83. Piston Rod
84. Pogo Stick
85. Poker
86. Pole
87. Poontanger
88. Pork Chopper
89. Pork Sword
90. Priapus
91. Prick
92. Privates
93. Prong
94. Pudend
95. Pudenda
96. Pulse
97. Putz
98. Red Cap
99. Red-Hot Poker
100. Rhubarb
101. Richard
102. Rod
103. Roger
104. Rupert
105. Rusty Rifle
106. Schlong
107. Schmuck
108. Schnitzel
109. Schwanz
110. Sexing Piece
111. She
112. Six inches
113. Skin Flute
114. Snake
115. Spout
116. Stalk

117. Stick
118. Sticker
119. Stinger
120. Stuff
121. Swanska
122. Sword
123. Tadger
124. Tallywhacker
125. Thing
126. Tommy
127. Tonge
128. Tongue
129. Tool
130. Wang
131. Weapon
132. Weenie

133. Wee-wee
134. Whang
135. Whelp
136. Whistle
137. White Meat
138. Wick
139. Wiener
140. Willie-whacker
141. Winkle
142. Wire
143. Worm
144. Yang
145. Yard
146. Ying-Yang
147. Zubrick

98 Synonyms for the Vagina

1. Ass
2. Bearded Clam
3. Bearded Lady
4. Black Velvet
5. Box
6. Bread
7. Bun
8. Bush
9. Bushy Park
10. Business
11. Cabbage
12. Cake
13. Canasta
14. Chuff
15. Cock
16. Cockpit
17. Conch
18. Cooch

19. Cookie
20. Crack
21. Cunnus
22. Cunt
23. Cush
24. Cut
25. Cuzzy
26. Dark Meat
27. Dead End Street
28. Dicky Dido
29. Dirty Barrel
30. Dog's Mouth
31. Fort Bushy
32. Fur
33. Furburger
34. Fur Pie
35. Futy
36. Garden
37. Gash
38. Geography
39. Gig
40. Gigi
41. Gonad
42. Groceries
43. Growl
44. Hair Pie
45. Hairy Ring
46. Hairy Wheel
47. Happy Valley
48. Hatchi
49. Hidden Treasure
50. Hole
51. Honey Pot
52. Hot Box
53. Jack-in-a-Box
54. Jaxy
55. Jelly
56. Jelly Roll
57. Jing-Jang
58. Joxy
59. Little Sister
60. Lollipop
61. Lower Deck
62. Meat
63. Mortar and Pestle
64. Moustache
65. Mowed Lawn
66. Muff
67. Nookie
68. Old Thing
69. One That Bites
70. Organ
71. Piece of Ass
72. Pink
73. Poontang
74. Pudendum
75. Puka
76. Punce
77. Pussy
78. Quiff
79. Quim
80. Rattlesnake Canyon
81. Scratch
82. She
83. Slash
84. Slit
85. Slot
86. Snake Pit
87. Snatch
88. Snippey
89. Split
90. Tail
91. Thing
92. Toolbox
93. Twat
94. White Meat
95. Wick Burner
96. X
97. Yoni
98. Zosh

7 Common but Frequently Misused Sex and Marriage Terms

1. *Polygamy*—refers to a plurality of either wives or husbands, not just wives.
2. *Polygyny*—refers only to a plurality of wives.
3. *Polyandry*—refers only to a plurality of husbands.
4. *Exogamy*—refers to marriage outside of the clan (the family).
5. *Endogamy*—refers to marriage inside the clan (the family).
6. *Tetragamy*—the Mohammedan law which purportedly permits four wives. Actually Mohammed had fourteen wives at one time and never really limited his subjects to four. The limit of four represents an interpretation.
7. *Pantagamy*—the practice in some societies in which every man is regarded as the husband of every woman, and vice versa.

9 Jamaican Sex Expressions

Morris Cargill is the managing director of Paradise, a Shangrila–like estate in Hope Bay on the island of Jamaica.

For twenty-five years he wrote a daily column for Jamaica's leading newspaper, *The Gleaner.* He also was a television commentator and has written several books. At one time he headed the Jamaican Banana Board.

Morris Cargill was a friend to Noël Coward, Ian Fleming and most everyone else who was anyone in Jamaica. Among his many accomplishments: he invented the liqueur *Tia Maria.*

These four words are synonyms for the female sexual organ:
1. Punny
2. Punani
3. Crotches
4. Fishy

These four words are synonyms for the male sexual organ:
1. Teapot

2. Wood
3. Pengelleng
4. The big bamboo

This word is used as a substitute for intercourse:
1. Rudeness
   Example: A man might ask a woman, "Will you do me a rudeness?" It is also used as a transitive verb, such as in "He rudenessed me."

—Contributed by Morris Cargill especially for The Book of Sex Lists

The 10 Most Popular Slang Words for Female Breasts

1. Balloons
2. Bazooms
3. Boobs
4. Bristols (British)
5. Grapefruits
6. Jugs
7. Kazongas
8. Knockers
9. Melons
10. Tits (or Titties)

36 Other Labels for Female Breasts

1. Bee Stings
2. Big Brownies
3. Boobies
4. Brace and Bits

6 FAMOUS BUXOM BEAUTIES WHO BARED THEIR BREASTS

These six famous ladies who have been photographed in the half-nude are but a sampling of several dozen. The collection is contained in "Celebrity Skin" which may be ordered for $5 postpaid from Dorjam Publications Inc., P.O. Box 3156, Grand Central Station, New York, NY 10163.

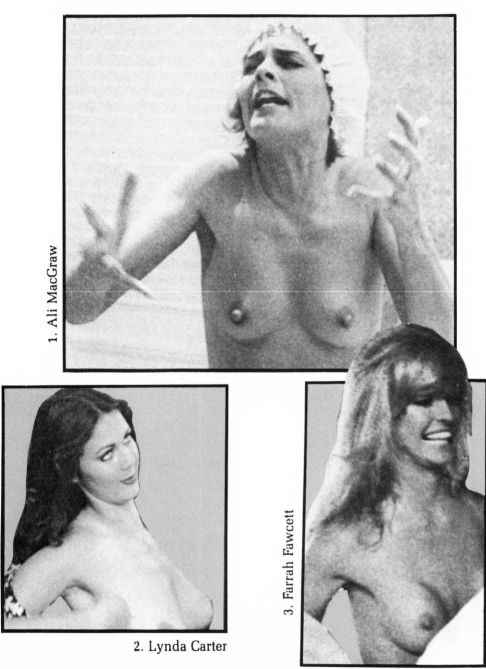

1. Ali MacGraw

2. Lynda Carter

3. Farrah Fawcett

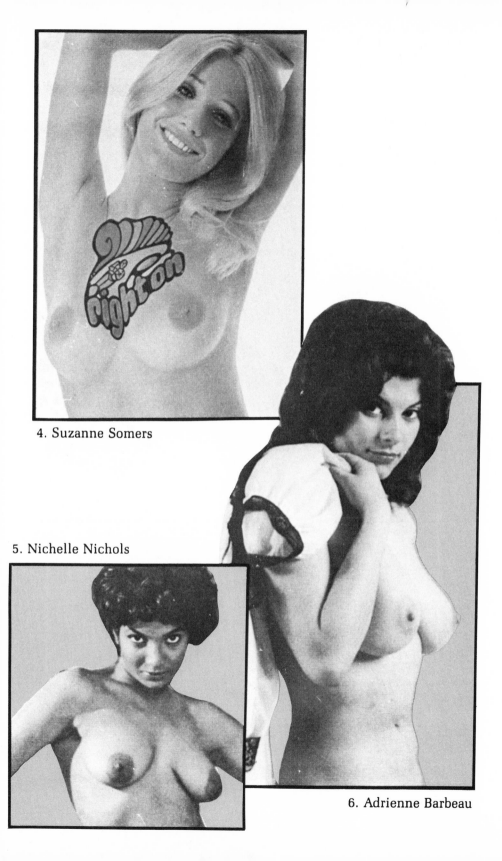

4. Suzanne Somers

5. Nichelle Nichols

6. Adrienne Barbeau

5. Bubbies
6. Bubs
7. Buds
8. Buffers
9. Bust
10. Chubbies
11. Droopers
12. Fore-buttocks
13. Globes
14. Headlights
15. Knobs
16. Lungs
17. Mammae
18. Mammary Glands
19. Manchesters
20. Maracas
21. Milkers
22. Milk Wagons
23. Mountains
24. Muffs
25. Muffins
26. Nay-nays
27. Nubbies
28. Pair
29. Silicones
30. Tabs
31. Teats
32. Topsides
33. Twin Hills
34. Twin Peaks
35. Upper Deck
36. Voos

10 Dirty Words and Their Substitutes

One aspect of the sediment of puritanism that still surfaces in our culture from time to time is the need for euphemisms to describe bodily functions—particularly sexual ones.

This residue of society's hostile attitude toward sex is evidenced in such a simple use of language so that one says what one wants to say without really using the words. The meaning is the same, but somehow some folks feel "cleaner" using the substitute.

Here are ten examples.

The word we use:	The word we mean:
1. nerts	nuts
2. weathervane	weathercock
3. son-of-a-bee	son-of-a-bitch
4. self-abuse	masturbation
5. cohabitated	screwed
6. foul up	fuck up
7. condom	scumbag
8. sleep with	to fuck
9. make love	to fuck
10. fornicate	fuck

9 Sex-Related Yiddish Words and Expressions

1. Tits—tzizkes
2. Penis—shmuck, schwanz, behn, der kleiner (the little one)
3. Ass—tochas
4. Fuck—trehn, shtoop
5. Kiss my ass—kiss mir in tochas
6. Suck a cock—leck a bein!
7. Cunt—loch (hole)
8. Shit—cock
9. Whore—nahfkeh, koorveh

7 "Indecent" Words

In 1973 George Carlin, a widely known satiric humorist, performed a 12-minute monologue before a live audience in a California theater. It was recorded. About 2 o'clock in the afternoon on Tuesday, October 30, 1973, a New York City radio station (WBAI) broadcast this monologue, now entitled "Filthy Words," as part of a program on language. A member of the listening audience sent in a letter of objection to the Federal Communications Commission (FCC).

The FCC found the language "patently offensive" and "indecent", but not obscene. It found the broadcast improper at 2:00 P.M., although there were indications that the Commission would not so hold for a broadcast at midnight, when young children would be unlikely to be listening.

Pacifica Foundation, the owner of the radio station, appealed to the Circuit Court of Appeals. That Court reversed the FCC, each of the three judges writing a separate opinion. Judge Tann said it was censorship prohibited specifically by the law. Chief Judge Bazelon rested on the First Amendment, and said that unless the language was "obscene" it could not be prohibited. Judge Leventhal dissented on the ground that the FCC could protect children.

The FCC petitioned the U.S. Supreme Court to hear the case and it did. On July 3, 1978, the high court reversed the Circuit Court of Appeals but could not agree on why.

Justice Stevens wrote an opinion joined in by Chief Justice Burger and Justice Rehnquist. They said the FCC could protect children by preventing "indecent" broadcasts. But the broadcast would be protected "in other contexts."

Justice Powell (joined by Justice Blackman) agreed in part, but emphasized that the Supreme Court had to decide when protected speech could be stopped.

Justice Brennan (joined by Justice Marshall) dissented on the ground that government had no constitutional power to engage in the "cleansing of public radio" of four-letter words. To do so would ban from radio the works "of Shakespeare, Joyce, Hemingway, Ben Jonson, Henry Fielding, Robert Burns and Chaucer." They could even suppress parts of the Nixon tapes and "certain portions of the Bible." (Citing and quoting specific lines.)

Justice Stewart (joined by Justices Brennan, White and Marshall) dissented squarely on the ground that the FCC could only prohibit obscenity and the Carlin monologue was not obscene.

Excerpts from the Monologue

"A guy . . . in Washington knew his phone was tapped so he used to answer it with "Fuck Hoover. . . . He don't know shit from

Shinola. Always wondered how the Shinola people felt about that."

The seven controversial words were:

1. cocksucker
2. cunt
3. fuck
4. motherfucker
5. piss
6. shit
7. tits

6

*Thoughts on sex are many and varied
and variety is the spice of life.
Here are some slices of that spice...*

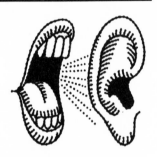

22 Selected Quotations on the Subject of Sex

1. The ultimate in intimacy between two people has been defined not as the sharing of sexual pleasure but the ability to fart in each other's presence.

   —Claire Rayner, *Related to Sex*

2. The orgy serves the useful purpose not only of providing relief from tension caused by abstinence, necessary or unnecessary, but also of re-arousing by contrast an appetite for the humdrum temperances which are an inevitable part of everyday life.

   —B. Partridge, *History of Orgies*

3. Prostitution is a necessary adjunct of morality just as a cesspool is necessary to a palace if the whole palace is not to smell.

   —Thomas Aquinas

4. Rape and incest characterized the sexual life of the Englishman in the first millennium of our era; homosexuality and hysteria the years that followed.

—G. Rattray Taylor, *Sex and History*

5. If people spend too much time indulging in sexual intercourse, and even more time thinking about it, other parts of our national life are bound to suffer. . . .
Research has shown that those who were most prominent in this campaign [against sex] tended to be married men who were finding it difficult to satisfy the sexual desires of their wives.

—*Report of the Committee on the Operation of the [British] Sexual Containment Act*

6. I could be content that we might procreate like trees, without conjunction, or that there were any way to perpetuate the world without this trivial and vulgar way of coition; it is the foolishest act a wise man commits in all his life.

—Sir Thomas Browne, *Religio Medici*

7. There is no greater nor keener pleasure than that of bodily love—and none which is more irrational.

—Plato, *The Republic*

8. When we will, they [women] won't; when we don't want to, they want to exceedingly.

—Terence, *Eunuchus*

9. 'Tis the Devil inspires this evanescent ardor, in order to divert the parties from prayer.

—Martin Luther, *Table Talk 732* (Luther's explanation of marriages which commence with excessive amorous ardor and end soon after in disgust)

10. The lustful longing which allures us to women seeks but to expel that pain which an earnest and burning desire doth possess us with, and desireth but to allay it thereby to come to rest and be exempted from this fever.

—Montaigne, *Essays*

11. It is a common proverb in Italy that he knows not the perfect pleasure of Venus that hath not lain with a limping woman.

—Montaigne, *Essays*

12. Morality in sexual relations, when it is free from superstition, consists essentially of respect for the other person, and unwillingness to use that person solely as a means of personal gratification, without regard to his or her desires.

—Bertrand Russell, *Marriage and Morals*

13. Sex-appeal is the keynote of our civilization.

—Henri Bergson, French philosopher

14. Q. What kind of sins are the greatest?
A. Adultery, fornication, murder, theft, swearing, witchcraft, sedition, heresies, or any the like.

—John Bunyan, *Instructions for the Ignorant*

15. The sanctity of the institution of marriage and the home shall be upheld. Pictures shall not imply that low forms of sex relations are the accepted or common thing. Miscegenation is forbidden.

—Motion Picture Code, March 31, 1930

16. If a woman hasn't got a tiny streak of a harlot in her she's a dry stick as a rule.

—D.H. Lawrence

17. Freud found sex an outcast in the outhouse, and left it in the living room as an honored guest.

—W. Beran Wolfe, American psychiatrist

18. I doubt that the lives of normal men, taking one with another, are much colored or conditioned, directly or indirectly, by purely sexual considerations.

—H.L. Mencken

19. All this humorless document [the Kinsey Report] really proves is: (a) that all men lie when they are asked about their adventures in *amour*, and (b) that pedagogues are singularly naive and credulous creatures.

—H.L. Mencken

20. Breathes there a man with a hide so tough
Who says two sexes aren't enough?

—Samuel Hoffenstein

21. Woman, observing that her mate went out of his way to make himself entertaining, rightly surmised that sex had something to do with it. From that she logically concluded that sex was recreational rather than procreational. (The small hardy band of girls who failed to get

this point were responsible for the popularity of women's field hockey.)

—James Thurber and E.B. White, *Is Sex Necessary?*

22. Anyone who knows anything of history knows that great social changes are impossible without feminine ferment. Social progress can be measured by the social position of the fair sex (the ugly ones included).

—Karl Marx

12 Amusing Differences Between the Sexes

1. There's approximately twice as much left-handedness among males as among females. About 8% of all males are left-handed and only 4% of females are port siders.

—M.M. Clark, *Left-Handedness*

2. Women have a better sense of future time orientation than men. They think more of the future and plan ahead better.

—Torgrim Gjesine, *Future Time Orientation* (A study at the University of Oslo)

3. Women are conformists to a degree almost twice that of men.

—J.L. Freedman, J.R. Charlsmith and D.O. Searn, *Social Psychology*

4. Women demonstrate a much higher degree of persuasibility than men.

—I.L. Janis and P.B. Field, *Behavioral Assessment of Persuasibility*

5. Women are more likely to express their emotions, to empathize with the emotions of others and to be compassionate.

6. Men are more skillful in space perception, mathematical ability and concepts and mechanical problems as contrasted with women, who scored higher in verbal ability.

7. Women are more anxious about the risk of failure in any undertaking and they blame themselves, while men are less anxious and they blame others.

> —For items 5 through 7 see Eleanor E. Maccoby and Carol N. Jacqueline, *The Psychology of Sex Differences.*

8. Women are more likely to disclose personal information than men. This includes their politics, religion, sexual activities and other information.

> — *"Sex Differences in Self-Disclosure During an Interview"—Journal of Social Psychology.*

9. From the moment of birth onward, females are more sensitive to sounds and are more disturbed by loud noises.

10. Females are more sensitive on the skin, particularly finger tips.

11. Females as infants speak earlier, rarely have speech defects, and have better linguistic abilities than males.

12. Boys, from birth, have superior visual ability and total body coordination.

> —For items 9 through 12 see Richard M. Restak, *The Brain: Last Frontier.*

5 Classes of Acceptance of a Partner for Sex

1. *Casual*—Anyone who is available at the time. (This category includes rapists, pedophiles, prostitutes, homosexuals who do it in toilets, and nymphomaniacs.)
2. *General*—All forms of recreational sex, featuring loose standards. Enthusiastic swingers are typical of this class.
3. *Selective*—Requires affection for the sex partner. Personalized sex.

4. *Affectionate*—Requires emotional attachment to the sex partner.
5. *Unique*—The "one and only" syndrome.

> —Adapted from Daniel L. Mosher, *Three Dimensions of the Depth of Involvement in Human Sexual Activity*

The 10 Sexual Activities Preferred by Heterosexual Women (in Order of Preference)

1. Gentle cunnilingus (on the clitoris) by a man (much emphasis on the "gentle")
2. Gentle finger stimulation of the clitoris (gentle!) by a man
3. Sexual intercourse on top of a man
4. Sexual intercourse in a variety of changing positions
5. Receiving cunnilingus (gentle, of course) while performing fellatio ("sixty-nine")

6. Massaging a man all over
7. Masturbating a man
8. Being petted, kissed, and stimulated manually and orally by two men, culminating in intercourse with one man while the other finger-strokes alternately gently the clitoris and the nipples
9. Masturbation
10. Performing simple fellatio

> —Prepared by the Association for Research, Inc., especially for *The Book of Sex Lists*

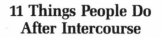

11 Things People Do
After Intercourse

1. Go to sleep
2. Smoke (legal or other variety)
3. Go to the bathroom
4. Eat something (food)
5. Kiss, hug and snuggle (this is the best thing to do)
6. Watch TV
7. Read *Mad* magazine
8. Read other books or periodicals
9. Telephone one's therapist
10. Go back to work (if sex was the lunch break)
11. Argue (this is the worst thing to do)

—Research by William M. Gaines, Anne
Griffiths and Carole Livingston

The 10 Sexual Activities Preferred
by Heterosexual Men

(in order of preference)

1. Fellatio by a woman to orgasm
2. Intercourse with a woman in a variety of positions, changing from time to time
3. Nude encounters with two women in a variety of activities, changing from time to time
4. Petting the breasts of a woman
5. Anal intercourse with a woman
6. Performing cunnilingus while the woman is performing fellatio ("sixty-nine")
7. Performing sadomasochistic acts (mild, not severe) upon a woman
8. Being masturbated by a woman

9. Performing simple cunnilingus

10. Masturbation

—Prepared by the Association for Research, Inc., especially for *The Book of Sex Lists*. For a slightly different list of nineteen activities see *The Kahn Report on Sexual Preferences*, by Sandra Kahn with Jean Davis.

7

Not all people express themselves eloquently
But people do express themselves!
You don't have to wear your heart on your
sleeve these days.
The front of a T-shirt will do....

50 Sexy Sayings Found on T-Shirts

1. A hard man is good to find
2. Put some fun between your legs (picture of motorcycle)
3. The word for the day is "legs": Spread the Word
4. Give me liberty or give me head
5. Ask me—I might
6. I used to hate it—until I ate it
7. Beer drinkers give better head
8. Dentists do it in the mouth
9. Bookkeepers do it with double entry
10. Teachers do it in class
11. Colonel Sanders does it with chickens
12. Photographers do it in the dark
13. Stewardesses do it in the sky
14. Librarians make novel lovers
15. Waitresses serve it on a tray
16. Secretaries do it at their desks
17. Lawyers do it in court

18. Mechanics have better tools
19. I am ready
20. Surety salesmen enjoy bondage
21. Boy Scouts tie it in knots
22. Hockey Players like to puck
23. Sailors do it on deck
24. Let the phone man put it in
25. Tonight's the night!
26. Stenographers do it by hand
27. I'm a Virgin (This is a very old T-shirt)
28. (On shorts) Home of the Whopper
29. Eat me
30. Sit on a Happy Face
31. Stay healthy: Eat your honey.
32. Nipple freak
33. Pussy hunter
34. *(For homosexual men, on the back of the shirt)* In case of rape, this side up.
35. FCK—The only thing missing is you
36. Lick me quickly
37. City of Brotherly Love
38. City of Sisterly Love
39. All purpose generic female. Suitable for general use.
40. Is that a gun in your pocket or are you just happy to see me?
41. I'll lick your problem
42. Five sleazy pieces
43. Premature evacuation *(picture of airplane)*
44. I'm so horny even the crack of dawn looks good to me
45. Class ass!
46. Starfucker!
47. Mechanics do it in cars
48. Be nice to boobs: They outnumber people 2 to 1
49. Go Fuck Myself Polish T-Shirt
50. Picnickers enjoy a piece on earth

8

*Sex can be fun and it also can be funny.
As for example . . .*

3 Sexy Names of Heroines
in James Bond Books

1. Pussy Galore (*Goldfinger*)
2. Kissy Suzuki (*You Only Live Twice*)
3. Holly Goodhead (*Moonraker*)

Roger Price's 10 Sexy Plants

Roger Price is a nationally known humorist who created the popular Droodles® line drawings in the 1950s. He has authored the Mad-Libs® series as well as such books as *J.G. the Upright Ape*, *The Great Roob Revolution*, *I'm for Me First*, and *The Theory of Avoidism*.

1. Tomato (only because it was known for years as the "love apple")
2. Cockleshell (why not?)
3. Lady Slipper (a favorite with fetishists)
4. Larkspur (popular with S & M folk)
5. Cactus (see Larkspur)
6. Pansy (suitable gift to a consenting adult)
7. Banana (needs no explanation)
8. Cucumber (see Banana)
9. Zucchini (see Cucumber)
10. Lantana (This plant is included for reasons of my own which are none of your business!)

—Exclusive for *The Book of Sex Lists*

Norman Corwin's List of 20 Terms That Sound Sexual and Are Not

Norman Corwin was the number-one writer in the golden days of radio. His "On a Note of Triumph"—a one-hour drama that was broadcast on the day of victory in Europe in World War II—was the most widely celebrated dramatic broadcast in radio history.

1. assole	to absolve from sin; also spelled assoil
2. beaver eater	a wolverine
3. bubbybush	a Carolina spice tree
4. cockarouse	an important person; honorary title of a chief among the early Indians of Virginia
5. cunctator	procrastinator
6. dingle	a small secluded valley
7. firkin	a small wooden barrel for butter
8. forcemeat	seasoned meat used for stuffing
9. hot box	a journal box overheated by friction
10. interrupted screw	a screw of uniform diameter with longitudinal slots
11. jactitation	loud bragging
12. lay shaft	a camshaft
13. organ action	the mechanism of an organ

14. prickmadam	a mosslike herb used in expelling intestinal worms
15. pumping jack	device for operating a pump in a deep well
16. right and left nut	a coupling formed with right-handed threads at one end and left at the other
17. snatch block	a nautical device
18. tittup	jumping or bouncing movement
19. twatter	to chatter
20. vug	a small cavity in a rock

—Exclusive for *The Book of Sex Lists*

16 of the World's Best Dirty Jokes

1.

A man was standing on a train platform seeing the train off, and he observed someone near him shouting at one of the departing passengers, "Goodbye! Your wife is a great lay! Your wife is a great lay!"

He was stunned.

After the train pulled away, he walked over to the man who'd done the shouting and asked, "Excuse me, sir. Did I hear you correctly? Did you tell that man his wife is a great lay?"

The other man shrugged. "Yes," he said, "but it isn't really true. I just didn't want to hurt his feelings."

2.

The Israeli army unit was crossing the desert and most of the men were on camels. Lt. Smith had a very stubborn camel, and finally it stopped dead in its tracks and refused to move another step.

The rest of the unit moved on, leaving Smith alone with his mulish camel.

Smith sat on the camel for three hours. He kicked the camel. He pleaded with the camel. He shouted curses at the camel. But still the camel wouldn't move.

He dismounted and was standing disconsolately at its side when a woman soldier drove up in a jeep. She asked Lt. Smith what the trouble was and he explained that the camel wouldn't budge.

"I can fix that," she said confidently. She sprang from her jeep and reached down, putting her hand under the camel's belly. The camel suddenly jumped up and down, up again, and then raced madly away at the rate of a mile a minute.

Lt. Smith was astounded. "Lady, what did you do? What's the trick?"

"It's simple, Lieutenant," she smiled. "I tickled his balls."

"Well, lady, you'd better tickle mine too—and quickly—because I've got to catch that camel!"

3.

It was their wedding night, and after the minister finished undressing in the bathroom, he tiptoed into the bedroom. He was surprised to see that his bride had already slipped between the sheets.

"My dear," he said, "I thought I would find you on your knees."

"Well, honey," she said, "I can do it that way too, but it gives me the hiccups."

4.

He was a junior bank executive and he had swindled one hundred thousand dollars from his bank—all of which he'd lost at the races. The bank examiners were coming next morning, and when he confessed the whole thing to his wife, she packed her luggage and left him. Despondent, he walked to the middle of the George Washington Bridge and stood at the rail, about to leap off and end it all.

Suddenly a voice called, "Young man, don't do that! There is no need to end your life! I'm a witch. I can help you!"

"I doubt it," he said sadly. "I've stolen a hundred thousand dollars from the bank, for which I'll probably be arrested tomorrow, and a few hours ago my wife left me."

"Young man, witches can do anything," she said. "I'm going to perform a witch miracle." She said, "*Alakazam!* The hundred thousand dollars has been replaced, and there's another fifty thousand in your personal safe deposit box! *Alakazam!* Your wife is back home again!"

He looked at her in obvious disbelief "Is this all true?" he asked.

"Of course," she said, "but to keep it true you must do one thing."

"Anything!" he said. "Anything!"

"Take me to a motel and make love to me."

He stared at her. She was an ugly old crone, dressed in rags. Nevertheless, he thought about the one hundred and fifty thousand dollars and agreed to her terms. He took her to a nearby motel and screwed her all night. In the morning, as he was getting dressed and combing his hair in front of the mirror, she lay on the bed watching silently. Finally, she asked, "Sonny, how old are you?"

"I'm thirty-two," he said.

"Tell me something," she said. "Aren't you a little old to believe in witches?"

5.

Goldstein had been with whores everywhere in the world, but in Hong Kong he met his undoing. He got under the sheets with a very sick Chinese prostitute and picked up so many venereal diseases that the doctors had difficulty separating and identifying them all.

He went to a prominent urologist in the American quarter who examined him and shook his head. "Bad news, Goldstein, you need immediate surgery. We've got to cut your cock off."

Goldstein went into traumatic shock at the prognosis. Pulling himself together, he hurried across the street to another American doctor. There he was told the same thing.

He wandered out into the street in a daze. Stumbling along, he found himself in the Chinese quarter, where he saw a sign identifying the office of a Chinese surgeon.

Deciding to get one more medical opinion, Goldstein went in. He told the Chinese doctor that he'd been to two American doctors and both of them wanted to perform immediate surgery to cut off his penis.

The Chinese surgeon examined Goldstein's penis. He consulted large medical books. Then he examined the penis again.

"Is there any hope, Doc?" Goldstein asked plaintively.

"Sure there is hope!" the doctor said. "I make complete examination. I know exactly what is wrong. You play with Chinese girl, but she very sick. You make mistake and go to Amelican doctor.

Trouble with Amelican doctors, all they think is cut, cut, cut and money, money, money."

Goldstein suddenly brightened up. "You mean I don't really need surgery? My penis doesn't have to be cut off?"

"Absolutely not!" the Chinese doctor said. "Go home, now. Forget surgery. Wait one, maybe two weeks. Pecker fall off all by itself!"

6.

Mrs. Russell Young had a very talented parrot. At her dinner parties he often was the center of attention, for she had trained him to repeat what the butler said when he announced the arriving guests.

The parrot had only one failing: he loved to fuck chickens. Every time he got the chance, he would fly over the fence into the yard of the farmer next door and fuck his chickens.

The farmer complained to Mrs. Young, and finally she laid the law down.

"Bertram," she said to the parrot, "you listen to me! If you go into Farmer Whalen's chicken coop one more time, you're really going to get it!"

The parrot hung his head to show he understood. But two days later, he couldn't resist temptation, and over the fence he went. He was deep into screwing his third hen when Farmer Whalen spotted him and chased him. Whalen complained again to Mrs. Young.

"Now you're going to be punished," she said. She got a pair of barber's shears and clipped all the feathers from the top of the parrot's head.

That night, Mrs. Young threw one of her gala parties. She put the parrot on top of the piano.

"Bertram," she said, "you've been a bad parrot. Tonight you're to sit here all night. No wandering around, and no playing the way you usually do!"

Feeling disconsolate, Bertram sat on the piano. As the butler announced the guests, Bertram performed his usual task of repeating the names. The butler said, "Mr. Arnold Levy and Lady Stella," and the parrot said, "Mr. Arnold Levy and Lady Stella."

The butler announced, "Mr. and Mrs. Robert Salomon," and the parrot echoed, "Mr. and Mrs. Robert Salomon."

Then two bald-headed men entered the room. Without waiting

for the butler to announce them, the parrot shouted, "All right, you chicken-fuckers, up here on the piano with me!"

7

An elephant was having a terrible time in the jungle because a horsefly kept biting her near her tail and there wasn't anything she could do about it. She kept swinging her trunk, but he was far out of reach.

Suddenly, a little sparrow observed this, flew down and snipped the horsefly in half with his beak.

"Oh, thank you!" said the elephant letting out a large sigh. "That was such a relief."

"My pleasure, ma'am," said the sparrow.

"Listen, Mr. Sparrow, if there's anything I can ever do for you, don't hesitate to ask."

The sparrow hesitated. "Well, ma'am—" he said.

"Speak up," said the elephant. "You needn't be shy with me."

"Well," said the sparrow, "all my life I've wondered how it would feel to fuck an elephant."

"Go right ahead," said the elephant. "Be my guest!"

The sparrow flew around behind the elephant and began to fuck away. Up above them, a monkey in the tree watched and the scene excited him. He began to masturbate. This shook a coconut loose, and it fell from the tree and hit the elephant smack on the head.

"Ouch!" cried the elephant.

At which point the sparrow looked over from behind and said, "Am I hurting you, dear?"

8.

Charlie was visiting an old friend and his wife for dinner. When the time came to leave, his car wouldn't start, and it was too late to call the local service station.

The husband urged Charlie to stay over. There was no spare bed in the house; there wasn't even a sofa. So Charlie would have to sleep with the husband and wife.

No sooner had the husband fallen asleep, than the wife tapped Charlie on the shoulder and motioned for him to come over to her.

"I couldn't do that," he whispered. "Your husband is my best friend!"

"Listen, sugar," she whispered back, "there ain't nothing in the whole wide world could wake him up now."

"I can't believe that," Charlie said. "Certainly if I get on top of you and screw you, he'll wake up, won't he?"

"Sugar, he certainly won't. If you don't believe me, pluck a hair out of his asshole and see if that wakes him."

Charlie did just that. He was amazed when the husband remained asleep. So he climbed over to the wife's side of the bed and fucked her. When he finished, he climbed back to his own side. It wasn't long before she tapped him on the shoulder and beckoned him over again. Again he pulled a hair to determine if his old friend was asleep.

This went on eight times during the night. Each time Charlie screwed the woman, he first pulled out one of the husband's asshole hairs.

The ninth time he pulled a hair, the husband awoke and muttered, "Listen, Charlie, old pal, I don't mind your fucking my wife, but for Pete's sake, stop using my ass for a scoreboard!"

9.

Lee and Larry were a pair of winos. They woke up with the shakes one afternoon to find they had only seventy-five cents between them.

Lee began to climb the walls, but Larry said calmly, "Look, old man, give me the seventy-five cents and I'll show you how we can drink free all day." So they went to a delicatessen, and Lee bought a frankfurter, which he stuck into Larry's fly.

Next, they visited a local bar and ordered drinks. When the bartender asked for his money, Lee got down on the floor and started sucking the frankfurter. The bartender screamed, "You fucking queers, get out of here!"

They repeated the scene in bar after bar until they had toured a dozen of them. Finally, Lee complained. "Listen Larry, it was a great scheme, but my knees are getting sore from hitting the floor so much."

Larry shook his head. "What are you complaining about?" he said, "We lost the hot dog after the second bar!"

10.

Jones took his nymphomaniac wife to the doctor for treatment. "This is one hot potato of a lady, doctor," he said. "Maybe you can do something for her? She goes for any man, and I get very jealous."

"We'll see," the doctor said. He directed Mrs. Jones into his examining room, closed the door behind him, and told her to undress. Then he told her to get onto the examining table on her stomach.

The moment he touched her buttocks, she began to moan and squirm. This was too much for the doctor to resist, so he climbed up on top of her and began to screw her.

Jones heard moans and groans coming from the examination room. Unable to control himself, he pushed open the door to be confronted by the sight of the doctor astride his wife and banging away.

"What are you doin', Doc?" he shouted.

The flustered doctor said, "Oh, it's you, Mr. Jones? I'm taking your wife's temperature!"

Jones opened his switchblade knife and began to hone it on his sleeve very deliberately. "Doc," he said, "when you take that thing out, it sure better have numbers on it!"

11.
He was on his way home when he came upon a woman standing in the street, sobbing hysterically. "What's the matter, lady?" he asked.

She could only cry, "Schultz is dead. Schultz is dead!"

He shook his head and continued walking. Suddenly he came upon another woman sobbing, "Schultz is dead! Schultz is dead!"

He couldn't get over it, because soon he came upon still another woman weeping over the same thing. He had never seen so many unhappy women. And then he came upon a scene that caused him to stop. A trolley car had run over a man and cut him into pieces. There, on the pavement next to the body, was this foot long penis, and a dozen women were standing around crying hysterically, "Schultz is dead! Schultz is dead!"

When he arrived home, he greeted his wife with, "I just saw the damnedest thing. A trolley car ran over a man and cut off his cock, and would you believe it, the cock was a foot long."

"Oh my God!" the wife cried. "Schultz is dead! Schultz is dead!"

12.

Once upon a time there was a sperm named Stanley who lived inside a famous movie actor. Stanley was a very healthy sperm. He'd do pushups and somersaults and limber himself up all the time, while the other sperm just lay around on their stomachs not doing a thing.

One day one of them became curious enough to ask Stanley why he exercised all day.

Stanley said, "Look, pal, only one sperm gets a woman pregnant. Well, when the right time comes, I'm going to be that one."

A few days later, they all felt themselves getting hotter and hotter, and they knew that it was getting to be their time to go. They were released abruptly and, sure enough, there was Stanley swimming far ahead of all the others.

Suddenly Stanley stopped, turned around, and began to swim back with all his might. "Go back! Go back!" he shouted. "It's a blow job!"

13.

The famous Greek shipowner, Ori Oristotle, was having a house built on his large estate in Greece. He said to the architect, "Don't disturb that tree over there, because directly under that tree is where I had my first sex."

"How sentimental, Mr. Oristotle," the architect said. "Right under that tree."

"Yes," continued Ori Oristotle, "and don't touch that tree over there either. Because that's where her mother stood watching while I was having my first sex."

"Her mother just stood there while you were fucking her daughter?" the architect asked.

"That's right," said the Greek shipowner.

"But, Mr. Oristotle, what did her mother say?"

"Baaaa."

14.

The judge came home and found his wife in bed with his very best friend.

"Hey you!" he shouted. "What do you think you're doing?"

"See," the wife said to the man beside her, "I told you he was stupid."

15.

The seedy-looking girl walked into a seedy-looking saloon. A couple of seedy-looking customers hovered at the bar.

"Gimme a Schlitz," she said.

She took the glass of beer and swallowed it in one gulp. Then she fell to the floor in a dead faint.

"Come, give me a hand," the bartender called. The two customers helped the bartender carry her into the back room. One of the men glanced around and said, "Listen, nobody'll know. How about we all give her a quick fuck?"

They did just that. An hour or so later, she came to and said, "Where am I? What time is it? I've got to get home." And out she went.

Next afternoon, there were six men hanging around the bar when the same girl came in, walked up to the bartender and said, "Gimme a Schlitz."

She drank it down in one gulp and then fell to the floor in a dead faint.

The men carried her to the back room and the fucking performance was repeated, except that now there were seven, including the bartender.

The next day when she came in, there were twenty-one men waiting.

"Gimme a Schlitz," she said. She swallowed it in one gulp, fell to the floor in a dead faint, and was carried to the back room, where all twenty-one men partook of her.

When she arrived on the fourth day, word had really spread, and there were more than seventy men in the bar, waiting eagerly with lustful eyes and eager cocks. As she walked up to the bar, the bartender pushed a glass of beer toward her.

"You want your Schlitz, Miss?" he said.

"No," she said. "You better give me a Miller. That Schlitz gives me a pain in the cunt!"

16.

Marilyn had a parrot for a pet, but the parrot would embarrass her whenever she came into the apartment with a man. He would shout all kinds of obscenities, always leading off with "Somebody's gonna get it tonight! Somebody's gonna get it tonight!"

In desperation, Marilyn went to her local pet shop and explained her parrot problem to the pet shop proprietor.

"What you need," he said, "is a female parrot too. I don't have one on hand, but I'll order one for you. In the meantime you could borrow this female owl until the female parrot arrives."

Marilyn took the owl home and put it near her parrot. It was immediately obvious that the parrot didn't care for the owl. He glowered at it.

That night, Marilyn wasn't her usual nervous self as she opened the door to bring her gentleman friend in for a nightcap. Then suddenly she heard the parrot screech and she knew that nothing had changed.

"Somebody's gonna get it tonight! Somebody's gonna get it tonight!" the parrot shrieked.

The owl said, "Whoo? Whoo?"

And the parrot said, "Not you, you big-eyed bitch!"

Roger Price's 10 Most Popular and Practical Sex Positions

1. Sixty-nine
2. Ninety-six
3. Sixty-six and ninety-nine (not recommended for beginners)

4. Thirty-three (sometimes known as "Rover's Delight" or "The Doggie Way")
5. Twenty-twenty (eyeball to eyeball)
6. Seven (for hermits and lonely people)
7. Seventy-one (a woman and a voyeur)
8. One hundred and twelve (don't ask)
9. Forty-two, eighty-one... hike! (popular with the Dallas Cowboys Cheerleaders)
10. Fifty-eight and a quarter (disgusting, forget it)

—Exclusive for *The Book of Sex Lists*

Roger Price

9

The wisdom of sex may be found in the Bible or on the wall of a men's room at New York City's Columbia University.
Here are some of the utterings of wise men!

---

9 Aphorisms of Sex

1. A stiff prick has no conscience.
2. The most beautiful woman in the room has pimples on her ass.
3. Beautiful tits do not a great lay make.
4. The man with the largest penis is not always the best lover.
5. Women, like black cats, all look alike in the dark.
6. When a girl is big enough, she's old enough.
7. A woman's "no" generally means "maybe" and her "maybe" always means "yes" if you play your cards right.
8. More than a mouthful (penis or breast) is wasted.
9. It's the man behind the gun that counts.

1 Short Essay on Sex

Sex is the most flexible and adaptable game in the world. One person can play alone. Two people play regularly. Three play and they call it a *menage à trois*. Four or more (unlimited numbers) play and call it an orgy. Men can play with women, and usually do.

Men can play with men, and sometimes do. Women can play with women, and sometimes do. You can play fast, as for example when you're double-parked. You can take hours on a lazy Sunday when it's raining outside and there's no football or baseball on the boob tube.

You can play it to silence or the best music in the world. There's no other game in the world that can use so many parts of the body. In handball or boxing you use both hands to hit with and both feet to get around. In a sex encounter you can use many organs of the body and get into every orifice of the body.

Sex is the only game played by the people of all nations, creeds, colors and sexes. Finally, you can play for keeps and bring life into the world, or play for fun and usually have it, or play for money and, if you're of the female gender, they'll call you a whore.

> —Compiled from correspondence between Bennett Cerf and the author.

6 Examples of Sexual Graffiti Found
on the Men's Room Walls at Columbia University

1. Tap toilet wall for blow job
2. Don't worry, everybody masturbates
3. Up yours, Anita Bryant
4. Black may be beautiful and tan may be grand, but a white prick is to lick
5. Live each day as if it were your last: Screw like crazy
6. It's better with Mary Jane

> —For analysis of graffiti, see John A. Bates and Michael Martin, "The Thematic Content of Graffiti as a Non Reactive Indicator of Male and Female Attitudes," *Journal of Sex Research*, vol. 16. no. 4, Nov. 1980. Also *Encyclopedia of Graffiti* by Robert Reisner and Lorraine Wechsler

10

Here are some of the stars of sex.

Allan J. Wilson's 10 Favorite Burlesque Stars

Allan J. Wilson has been a burlesque fan from the days when a burlesque performer would graduate from the Hudson Burlesque Theatre in Union City, New Jersey, to the loud, flashy emporiums on 42nd Street between Broadway and 8th Avenue.

Here are his ten favorite strippers. These aren't alphabetical because Sir Allan wanted the list to reflect the true order of his preference.

1. Lillian Murray
2. Margie Hart
3. Gypsy Rose Lee
4. Ann Corio
5. Lois DeFee
6. Georgia Southern
7. Carrie Finnell
8. Sherry Britton
9. Lili St. Cyr
10. Rita Royce

Lili St. Cyr

Not on this list are dozens of others including Tempest Storm, Liz Renay, Marilyn Chambers, Sally Rand and Candy Barr.

Al Goldstein's 10 Best Porno Actresses

(Based on a combination of sexuality and acting ability)

1. Marilyn Chambers
2. Seka
3. Georgina Spelvin
4. Marlene Willoughby
5. Veronica Hart

6. Annette Haven
7. Gloria Leonard
8. Tiffany Clark
9. Linda Lovelace
10. Samantha Fox

John Springer's 13 Sex Symbols
of the Movies
Plus 13 Beautiful (but Not
Necessarily Sensual) Lovers

There's nothing more personal than one's own list of "sex symbols." What is sexy to you may be Jean Harlow to me—and Jean Harlow to me was funny and rowdy but more of a parody of sex appeal (like Mae West) than the real thing.

Louise Brooks

So here they are—my own idea of the (baker's) dozen sexiest sirens of the silver screen. No, there's no Farrah Fawcett here, no Jessica Lange, not even a Miss Piggy. Maybe the lack of new sex bombs is my own hangup. Then so be it. And keep in mind—the key word is personal. And I wouldn't dare pick them in any order except alphabetical!

1. *Louise Brooks.* If one thought about her at all when she was making movies—and not very many did—it was as a pert flapper with a distinctive black patent-leather helmet of hair. It wasn't until long after her heyday that her almost unknown great Pabst German films, *Pandora's Box* and *Diary of a Lost Girl*, were given limited circulation in this country. And Louise Brooks in those films was the epitome of sheer sex.

2. *Nancy Carroll.* She may have been thought of more appropriately as "Sweetie" or "Honey"—but Nancy Carroll was "sexy" to this kid. Up until she came onto the scene, movie stars meant Douglas Fairbanks and Tom Mix. Nancy Carroll changed all that. She was probably the prettiest girl in movies and in those days, "pretty" to me was synonymous with "sexy."

3. *Jane Fonda.* She had her deliberately sexy period in the Vadim-*Barbarella* era. But today's Fonda with her more mature beauty, her crisp and forthright personality—she's the girl who makes the list.

4. *Rita Hayworth.* Of the vaunted "sex goddesses" of the thirties and forties, Ava Gardner and Lana Turner both had their moments. But, in this corner, Rita Hayworth was it. Hayworth emanated sex appeal even when she was a squeaky-clean *Cover Girl* or a drab street girl (in *Angels Over Broadway*). And when she really worked at it—as *Gilda*, for instance—wow!

5. *Lena Horne.* Even when they just posed her leaning on a column and singing for scenes that could be cut out for the South, Lena Horne provided excitement. The eyes still blaze, the teeth still flash and the years only add to the voltage.

6. *Janet Leigh.* Alfred Hitchcock had the knack of bringing out the sex appeal in cool blonde beauties like Madeleine Carroll and Grace Kelly, but his best step in that direction was Janet

Leigh in *Psycho* right up to the moment she got into the shower. Most of her movie roles didn't give her that much chance to show it, but the sex was there, and trust Old Master Hitchcock to bring it out!

7. *Sophia Loren*. Ah, Sophia Loren! Ah, Mama mia! All woman and all sex.

8. *Myrna Loy*. Is there sex after marriage? Take a look at Myrna Loy, so cool and yet so warm. She served her apprenticeship as Oriental vamps, but it was when she became the movies' "perfect wife" to the likes of Powell, Gable, March, and Grant that she showed you what wedded sex was all about.

9. *Marilyn Monroe*. On and off screen, Marilyn Monroe radiated sex as naturally as she breathed and there was always that vulnerability added to it that her competitors could never achieve. It's the thing that launched her, put her on a pedestal and eventually destroyed her. But it's why she'll never be forgotten.

Marilyn Monroe

10. *Maureen O'Sullivan*. No wonder Tarzan was the fantasy here of millions of men—with someone like Jane to swing home to. Sorry, Bo—we mean Maureen O'Sullivan.

11. *Sylvia Sydney*. She spent too much movie time in tenements and prisons, but nobody had more earthy sensuality than *Sylvia Sidney*. And nobody kissed more passionately.

12. *Simone Signoret*. Brigitte Bardot was just a sex kitten; Simone Signoret was the cat. Even grown uncaringly older and fat, you still catch the sparks that flamed up in those *Casque d'Or* days.

13. *Tuesday Weld*. When we first saw her, Tuesday Weld was the right age to play *Lolita*—and what a shame she didn't. She's now frequently cast as a faded woman (*Who'll Stop the Rain?*, *Thief*), but the sex excitement she generates is as strong as it ever was.

And a postscript:

"Beautiful" isn't always "sexy" but there's joy—not necessarily sensual—in just looking at the screen faces. Of course, to this fellow, all those sexy ladies are beauties and all of the following beauties are sexy—but in different degrees. Only one, Lana, makes both lists.

I happen to adore the faces of Katharine Hepburn, Audrey Hepburn, Liv Ullmann, Barbara Stanwyck, and Margaret Sullavan. However, I know they are not conventional beauties.

I'm a pushover for the curly-nosed Irish-eyed freshness of Marsha Hunt, but I suppose she's like a couple of my sexy ladies in that you could call her "pretty," "the prettiest" but not necessarily "beautiful." There is a difference—subtle but it exists.

Some bona fide beauties—Vanessa Redgrave, Julie Christie, Jean Muir—do everything possible to downgrade their looks. There are those—Gene Tierney, Frances Farmer, Arlene Dahl, and even Loretta Young—who are raving beauties in one setting but not at all much to look at the next time around.

So here, with apologies to many—from Banky to Bennett to Bergen and Bisset, is the John Springer list of candidates for inclusion in my "Hall of the Most Beautiful Movie Actresses. (In alphabetical order, of course!)

I'll have to leave those Caroles and Claudettes and Judys and Joans, Brookes and Barbras to your personal list.

Elizabeth Taylor

 1. Mary Astor
 2. Ingrid Bergman
 3. Madeleine Carroll
 4. Dolores Del Rio
 5. Marlene Dietrich
 6. Greta Garbo
 7. Ava Gardner
 8. Lena Horne
 9. Vivien Leigh
10. Maureen O'Hara
11. Jean Seberg
12. Gloria Stuart
13. Elizabeth Taylor

—exclusive for *The Book of Sex Lists*

11

And here is something about you and the stars and the stars and the stars.

The 12 Astrological Signs
and Their Sexual Significance

ARIES—Birthday: 3/21 to 4/19
You are an arrogant and self-centered lover. Your pleasure and gratification must come first. Your sexual creativity is truly innovative and original but it is designed to further your own self-satisfaction. Choose your partners from those who prefer to be dominated.

WARREN BEATTY and ALI MacGRAW

TAURUS—Birthday: 4/20 to 5/20
You tend to set your lover on a pedestal without analyzing the reasons for doing so. However, if your lover tries to fence you in in any way, you'll kick up your heels and run. You know you're a faithful lover and you resent anyone trying to hold you or force you. You need a permanent relationship for your own emotional security.

JILL CLAYBURGH and RICKY NELSON

GEMINI—Birthday: 5/21 to 6/21
You are a rebel, not content to enjoy conventional relationships. Your lover must be content to accept what you offer freely while you always retain that untouched personal inner core. Left to explore, you develop heights of sexual creativeness.

BROOKE SHIELDS and DENNIS WEAVER

CANCER—Birthday: 6/22 to 7/22
You crave security in your emotional life. You may be clinging or independent, depending on how you react to what your lover promises. You defend your mate fiercely. You are at all times an emotionally sensitive person which makes you a difficult lover.

SYLVESTER STALLONE and KAREN BLACK

LEO—Birthday: 7/23 to 8/22
You require approval to a degree that may interfere with complete fulfillment of your love relationships. Remember, your mate needs a pat on the head also. You'd achieve greater satisfaction in a love affair if you could occasionally lose yourself in it. You have no problems of conscience, so for you love may well be unconventional, but it will always be discreet. You will strive mightily to obtain your lover's approval of your performance.

ROBERT DeNIRO and LUCILLE BALL

VIRGO—Birthday: 8/23 to 9/22
Your single-minded absorption in each thing you do makes you an intense and exciting bed partner. With the right partner or even the wrong one, you seek satisfaction to the exclusion of all outside circumstances. Lucky the sex-mate who has you in bed!

JACQUELINE BISSET and SEAN CONNERY

LIBRA—Birthday: 9/23 to 10/23
Your carnal passions are bestowed only on those who are available! But you can also lead a lover on and give nothing. You can lose yourself totally in the sex act as long as you don't feel threatened by an overly dominating partner. If that happens, you turn cold and withdraw completely.

LARRY HAGMAN and ROMY SCHNEIDER

SCORPIO—Birthday: 10/24 to 11/21
You are a devil and you are an angel. You won't hesitate to explore the depths of sexual experiences with your partner, but then, with bewildering inconsistency, you turn puritanical. Somehow you move to satisfy yourself without offering equal satisfaction to your partner.

SALLY FIELD and RICHARD DREYFUS

SAGITTARIUS—Birthday: 11/22 to 12/21
You rush into relationships eagerly, hungry to taste whatever your new partner has to offer. But woe to the mate who expects to hold on to you. The next warm bed that offers a new experience will find you a ready taker, eager to taste new fruits. However, you won't stay around to seek the depths of sex or love. A quick roll in the hay and off you go again.

FRANK LANGELLA and ELLEN BURSTYN

CAPRICORN—Birthday: 12/22 to 1/19
Your sex life is safe and stable, rarely rising to great heights. You may be free with sex, but when it comes to marriage you'll choose carefully, selecting a "suitable"mate. You believe it's just as easy for love to live in the same house with money. Your responses to sexual advances by your partner are instinctive rather than studied. You give little thought to pleasing your sex-partner as long as you are satisfied yourself.

DOLLY PARTON and JOHN DENVER

AQUARIUS—Birthday: 1/20 to 2/18
You like to live in a crowd and carry this into group sex experiences. Sex is a social outlet. You are an affectionate, unconventional partner and rarely lack willing companionship in your exploits.

FARRAH FAWCETT and JOHN TRAVOLTA

PISCES—Birthday: 2/19 to 3/20
You set your sights high in love as in life, and you never quite reach your goal. How can your partner live up to your expectations when even you don't know what it is you really want? You can be a warm, tender, satisfying partner if you just forget what you want and concentrate on your mate's desires instead.

RON HOWARD and LIZA MINNELLI

12

Sex is sometimes something to sing about

2 Operas That Are Sexy Because of Their Content and Because of the Aural/Visual Erotic Stimulation They Provide

1. *Samson et Dalila* by Camille Saint-Saëns—Dalila's aria "Mon coeur s'ouvre a ta voix" is heard to the accompaniment of a light rainfall whose insistent drumming has a powerfully erotic evocative effect.

2. *Thaïs* by Jules Massenet—At this opera's world premiere an appropriate accident happened to Thaïs as interpreted by Sibyl Sanderson: One of her shoulder straps broke, revealing her breasts. The spectators were delirious.

> —exclusive for *The Book of Sex Lists* by Alfonso Tornusciolo, M.D., P.C., a New York City psychoanalyst who loves opera.

3 Operas in Which the Music Alone
Conveys Sexuality

1. *The Marriage of Figaro* by W.A. Mozart (the personal preference of the list donor)—The carrying on is continuous. Cherubino is one of the most lustful personages in opera and when he sings that he is in love with love, he is referring to a very physical condition and not to a platonic feeling.

2. *Manon* by Jules Massenet—What real man could resist Manon's temptation to the music of Massenet in the scene at St. Sulpice?

3. *Tristan und Isolde* by Richard Wagner—The love duet is probably the best musical rendition of climaxing love.
   —exclusive for *The Book of Sex Lists* by
   Alfonso Tornusciolo, M.D., P.C.

12 Sexiest Metropolitan Opera Sopranos
(From 1950 to the Present)

Nick Meglin is an editor at *Mad* magazine. He is also an opera lady lover. Here are a dozen of his favorite chirping damsels.

1. Maria Callas, *Tosca*
2. Carol Neblett, *L'Incoronazione di Poppea*
3. Anja Sylia, *Salome*
4. Grace Bumbry, *Salome*
5. Gwyneth Jones, *Salome*
6. Risë Stevens, *Carmen*
7. Frederica von Stade, *Il Ritorno D'Ulisse in Patria*
8. Marilin Niska, *The Makropoulos Affair*
9. Anna Moffo, *La Traviata*
10. Shirley Verrett, *Samson et Delila*
11. Gail Robinson, *Il Barbiere di Siviglia*
12. Patrice Munsel, *Die Fledermaus*

I haven't included films based on operas, or I'd surely mention how delicious Gina Lollobrigida looked as Nedda in a film version of *Pagliacci* and Sophia Loren in *Aïda*.

It seemed fitting that 3, 4 and 5 be used for the 3 sexy Salomes. The role seems to bring out the best in the ladies as they play up to the Johns.

—Nick Meglin especially for *The Book of Sex Lists*

Mitch Miller's 8 Love Songs to Have Sex By

1. "All the Things You Are," Jerome Kern
2. "Bewitched, Bothered and Bewildered," Richard Rogers
3. "Easy to Love," Cole Porter
4. "I Only Have Eyes for You," Harry Warren

5. "I've Got My Love to Keep Me Warm," Irving Berlin
6. "The Man That Got Away," Harold Arlen
7. "September Song," Kurt Weill
8. "Stormy Weather," Harold Arlen

A 6-Pack of Sex-Packed Songs

1. "Let's Put Out the Lights and Go to Bed" by Herman Hupfield (1931). Hupfield also wrote "As Time Goes By," which was published a year earlier, recorded by Rudy Vallee, and faded into obscurity until it was used in the film *Casablanca*. "Let's Put Out the Lights..." was also recorded by Rudy Vallee at the Atlantic City Steel Pier. It became a favorite during the Depression, but when played on radio it was called "Let's Put Out the Lights and Go to Sleep."

2. "Do It Again" (1922) had a George Gershwin melody with a Buddy De Sylva lyric. The song was banned from the airwaves because of its suggestive lyrics, which were chock full of double entendres.

3. "You Took Advantage of Me" was a Rodgers and Hart hit (1928). To make it palatable to the radio public, the line "I'm so hot and bothered that I can't tell my elbow from my ass" was changed to "...my elbow from my ear."

4. "I'm Forever Blowing Bubbles" was published in 1919 and smoothly got past all the censors. It sold two and a half million copies of sheet music. And made any girl named "Bubbles" the butt of lots of kidding.

5. "I'm Coming, Virginia" by Spud Murphy and Donald Heywood, published in 1925, became a jazz standard. Jazz itself was a word that originated in the cathouses of New Orleans as a euphemism for sex. "Honey, you want to jazz me? You got to dig me deep, man, 'cause I'se a long-bodied woman" was a common approach from the working girls on the streets of the French Quarter.

6. "Clap Hands, Here Comes Charlie" was written by Billy Rose in honor of a local chorine, first named Charline, who had given many of the music publishers' contact men (song pluggers) cases of gonorrhea—a venereal disease commonly known as "the clap."

Nat Hentoff's 12 Albums to Make Love By

Nat Hentoff is a jazz critic and columnist. In the February 1981 issue of *Cosmopolitan*, he selected these 12 albums for "aural sex."

1. Miles Davis, *Sketches of Spain*, Columbia
2. Jimmy Rowles, *We Could Make Such Beautiful Music Together*, Xanadu
3. Sarah Vaughan, *How Long Has This Been Going On?* Pablo
4. The Eagles, *Hotel California*, Capitol
5. Bob Seeger, *Night Moves*, Capitol
6. Frank Sinatra, *In the Wee Small Hours*, Capitol
7. Johnny Duncan, *See You When the Sun Goes Down*, Columbia
8. Peter Rowan, *Peter Rowan*, Flying Fish
9. Joan Baez, *Diamonds and Rust*, A & M
10. Bach, *The Art of the Fugue*, Philips.
11. The Guarneri Quartet, Debussy, *String Quartet;* Ravel, *String Quartet*, RCA Victor
12. Ravi Shankar, *Ragas*, Fantasy

Wolfman Jack's 12 Famous Songs with Dirty Lyrics

Wolfman Jack is a popular disc jockey. He is also a television personality, hosting the late-night concert series *The Midnight*

Special and producing and starring in his own internationally syndicated program.

Wolfman has appeared in such TV series as *The Odd Couple*, *Vega$*, and *Wonder Woman*. He played himself in the hit movie *American Graffiti*.

1. "Work with Me, Annie" (Hank Ballard and the Midnighters)
2. "Annie Had a Baby" (Hank Ballard and the Midnighters)
3. "Love to Love You, Baby" (Donna Summer)
4. "You're Breakin' My Heart" (Harry Nielsen)
5. "Mickey's Monkey" (Smokey Robinson and the Miracles)
6. "Tell Me Somethin' Good" (Rufus)
7. "Honky Tonk Women" (The Rolling Stones)
8. "Lay Lady Lay" (Bob Dylan)
9. "Dance with Me, Henry" (Etta James)
10. "Got My Mojo Working" (Muddy Waters)
11. "Rock and Roll Hootchie-Coo" (Rich Derringer)
12. "Louie Louie" (The Kingsmen)

—Exclusive for *The Book of Sex Lists*

Wolfman Jack's 12 Sexiest Popular Singers

1. Frank Sinatra
2. Elvis Presley
3. Engelbert Humperdinck
4. Tom Jones
5. Linda Ronstadt
6. Rudy Vallee
7. Vic Damone
8. Bing Crosby
9. Dean Martin
10. Lola Falana
11. Gladys Knight
12. Donna Summer

—exclusive for *The Book of Sex Lists*

4 Famous Homosexual Songwriters

1. Noël Coward ("Mad About the Boy")
2. Cole Porter ("I'm in Love with a Soldier Boy")
3. Lorenz Hart ("Take Him")
4. Ivor Novello ("We'll Gather Lilacs in the Spring Again")

Sir Noël Coward

12 Suggestive Double-Entendre Songs

Dick Manning is one of America's most successful songwriters. His hits include *Takes Two to Tango, Fascination, Hawaiian Wedding Song, Allegheny Moon, Papa Loves Mambo,* and *The Pussy Cat Song.*

These are his choices as the songs with the most sparkling double-entendre lyrics:

1. *All of You*—Cole Porter (*Silk Stockings,* 1935)
2. *But in the Morning*—Cole Porter (*DuBarry Was a Lady,* 1929)
3. *Doin' What Comes Naturally*—Irving Berlin (*Annie Get Your Gun,* 1946)

4. *Ev'ry Little Movement Has a Meaning All Its Own*—Otto Harbach and Karl Hoschna (*Madame Sherry*, 1910)
5. *I said "No." He said "Please."* (Last lines: "Then at last I confess, I said 'Yes, yes, yes, yes.' That's how I subscribed to Esquire magazine.")
6. *The Lady Is a Tramp*—Richard Rodgers and Lorenz Hart (*Babes in Arms*, 1937)
7. *Let's Do It*—Cole Porter (*Paris*, 1928)
8. *Love for Sale*—Cole Porter (*The New Yorkers*, 1930; banned from radio because of its suggestive lyrics)
9. *Mademoiselle from Armentieres*—Anonymous (1918)
10. *She Had to Go and Lose It at the Astor*—Hughie Prince and Don Ray (1939)
11. *She Wouldn't Do What I Asked Her To*—Sidney D. Mitchell, Sam Gottlieb, Philip Boutelje and Al Burt (1923)
12. *Wouldja For a Big Red Apple?*—Johnny Mercer (sung in Monette Moore's club in Harlem by Billie Holiday, 1933)

—exclusive for *The Book of Sex Lists*

3 Obscene Song Lyrics

1. *"The Girl Ran Down the Burning Deck"*

The Girl ran down the burning deck;
The Captain, he pursued her.
The white of egg ran down her leg....
The Captain, he had screwed her.

2. *"A Gassing Young Girl from St. Paul"*

A gassing young girl from St. Paul
Wore a newspaper dress to a ball.
Her dress caught on fire
And burned her entire
Front page, sporting section and all.

3. *"Screwy Dick"* (A favorite of mechanics and engineers)

Here lie the bones of Screwy Dick,
Born to the world with a spiral prick.
He searched the world with might and main,
But all his searching was in vain
Until, with the help of Alan Funt,
He found a girl with a spiral cunt.
One look and the poor guy dropped stone dead
For the Goddamn thing had a left-hand thread!

—Selected by Dick Manning especially
for *The Book of Sex Lists*

105

13

Money makes the world go 'round. Power corrupts. Love is everywhere.
But s-e-x can be bought for cash, secured through power and persuaded with love.
Sex makes the universe stop and go! Here some literary light is thrown on the subject.

9 Great Writers of Sexy Letters

1. *Louis Armstrong*—His candid letters sizzle with passion and he could play on a woman's emotions as adroitly as on a trumpet. His nickname, *Satchmo*, is short for Satchelmouth, a perfect piece of equipment for a sensual lover.

2. *Napoleon Bonaparte*—His amorous letters to Josephine during the Italian campaign were literal "hot line" to Paris. A typical comment: "I long to cover you with a thousand kisses."

3. *Robert Browning*—This sedately bearded and seemingly staid Victorian poet was an ardent suitor, as his beautiful love letters to Elizabeth Barrett (later his wife) testify. But to another woman he wrote: "If you will let me visit you again, I promise to make my hands behave." A Browning buff bought this incriminating note for $500 and then burned it, observing: "No one must ever know this about Browning."

4. *George A. Custer*—The future Indian fighter's love letters to his sweetheart, Mollie J. Holland of Cadiz, Ohio, mostly signed "Bachelor Boy," were so impassioned that Mollie cut out many passages with her sewing scissors, leaving only such relatively modest remarks as, "When are we going to get into the trundle bed?"

5. *Salvador Dali*—The celebrated surrealist wrote torrid letters in fractured French, often enriching them with erotic sketches.

6. *John Keats*—His immortal love letters to Fanny Brawne reveal the fierce passion of the poet who so desired intense sensations that he sprinkled cayenne pepper on his tongue before sipping claret.

   To Fanny he wrote: "Love is my religion. You have ravished me away by a power I cannot resist. I cannot breathe without you."

7. *John F. Kennedy*—The intimate, unpublished correspondence of our thirty-fifth President abounds in four-letter words and sexy comments. To the sweetheart who rejected his proposal of marriage only six months before he was wed to Jacqueline Bouvier, Kennedy wrote a passionate letter, pleading that she reconsider, adding: "You are the only woman I have ever loved or ever will love."

8. *Wolfgang A. Mozart*—The famed composer was a passionate lover and delighted in using explicit language in his letters, thus putting his modern editors to the embarrassment of censoring his uninhibited vocabulary.

9. *Giacomo Puccini*—An acknowledged master of the four-letter word, the great composer wrote poems in his letters to his mistresses that are so explicit they would bring a blush to the cheeks of a seasoned courtesan. Puccini had scores of lovers and once observed that he might have written many more operas if he hadn't spent so much of his life horizontal.

   —Prepared by Charles Hamilton exclusively for *The Book of Sex Lists*

7 Literary Works About Women
Who Loved Women

1. *Here Lies the Heart*, by Mercedes de Acosta. Its author claims in this autobiography that she bedded down both with Marlene Dietrich and with Greta Garbo.

2. *The King of a Rainy Country*, by Brigid Brophy. A teenage girl finds a schoolmate's naked photo in a porno book and searches her out, finally seducing her from the arms of a vocalist in Venice.

3. *Going Down with Janis*, by Peggy Caserta. Scenes of the physical love between the author and singer Janis Joplin.

4. *The Well of Loneliness*, by Radclyffe Hall. Published in 1928, this was a breakthrough book. It describes an upper-class English lady who agonizes before accepting her own lesbianism. An international best seller, though rather tame by today's standards.

5. *The Killing of Sister George*, by Frank Marcus. An English play in which the star of a soap opera is deprived both of her role and of the young girl she loves by another woman.

6. *Choices*, by Nancy Toder. A straightforward novel about love between women and the fear and confusion of a woman coming to terms with her sexual and emotional attraction to other women.

7. *Rubyfruit Jungle*, by Rita Mae Brown. A comic view of growing up and an offbeat positive look at lesbianism.

20 Novels, Plays and Films in Which
the Central Character Was a Prostitute

1. *Anna Christie* by Eugene O'Neill (1922)—The daughter of an old seafaring captain earns her living through the oldest profession. Her love for an Irish deckhand reforms her. The play gave Garbo her talking-film debut.

2. *Butterfield 8* by John O'Hara (1935)—The story of Gloria Wandrous (based on a society courtesan named Starr Faithful) and her career as a high-society call girl. Elizabeth Taylor played Gloria in the successful film.

3. *Camille* by Alexander Dumas fils (1852)—Marguerite Gautier was the dramatic character based on the life of Alphonsine Plessis, the legendary courtesan who wore white camillias nightly except for her "unwell" evenings, when she wore red ones.

4. *For Men Only* by Beth Brown (1932)—The story of Lily Love, former whore and the Madame of New Orleans' fanciest brothel. The book was considered daring for its time and sold nearly two million copies in various editions.

5. *Irma la Douce* by Alexander Breffort and Marguerite Monnot (1956)—First produced on Broadway in 1960, the play revolves around the Paris underworld and Irma, its most successful whore. A policeman pretends to be a pimp when he falls in love with Irma.

6. *Mrs. Warren's Profession* by George Bernard Shaw (1893)—The great Irish writer's impassioned attack against Victorian attitudes toward prostitution. The heroine's mother is a lady of beauty and intellect despite her youth as a whore.

7. *Nana* by Emile Zola (1880)—a drunkard's daughter grows up to be a third-rate actress in the Paris theater. Her main talent is a lethal sexuality, which she uses to attract and destroy rich men.

8. *Never on Sunday* by Jules Dassin (1960)—This film featured Melina Mercouri as a warm-hearted Greek whore who refuses to entertain patrons on Sundays.

9. *Rain* by John Colton and Clemence Randolph (1927)—A minister lectures Sadie Thompson, the San Francisco whore who sets up shop in the South Sea island of Pago Pago. He commits suicide after having sex with her, leaving Sadie with the deathless line: "Men! They're all pigs!" Adapted from the Somerset Maugham short story "Miss Thompson" and recreated on stage and screen by such actresses as Jeanne Eagels, Gloria Swanson, Joan Crawford, Rita Hayworth, June Havoc, and Gwen Verdon.

Greta Garbo

10. *The Respectful Prostitute* by Jean-Paul Sartre (1947)—Sartre's story of an American whore who befriends a man unjustly accused of rape and about to be lynched by an angry mob. Meg Mundy starred in the American premiere.

11. *Sex* by Mae West (1926)—Mae West's great Broadway success in the role of Margie La Mont, Montreal prostitute, who gets revenge on a society woman whom she had befriended and who accuses her of robbery, by threatening to marry the society matron's son. Miss West went to jail for this one!

12. *Waterloo Bridge* by Robert E. Sherwood (1930)—One of the best modern dramas, this deals with a ballerina's love affair with a society soldier. When the officer is reported missing, the dancer supports herself through prostitution.

13. *The Fortunes and Misfortunes of Moll Flanders* by Daniel Defoe (1722)—Born in prison, Moll Flanders was married at an early age to a man who deserted her. She then passed from man to man, hoping to better herself with each new liaison. This novel is considered the first social novel of modern times.

14. *Roxana, the Fortunate Mistress* by Daniel Defoe (1724)—A sort of sequel to *Moll Flanders*, this novel tells the story of a beautiful young woman who marries early, lives with her husband for eight years, and gives birth to five children. When her husband deserts her, Roxana hits the skids and comes to a bad end.

15. *Of Human Bondage* by W. Somerset Maugham (1915)— Mildred Rogers, a tough, vulgar London waitress, becomes the object of Philip Carey's affection, though she treats him miserably. Finally, Philip frees himself from Mildred's hold while she sinks into prostitution and degeneracy.

16. *Klute* by Alan J. Pakula (written by Andy K. Lewis and Dave Lewis) (1971)—An extremely bright call girl (brilliantly portrayed by Jane Fonda) becomes involved in a murder case and is almost killed. Released by Warner Bros.

17. *Forever Amber* by Kathleen Winsor (1947)—One of the big, bestselling romantic novels of the forties. Amber St. Claire bounced "from bed to bed," as a contemporary review described it.

111

18. *Fanny Hill: Memoirs of a Woman of Pleasure* by John Cleland (1749)—Fanny begins her brothel career at the age of fifteen and continues it for the rest of her life. Long banned in Britain and America, this book has finally been recognized as a witty masterpiece—which contains not one vulgar word.

19. *The Best Little Whorehouse in Texas* by Larry L. King and Peter Masterson, with music and lyrics by Carole Hall (1978)— Miss Mona, who spent her youth as a popular hooker, becomes the proprietor of a popular brothel, mothering her girls and enjoying her own love affair with the town sheriff until a "moral majority" group shuts her down.

20. *The Rise and Fall of the City Mahagonny* by Kurt Weill and Bertolt Brecht (1930)—Jenny, one of the Widow Begbick's most popular whores, falls in love with the prospector Jimmy Mahoney until he runs out of money. In Mahagonny, all is permitted except poverty. One of the great Weill-Brecht operas.

3 Respectable Movies That Broke Sex Taboos

Film taboos have existed since the formation of the first movie-land-sponsored censorship board of review. In recent years, as attitudes have changed, sex in films has become more real. The establishment major movie companies have included scenes that would once be found only in under-the-counter porn films. And porn film producers have begun to use better plots and thus move closer to establishment films.

The following is a selection of "respectable movies" which shocked or titillated audiences because of a scene or two.

1. *Cleopatra* (1934) with Claudette Colbert. In this Cecil B. De Mille spectacular, the Paris-born Claudette took a bath in a large pool. And as she bathed, her breasts bobbed up and down in the water. This was actually Claudette Colbert's second sexy film bath. In De Mille's *Sign of the Cross* she was Nero's wicked

consort, Poppaea, and bathed in asses' milk. This followed her 1931 role in which she sang to Miriam Hopkins, "You've got to jazz up your lingerie." Thereafter, Ms. Colbert stopped playing sex sirens and turned to comedy.

Hedy Lamarr
in Ecstasy

2. *Ecstasy* (1933) was a Czech-made film that featured an un-known Viennese teenager named Hedwig Kiesler. She became better known as Hedy Lamarr. The film achieved notoriety when Ms. Lamarr swam and then ran through the woods in the nude. She was seduced, and the closeups of her face during the sex scene gave the film its title. It is said that the expressions of ecstasy on her face were prompted by pins being stuck in her buttocks, a technique created by her director.

Hedy Lamarr married a wealthy manufacturer who attempted to remove the film from the market by buying up all prints. But as quickly as he paid for one, two more would appear. When Hedy left this husband for film stardom and her new name in

America, she was followed to these shores by *Ecstasy*, which was exhibited in movie houses in 1940, and has continued to be shown ever since.

3. *Last Tango in Paris* (1973), with Marlon Brando, was a shocker when first released. It involved full nudity, with Brando playing an aging American widower who is involved with the voluptuous Maria Schneider. This explicit film received lots of attention and made lots of money. Comedians referred to it as "Butter Fingers" because of a scene in which Brando uses butter as a lubricant while he and Ms. Schneider engage in anal intercourse.

The Real Names of the Authors Of 2 Best Selling Sex Books That Were Written Under Pseudonyms

1. *The Sensuous Woman* by "J" was written by a former press agent who was known as Terry Garrity. She departed a publishing house where she'd been in charge of publicity because, although she was excellent at coaching authors for appearances on radio and television, she was unable to write press releases.

One day, while she was unemployed, the publisher Lyle Stuart phoned her to ask how she was doing.

"Terribly!" she said. "It's the middle of the month and I haven't paid my apartment rent. And I think I need some surgery and don't have any medical insurance."

She mentioned that in an hour she would be going to another publishing house for an employment interview.

"Terry, be in front of your door in thirty minutes. I'm coming uptown in a taxi and I'll drive you to your interview."

"You don't have to do that, Lyle," she said. "It's only eight blocks away."

"Terry," he said, "I'm going to change your life."

When Stuart picked her up and told her that he wanted her to write a book, she didn't conceal her disappointment. Her face fell. "Don't you remember," she said. "I left your employ because I couldn't write press releases."

"I want you to write a sex book for women," he said.

"Do you mean like the books of Dr. [Albert] Ellis?"

"No, I want you to write the way you talk. Terry, I want you to make cocksucking respectable in America."

They drove for a few minutes in silence, and then he said, "Give me a chapter and an outline and I'll give you an advance to cover your rent. We can make a lot of money together with this book."

"I'll try," she said, sounding not very confident.

When a chapter and outline were delivered, though, Stuart saw that Terry Garrity had grasped exactly what he wanted. He gave her a contract that provided for $300 on signing and additional amounts of money as the script was delivered for a total of $1,500.

The Sensuous Woman became a number one best seller in America, selling some 600,000 copies in cloth. The Dell paperback sold more than 10 million copies and is still selling.

The book was published in more than a dozen foreign language editions including French, Spanish, Italian, German, Japanese, Hebrew, and Dutch. It "made cocksucking respectable" not only in America but throughout the Western world.

Terry Garrity didn't want to use her real name as author because she was afraid it would embarrass her mother. Stuart suggested that she use an initial rather than a pseudonym and she submitted the script with the name "K."

Publisher Stuart didn't like that one because it reminded him too much of a Kellogg's breakfast cereal.

"Terry, what's your real name?" he asked.

"Joan," she said.

"Then let's call the author 'J.'"

Joan Garrity appeared on radio and television shows, and her identity became known to her mother. By this time her earnings were several hundred thousand dollars and her mother was very proud of her.

2. *The Sensuous Man* by "M" was a natural companion book to *The Sensuous Woman*. It too became a number one best seller, selling approximately 350,000 copies in cloth and 3.5 million in paperback.

Here the author was "M" (for "man").

Newspaper ads appeared in *The New York Times* to assure the public that the rumors that the book was written variously by Artie Shaw, Hugh Hefner, Lyle Stuart and others were simply not true.

The writer? Although the author had help from some acquaintances, *The Sensuous Man* was produced by the same person who wrote *The Sensuous Woman*: Joan "Terry" Garrity.

To date Ms. Garrity has been paid more than $1.8 million in royalties and lives in Palm Beach, Florida.

5 Popular Books with Double-Entendre Titles

1. *There I Stood With My Piccolo in My Hand* by Meredith Willson
2. *Every Frenchman Has One* by Olivia De Havilland
3. *Emily Is Easy* by Derrick Banger
4. *Rest Your Head Upon These Two* by Evelyn Hamlin
5. *Come Play in My Tunnel* by Dorothy Aaronson

10 Books Deemed Objectional by Various Censorship Groups

Censorship groups have forever been raging against literature when it contains sexual material. The theory seems to be that these groups are smart enough to decide what other people shouldn't read.

Some examples of the variety of books that have been attacked and removed from some library shelves over the years:

1. *The African Queen* by C.S. Forester
2. *A Farewell to Arms* by Ernest Hemingway
3. *Kitty Foyle* by Christopher Morley
4. *The Man with the Golden Arm* by Nelson Algren

5. *Pleasure Was My Business* by Madam Sherry
6. *Tales of the South Pacific* by James Michener
7. *The 42nd Parallel* by John Dos Passos
8. *Tropic of Cancer* by Henry Miller
9. *Ulysses* by James Joyce
10. *Where Did I Come From?* by Peter Mayle

Source: Sex, Pornography & Justice by
Albert B. Gerber

10 of the Best Selling Sex Books of All Time

1. *The ABZ of Love* by Inge and Sten Hegeler
2. *The Art and Science of Love* by Dr. Albert Ellis
3. *Everything You Ever Wanted to Know about Sex (But Were Afraid to Ask)* by Dr. David Reuben
4. *Ideal Marriage* by Theodore H. van de Velde
5. *The Joy of Sex* by Dr. Alex Comfort (more than 375,000 cloth edition and 5.4 million paperbacks)
6. *Love Without Fear* by Eustace Chesser
7. *A Marriage Manual* by Hannah and Abraham Stone
8. *A Sane Sex Life* by H.W. Long
9. *The Sensuous Man* by "M" (more than 300,000 cloth edition and more than 3.5 million paperbacks)
10. *The Sensuous Woman* by "J" (more than 600,000 copies of the cloth edition and 10 million paperbacks)

—Prepared by Morris Sorkin especially
for The Book of Sex Lists

Greg Nash's 6 Sexiest Comic-Book Heroes

Greg Nash has been an avid reader and collector of "superhero" comic books for more than twenty years. At one time his inventory totalled more than three thousand comic books. Nash is coauthor of *The Star Trek Make-a-Game Book* and is presently working on his own super-hero comic-book creation.

1. *Superman* (who else?). Just keep off the kryptonite panties.
2. *Wonder Woman.* Anyone who's into bondage beware! Chain her wrists to the bedpost and you're in for a very boring evening.
3. *The Flash.* For those who prefer "quickies."
4. *The Incredible Hulk.* Brute raw sex all the way. Don't forget to catch him while he's mad or you'll wind up with his puny alter-ego.
5. *The Silver Surfer.* And you thought doing it on a waterbed was fun!
6. *Batman and Robin.* For all the kinky ones who think "three's company."

—exclusive for *The Book of Sex Lists*

12 Famous People Who Wrote Secret Pornographic or Scatological Things

1. *Benjamin Franklin* (1706–1790). American stateman, writer, printer, diplomat, and scientist. Essay: "Advice to a Young Man on Choosing a Mistress."
2. *Eugene Field* (1850–1895). American poet and journalist. Short story: "Only a Boy." Poem: "Little Willie."
3. *David Herbert Lawrence* (1885–1930). English author. Novel: *Lady Chatterley's Lover.*
4. *Frank Harris* (1856–1931). American author and editor. An unusually frank autobiography: "My Life and Loves" (4 volumes).
5. *George Gordon Noel Lord Byron* (1788–1824). English poet. Poem: "The Bridal Night."
6. *Samuel Langhorne Clemens (Mark Twain)* (1835–1910). American author and humorist. Satires: "1601" and "The Science of Onanism."
7. *Theophile Gautier* (1811–1872). French poet, novelist and critic. Essay: "An Obscene Letter to the President."

8. *George Norman Douglas* (1868–1955). English novelist and essayist. Bawdy limericks.
9. *François Marie Arouet de Voltaire* (1694–1778). French author and philosopher. Poem: "Maid of Orleans."
10. *Sir William Schwenck Gilbert* (1836–1911) and *Sir Arthur Seymour Sullivan* (1842–1900). Collaborators in comic operas. Bawdy opera: "The Sod's Opera."
11. *Paul Verlaine* (1844–1896). French poet. Poem: "Women."
12. *Alfred de Musset* (1810–1857) French poet, novelist and dramatist. Poem: "Gamiani."

The Best Parts of 9 Novels

Gore Vidal, in his book *The Judgment of Paris*, says that "part of the pleasure of reading novels is the inevitable moment when the hero beds the heroine or, in certain advanced and decadent works, the hero beds another hero in an infernal glow of impropriety. The mechanical side of the operation is of intense interest to everyone. Partly, of course, because so few of us get entirely what we want when it comes to this sort of thing, and, too, there is something remarkably exciting about the sex lives of fictional characters."

Robert Reisner prepared a reader's guide to sex in literature titled *Show Me the Good Parts*. It cited the pages and described the action in more than 300 widely known books. The following is but a sampling.

1. *The Future Mister Dolan*, by Charles Gorham. Dolan picks up a woman in a movie theater. She takes him home and has an intense fifteen-minute sexual encounter with him. Later he returns and she acts as though she doesn't know him and orders him off the premises. Pages 93–97.

2. *A Charmed Life*, by Mary McCarthy. A pair of remarried former mates try sex again for old times' sake. He gets her excited but not enough for her to forget to worry about the safety of her good sofa. Pages 197–204.

3. *Desire and Other Stories*, by Clement Wood. Two sisters lose their virginity on separate dates. One describes the experience to her uncle. He performs oral sex on her. This enthralls her so that when the uncle comes wandering into the room at night to do it again, she switches places with her sister so her sister can share the same ecstasy. Pages 107–130.

4. *Lolita*, by Vladimir Nabokov. Humbert Humbert manages to masturbate his nymphet in a very devious manner. Pages 60–63.

5. *Thunder in the Heart*, by James Lee Weldon. A mother forces a young black man to have sexual intercourse with her while her daughter secretly watches in silence. Pages 52–56.

6. *Campus Love Club*, by David Challon. Marge is supposed to be the easiest conquest on the campus. Jeff takes her to his room and she says OK even before he can finish asking her. Pages 50–56.

7. *Studs Lonigan*, by James T. Farrell. A woman tries to recover some of the money she lost at the race track by selling her body to several men. Pages 231–240.

8. *Return to Peyton Place*, by Grace Metalious. A vivid and shocking description of a woman's rape-filled past. Pages 154–158.

9. *By Love Possessed*, by James Gould Cozzens. A young lady who gives herself to men freely has a young man arrested for rape. The defense attorney questions her in detail about how people can "do it" in the back seat of an automobile. Pages 148–159.

Michael Perkins' 10 Favorite Erotic Novels

Michael Perkins is America's foremost critic of erotic writing. He has reviewed pornographic books for *Screw* since its inception and is the author of the definitive survey *The Secret: Modern Erotic Literature*. His own erotic novel, *Evil Companions*, has just been published in England.

1. *Story of the Eye*, by George Betaille
2. *Irene*, by Albert De Routisie
3. *Story of O*, by Pauline Reagé
4. *Lolita*, by Vladimir Nabokov
5. *Helen and Desire*, by Alexander Trocchi
6. *The Real Thing*, by William Carney
7. *Justine*, by D.A.F. de Sade
8. *Memoirs of a Woman of Pleasure*, by John Cleland
9. *The Image*, by Jean de Berg
10. *Evil Companions*, by Michael Perkins

11 Famous Anonymous Classics of Hard-Core Pornography

1. *The Lustful Turk*
2. *The Autobiography of a Flea*
3. *Miss High Heels*
4. *Fifteen Plagues of a Maidenhead*
5. *The Story of a Dildo*
6. *The Lascivious Hypocrite, or The Triumph of Vice*
7. *My Cunt Is My Fortune*
8. *My Secret Life (4 volumes)*
9. *The Whore's Rhetorick*
10. *Lustful Stories*
11. *Raped on the Elevated*

—Prepared by Arnold Bruce Levy especially for *The Book of Sex Lists*

14

Sex has always been natural, but it hasn't always been easy.
From Lenny Bruce to the lady who first removed the fig leaf from the nude statue of Apollo—many of the more daring men and women of our time have had to spend time before judges and juries defending their words and deeds.

20 Landmark Obscenity Cases

1. *Le Roy* v. *Sedley* (England, 1663). Sir Charles Sedley (an intimate of King Charles II), Lord Buckhurst, and Sir Thomas Ogle got drunk and staged an uninhibited performance on the balcony of a public house. They undressed and pantomimed indecent proposals to the public and finally urinated in the bottles from which they had drunk and threw them at the audience. They were arrested and tried, and Sedley "was fined 2,000 marks, committed without bail for a week, and bound to his good behavior for a year, on confession of information against him, for showing himself naked in a balcony and throwing down bottles [pissed in] ... contra pacem and to the scandal of the government." (This is regarded as the first case of criminal obscenity under the common law.)

2. *Regina* v. *Read* (England, 1708). A publisher was arrested and charged with publication of an obscene pamphlet, *The 15 Plagues of a Maiden-head*. The court held that this was no offense at the common law and jurisdiction was in the ecclesiastical courts.

3. *Rex* v. *Curll* (England, 1727). Edmund Curll, a printer and bookseller, was indicted, tried and convicted for the sale of obscene literature, newly found as a common law crime. The item was *Venus in the Cloister, or the Nun in her Smock*. In addition to being colorful and explicit, the book had anti-Catholic overtones.

4. *Commonwealth* v. *Sharpless* (Pennsylvania, 1815). Upheld the conviction of the defendant for displaying an obscene picture which depicted a man in a sexual position with a woman.

5. *Commonwealth* v. *Holmes* (Massachusetts, 1821) This was the first instance in which an American state court banned a book. The Supreme Court of Massachusetts held that John Cleland's *Memoirs of a Woman of Pleasure (Fanny Hill)* was obscene and therefore deserved to be banned in Massachusetts.

6. *Regina* v. *Hicklin* (England, 1868). Possibly the most important obscenity case in Anglo-American law. The actual item involved was *The Confessional Unmasked: Showing the Depravity of the Romish Priesthood, the Inequity of the Confessional and the Questions put to Females in Confession*.
   In this case, Chief Justice Cockburn laid down the first and probably the most famous test for obscenity: "I think the best test of obscenity is this, whether the tendency of the matter charged as obscenity is to deprave and corrupt those whose minds are open to such immoral influences, and to whose hands a publication of this sort may fall."

7. *United States* v. *Rosen* (U.S. Supreme Court, 1896). This case marked the first time the United States Supreme Court sustained a conviction under the Comstock Act. Lou Rosen was the publisher of a periodical *Broadway*, which included photographs of near-nude females. This case established the constitutional legality of the doctrine of banning allegedly obscene books, magazines and newspapers in the United States.

8. *United States* v. *Kennerly* (New York Federal Court, 1913). For the first time in almost a century, a respected judge questioned the doctrine of obscenity. He sustained a law but stated: "I question whether in the end men will regard that as obscene which is honestly relevant to the adequate expression of innocent ideas, and whether they will not believe that truth and beauty are too precious to society at large to be mutilated in the interest of those most likely to pervert them to base uses.

   "Indeed, it seems hardly likely that we are even today so lukewarm in our interests in letters or serious discussion as to be content to reduce our treatment of sex to the standard of a child's library. . . ."

9. *Commonwealth* v. *Friede* (Massachusetts, 1930) The highest court in Massachusetts upheld the conviction of a bookseller for the sale of one of America's best novels, Theodore Dreiser's *An American Tragedy*. (Many consider this the highwater mark in America for stupid censorship.)

10. *United States* v. *Dennett* (New York Federal Court of Appeals, 1930). Reversed a lower court conviction of Mary Ware Dennett for writing and circulating a pamphlet on sexual education for youngsters. The case makes the important point that obscenity is essentially a legal doctrine and that a jury's findings that a pamphlet was obscene and the jury's conviction of the defendant may be reversed by the court as a matter of law.

11. *United States* v. *One Book Called "Ulysses"* (New York Federal Court, 1934). United States customs authorities seized the book *Ulysses*, and it became a legal issue as to whether the book was obscene in law. The book contains explicit words such as "fuck."

    Federal District Judge John M. Woolsey held the book to be not obscene and established a new test: "Whether a particular book would tend to excite [sexual] impulses and thoughts must be tested by the court's opinion as to its effect on a person with average sex instincts—what the French would call *L'homme moyen sensuel*—who plays in this branch of legal inquiry the same role of hypothetical reagent as does the 'reasonable man' in a law of torts and 'the man learned in the art' on the questions of invention in patent law."

This decision established the principle that a book must be treated as a unit and may not be judged by individual passages taken out of context.

12. *Butler* v. *Michigan* (U.S. Supreme Court, 1957). A Michigan obscenity statute was found unconstitutional because it tested books by their possible influence upon youth.

   The Supreme Court said, "Surely, this is to burn the house to roast the pig." It was also the first time the United States Supreme Court undertook to decide the constitutionality of obscenity legislation.

13. *Roth* v. *United States* (U.S. Supreme Court, 1957). Here, the Supreme Court laid down the first test of obscenity: "Whether to the average person, applying contemporary community standards, the dominant theme of the material taken as a whole appeals to prurient interests."

14. *Smith* v. *California* (U.S. Supreme Court, 1959). Held that a bookseller could not be convicted of selling an obscene book without proof that he had knowledge of the contents.

15. *Ginzburg* v. *United States* (U.S. Supreme Court, 1966). This highly publicized case added the doctrine of "pandering" into the law on obscenity, in effect stating that whether an item is obscene depends a great deal upon how it is sold or advertised.

16. *Redrup* v. *New York* (U.S. Supreme Court, 1967). This reversed New York's holding of some paperback books as obscene and created a broad protection for all sexual matters limiting obscenity to materials that were either pandered, sold to minors, or forced upon an unwilling audience. Many regarded this case as eliminating obscenity problems from the courts for all time.

17. *Stanley* v. *Georgia* (U.S. Supreme Court, 1969). Established the rule that a man could not be prosecuted for possessing obscene material in his own home.

18. *Kaplan* v. *California* (U.S. Supreme Court, 1973). This ruling, with other cases decided the same day, completely reversed all the liberalizing decisions of the Warren Court and established the principle that the application of local community

standards was constitutionally proper. It also eliminated the need for the prosecution to use expert testimony.

19. *Miller* v. *California* (U.S. Supreme Court, 1973). Established new guidelines for what constitutes obscenity. These are very broad. Almost anything could be designated as obscene. The new rule is (a) whether "the average person, applying contemporary community standards" would find that the work, taken as a whole, appeals to the prurient interest, (b) whether the work depicts or describes, in a patently offensive way, sexual conduct specifically defined by the applicable state law, and (c) whether the work, taken as a whole, "lacks serious literary, artistic, political or scientific value."

20. *Schad* v. *Mt. Ephraim* (U.S. Supreme Court, 1981). Nude dancing may contribute a form of expression under the first amendment to the United States Constitution, and a law absolutely prohibiting nude dancing is unconstitutional.

25 States Where Any Sexual Act Between Consenting Adults Is Legal

1. Alaska
2. California
3. Colorado
4. Connecticut
5. Delaware
6. Hawaii
7. Illinois
8. Indiana
9. Iowa
10. Maine
11. Massachusetts
12. Nebraska
13. New Hampshire
14. New Jersey
15. New Mexico
16. New York
17. North Dakota
18. Ohio
19. Oregon
20. Pennsylvania
21. South Dakota
22. Vermont
23. Washington
24. West Virginia
25. Wyoming

States With the Highest and Lowest Rape Rates

1. Alaska has the highest rape rate with 55.6 rapes per 100,000 population
2. North Dakota has the lowest rape rate with 8.9 rapes per 100,000 population

Source: 1981 *World Almanac*

10 Cities in the USA Where You Have Your Best Chance to Be Raped

City metropolitan area	Rate per 100,000 population
1. Tallahassee, FL	75.1
2. Las Vegas, NV	67.7
3. Los Angeles–Long Beach Area, CA	66.9
4. Savannah, GA	62.6
5. Lubbock, TX	62.6
6. Gainesville, FL	62.2
7. Orlando, FL	61.7
8. Little Rock, AR	61.3
9. Pensacola, FL	59.0
10. Daytona Beach, FL	57.8

Source: Justice Department's Uniform Crime Reports

12 Important Sexual-Freedom Decisions Handed Down by the U.S. Supreme Court

1. *Griswold v. Connecticut* (1965)

    Court declared unconstitutional Connecticut law banning use of drugs, medical articles, or instruments for the purpose of preventing conception and making it a crime to assist in contraception. The executive director and medical director of Planned Parenthood were both fined one hundred dollars for violation of the law. Court upheld that the relationship between husband and wife lies within the zone of privacy created by fundamental constitutional guarantees.

2. *Boutilier v. Immigration and Naturalization Service* (1967)
The Court upheld the classification of homosexuals as psychopathic personalities thereby permitting them to be barred from entry into the United States.

3. *Loving v. Virginia* (1967)
The Court declared interracial marriage laws invidious racial discrimination and a violation of due process, hence uncontstitutional.

4. *Eisenstadt v. Baird* (1972)
The Court declared unconstitutional a Massachusetts law making it a felony to give out any contraceptive drug, medicine, or article except by a doctor or pharmacist (by prescription) to a married person. The Court held, under *Griswold*, that no rational reason exists to accord different treatment to married and unmarried persons; hence, law violates the First Amendment.

5. *Roe v. Wade* (1973)
In a class action suit by a pregnant single woman, the Court declared unconstitutional a Texas statute making it a crime to procure or attempt an abortion unless to save the life of the mother.

6. *Doe v. Boulton* (1973)
The Court declared invalid a Georgia law making abortion a crime unless judged by a physician to be necessary.

7. *Cleveland Board of Education v. La Fleur* (1974)
Court declared unconstitutional Cleveland's mandatory termination provision for teachers who become pregnant. Provision required teachers to take five months' unpaid maternity leave before birth and did not permit reinstatement until start of next term after child was three months old. Such a provision, varying the amount of time for no sound reason and acting as an irrefutable presumption, violates the 14th Fourteenth Amendment's due process provision.

8. *Doe* v. *Richard* (1976)

Court upheld a Virginia statute making sodomy a felony. Two males, consenting adults acting in private, were not entitled to the constitutional protections of marriage, family and home.

9. *Planned Parenthood of Central Missouri* v. *Danforth* (1976)

In a suit by two doctors asserting the rights of their patients, the Court declared unconstitutional a Missouri law requiring the consent of the spouse, and for minors, that of the parent, before abortion may be performed.

10. *Carey* v. *Population Services International* (1977)

The Court struck down a New York law restricting the sale of contraceptives. Law provided penalty for anyone selling or distributing contraceptives to anyone under the age of sixteen or for anyone other than a physician or licensed pharmacist to distribute to anyone and for anyone who advertised or displayed contraceptives. The Court held that the state may not limit the sale of contraceptives other than prescription types for medical reasons. The state may not limit advertising of anyone licensed to sell.

11. *Michael M.* v. *Sorona City* (1980)

California statutory rape law which punishes only the male is a legitimate exercise of state power in that its purpose is to prevent teenage pregnancies.

12. *Harris* v. *McRae* (1980)

States are not required to fund abortions for low-income mothers.

—Compiled by Lynne Gerber Saionz especially for *The Book of Sex Lists*

The High Cost of Defense in 4 Pornography Trials

1. *United States* v. *Al Goldstein, Jim Buckley and Milky Way Productions* (1973–1977)—The government charged that the weekly magazine *Screw* was obscene and, when mailed, vio-

lated federal law. The first trial was held in Wichita, Kansas, and lasted more than one month. A jury verdict to convict was vacated because of misconduct by the prosecution. The case was then moved to Kansas City, Kansas, and retried. This time there was a hung jury with nine for acquittal and three for conviction. The government finally dismissed all charges.

The cost of defense, including attorney's fees, travel expenses, living costs, printing and duplicating costs, etc., exceeded $400,000.

Counsel: Herald Prince Fahringer, Paul Cambria, Arthur Schwartz

2. *State of Ohio v. Hustler Magazine, Larry Flynt and others*—Charged with publishing and distributing obscene material and with violation of Ohio organized crime statute. The trial lasted five weeks. *Hustler* and Larry Flynt were convicted of felonies. On appeal, the Court of Appeals reversed and remanded the case for trial as a misdemeanor. The case was still pending as of August 1981.

Cost of defense: $250,000
Counsel Herald Price Fahringer, Paul Cambria

3. *United States v. Hamling* (1972 to 1975)—This case involved the alleged criminal obscenity of the illustrated version of *The Report of the President's [Nixon's] Commission on Obscenity* and a brochure advertising it. A trial in San Diego lasted three months. Conviction was sustained by 9th Circuit Court of Appeals and U.S. Supreme Court. The case was returned to lower courts for further proceedings and further appeals. The U.S. Supreme Court refused to review the case a second time.

Cost of defense: $200,000
Counsel: Stanley Fleischman

4. *United States v. Bernstene* (1981)—Case grew out of the "sting operation" conducted by the Justice Department's Federal Bureau of Investigation. Some forty-five defendants throughout the United States were indicted after the massive seizure of thousands of sex books, magazines and films. Defense lawyers were able to get the first general indictment dismissed for constitutional defects. The government then indicted again

130

individually. One of the first trials, the case against Bernstene, resulted in a hung jury. Bernstene was tried a second time and acquitted by a jury. His case involved the films "Deep Throat" and "Debbie Does Dallas."

Cost of defense: $200,000

Counsel: Robert Eugene Smith

15

If you know how to do it,
you'll want to know where to find it.

9 Swingers' Clubs in New York City
Where You Can Have Sex on the Premises

1. *Plato's Retreat.* 509 West 34th Street (between Tenth and
   Eleventh Avenues), New York City. Phone: (212) 947-0111. This
   is fantasy land for swingers come true. The club has almost
   25,000 square feet of space and can accommodate 1,000 people
   at one time.

   There is a marble disco dance floor with a sound and light
   system as good as anything around. This is operated by a live
   D.J. from opening time in the evening until the late hours of the
   morning.

   There's a large room with mats on the floor used for commu-
   nal sex. For those who want privacy, there are 32 private rooms.
   There are projection TVs, a game room, juice and snack bars
   and a buffet.

   The club has a sauna and whirlpool, but as of this writing the
   authorities of the City of New York have not permitted it to be
   turned on. Showers are working. The club is open every night

except Monday. Opening time is 9:00 P.M., and the club remains open until early morning if people want it.

Men are not admitted without a female companion. Single females are generally admitted without argument although this may not hold true if the place is crowded.

The price for admission of a couple is $50, which includes a $15 membership fee good for six weeks. For these six weeks, admission becomes $35. Swinging is common even among strangers. Most people walk about in the nude, though this is not required. Discreet voyeurs are not objected to.

Towels and a locker are included in the price of admission. Plato's Retreat marks the return of the public orgy.

2. *Le Trapeze.* 17 East 27th Street (between Fifth and Madison Avenues), New York City. Phone: (212) 532-0298. A clean well-kept club for couples only. Has a small disco, an operational whirlpool, lockers, and showers. The buffet is superior and there are soft drinks. Admission price is $25 Monday through Thursday and $35 on Fridays and Saturdays. Initially, there is a $15 membership fee good for three months. Opens at 9:00 P.M. Closed on Sunday.

3. *Screwples.* 133 West 19th Street (between Sixth and Seventh Avenues), New York City. Phone: (212) 243-9519. A swinging club that caters to younger people. At Plato's and Le Trapeze you'll find people from their teens to the geriatric set. But this one caters to people under 50 and most are under 40.

This is one of the clubs that permits either couples or singles; however, it is only open Wednesday nights at 9:00 P.M. Admission is $35 for a single man and $5 for a single woman, but $15 for a couple. Each charge includes a one month membership fee of $5. A logistics problem with this club is that on some evenings men will outnumber women three or four to one.

4. *Midnight Interlude.* This club has asked that its address not be published; therefore, if you want to go, write in advance or call. The mailing address is P.O. Box 6969 (is that number a coincidence?), Grand Central Station, New York, NY 10163. The phone number is (212) 532-0257. This is one of the few clubs that caters (except Saturday nights) to a singles crowd.

The location is a luxurious private residence with an excellent open swinging area, a sauna and some private rooms. (The atmosphere is good, but voyeurs are not welcome. If you don't intend to take your clothes off, don't show up.) From Mondays to Fridays, the charge for men is $75 and for women $5. Couples are charged $25 at all times. In addition, there's a three-month membership charge of $5.

5. *The Zoo.* 710 Seventh Avenue (between 48th and 49th Streets), New York City. Phone: (212) 245-0134. This is another club that admits singles, either men or women. It is well designed and has a cozy atmosphere. The club claims to be the first to have projection equipment and shows porno films. At our last inspection, the projection room was not completed. It opens earlier than most clubs, at 4:30 P.M., and closes at 2:00 A.M. Admission for single men is $60, which includes a $20 one month membership fee. No charge for women.

6. *Xtazy.* 143 West 44th Street (between Sixth and Seventh Avenues), New York City. Phone: (212) 944-1913. This is another club that caters to singles. It operates on two floors and you go up and down as you please. It has a disco dance floor, a bathing fountain, and standard checking facilities. It opens at 5:30 P.M. and goes to 3:00 A.M. every night of the week. Admission for single males or couples is the same, $40. Women are admitted

free. A complaint about Xtazy is that the ratio of men to women is very high.

7. *Chateau 19*. 133 West 19th Street (between Sixth and Seventh Avenues), New York City. Phone: (212) 243-9519. This club is slightly on the offbeat side. Theoretically, the operators intend to emphasize sadism and masochism, and there is S & M gear on the premises. Open Tuesdays and Thursdays from 8:00 P.M. on. Most of the people are younger than at the other clubs. Admission is only $10 for men and $3 for women, which includes two free drinks.

8. *Club O.* 31 West 21st Street (between Fifth and Sixth Avenues), New York City. Phone: (212) 620-0807. This club also features an S & M theme, and gear is available. Some use it; most don't. The club is open on Wednesdays and Thursdays from 8:00 P.M. Theoretically on those nights it is open only to couples. The charge is $20 per couple. On Fridays and Saturdays, the club opens at 9:00 P.M., and couples and singles are all admitted at $25 each. This is one of the few places with convenient parking.

9. *Hell Fire*. 28 Ninth Avenue. Just below 14th Street. Rates are the most reasonable in New York City and this is a very popular club with the S&M in-crowd. Singles, couples, and gays are all welcome and mix well together, but the place is very dirty. Wear your oldest, most washable clothes because no one ever seems to clean this place. In spots the dirt can be several inches thick. Don't get into anything here unless anything goes. If a scene is in progress anyone passing by usually joins in, whether you wish them to or not.

4 Unusual Correspondence Clubs

1. *Continental Spectator*—147 West 42nd Street, Room 603, New York, NY 10036. One of the oldest of the correspondence clubs. Operated by a husband and wife team who seem to be honest.

They know many of their advertisers personally. $24.00 for six issues and well worth it.

2. *Corporal*—Esoteric Press, Inc., P. O. Box 162, Great Neck, N.Y. 11022. They are honest, but disorganized. Mail is forwarded quickly, thanks to a computer. They also host frequent parties so that you can get to meet others face-to-face. They also publish other S&M-oriented magazines and newspapers, all containing coded ads.

3. *House of Milan Corp.*—P. O. Box 25304, Chicago, IL 60625. This company publishes several correspondence magazines with a different S&M theme in each. It was recently sold to new owners. In the past mail forwarding was slow, but reliable.

4. *Slave*—Published by Slave Productions, P. O. Box 356, Ronkokoma, NY 11779. New, so we have no reports about this organization.

7 Ways a Woman Can Meet a Man

1. Carry a visible copy of *Sports Illustrated*.
2. Walk a small, cute dog.
3. Wear a T-shirt or a button with an obscene message.
4. Take sightseeing bus tours.
5. Have breakfast alone at a table in the coffee shop or dining room of a hotel in which a convention is taking place.
6. Fly first class.
7. Put interesting ads in the personal columns of newspapers.

—From an adult education class held in New York City

10 College Campuses That Have Reputations for Wild Undergraduate Sex

1. University of California at Berkeley
2. Tyler School of Art (Temple University), Elkins Park, Pennsylvania

3. Indiana University—Bloomington campus
4. University of Colorado at Boulder
5. Beaver College, Glenside, Pennsylvania
6. Northwestern University, Evanston and Chicago campuses, Illinois
7. University of Massachusetts at Amherst
8. University of Hawaii, Honolulu campus
9. Emory University, Atlanta
10. George Washington University, Washington, D.C.

25 Apartments in New York City Where Men Can Buy Sex with Women

Most of these places are on the East Side of Manhattan in apartment houses that range from middle-class to ritzy. Try to get rates on the phone although many will refuse. They want to see you to make sure you're not the police. Rates average $50 a session although a $100 fee in these inflation-ridden days is not unusual.

Don't double-park; in many places, if they're busy you'll have to sit in the parlor and wait. If you're lucky, you'll get an early next.

Name	Telephone	Comments
1. Cheree	(212) 573-9017	Advertises all forms of straight sex
2. Kathy	(212) 599-1782	All forms; closes at 11 p.m.
3. Beverly	(212) 570-2166	$100
4. Seductive Girls	(212) 684-2905	Offers a drink to relax you
5. Jill	(212) 254-3700	Offers to accept chastisement
6. Sexy Girls	(212) 684-2905	Supposedly young girls
7. The Coed Dormitory	(212) 697-2298	Advertises amateurs.
8. Lady Margaret or Chris	(212) 486-1229	Will cater to fetishes

9. Gina	(212) 683-8182	
10. Mother's Milk	(212) 750-9618	Claims to have pregnant girls
11. Housewife House	(212) 697-2409	Advertises moonlighting housewives.
12. Mei-Lin or Gail	(212) 677-6882	Advertises young; Polynesians also available
13. Susan	(212) 679-4860	Oriental girls available
14. Lora	(212) 697-9791	Near Grand Central
15. Andrea	(212) 420-1858	$75
16. Caroline or Holly	(212) 980-6740	Quite young
17. Brooklyn	(212) 284-6359	Offers drinks, massages and movies
18. Candlelight	(212) 750-9183	Advertises a $45 special
19. Randy	(212) 980-6740	Young girls
20. Roxanne	(212) 254-3700	
21. Elizabeth	(212) 684-1077	
22. Nicole	(212) 599-1782	A penthouse with a view
23. Marie	(212) 591-0235	Located in Flushing
24. Britt or Tara	(212) 754-1264	
25. Vicki	(212) 750-9617	$45˙

10 Hot Gay Spots Throughout the World

1. The Saint, New York City
2. St. Marks Baths, New York City
3. The Mine Shaft, New York City
4. The Ice Palace, Cherry Grove, Fire Island
5. Meat Rack, Fire Island
6. 8709, Los Angeles
7. Heaven, London
8. Palace, Paris
9. L'Opera Baths, Paris
10. The Hot House, San Francisco

4 Sexy Things to Do While in Las Vegas

1. See a male strip show at Bogies Steak House Restaurant, 4375 Las Vegas Boulevard South. (702) 736-0668. Weekdays at 9 P.M. and Fridays at 8 P.M.
2. Watch the actual "Love Act" at Cabaret Burlesque Palace at 4416 Paradise Road (between Flamingo Road and Tropicana Avenue) with continuous shows Mondays through Saturdays, 8:30 P.M. until dawn. (702) 733-8666.
3. Enjoy a total nude show at the Satin Saddle at 1818 Las Vegas Boulevard North (one block south of the Palomino) with shows Tuesdays through Sundays.
4. Smile back at the sexy topless dancers at the Crazy Horse Saloon (no relation to the famous Paris saloon) at 4034 Paradise Road at Flamingo, where the action goes on 24 hours a day.

10 Foreign Nude Recreation Opportunities

1. *Four Seasons,* P.O. Box, Freelton, Ontario, Canada, is one of the most luxurious clothes-optional resorts in North America. It is located about ten miles from Hamilton.
2. *Unicamp,* Honeywood, Ontario, Canada, is a Unitarian Universalist church facility offering human potential workshops all summer.
3. *Yacht Taurus* organizes nude cruises in the Bahamas. Write Box 163, Crownsville, MD 21032.
4. *Sainte-Anne, Guadaloupe.* Plage Caravelle is the finest white sand beach in Guadaloupe and is also the home of Club Med Caravelle, although the beach is public and open to all. If you prefer not to stay at Club Med, try Mme. Giroux, 4, rue Bebian, F-97110 Ponte-a-Pitre, Guadaloupe, French West Indies. She has bungalows for rent. There is also the Motel de Sainte-Anne, F-97180, Guadaloupe, F.W.I.
5. *Denmark.* Most Danish beaches are open for clothes-optional sunning and swimming. Best bet for a fine map of locations is the Danish Tourist Office near you.

6. *Nautena.* A French Naturist organization devoted to yachting and water sports. Write to Mme. Dratz, 9, rue Bechant-le-Sarron, F-75009 Paris, France.
7. *Biking.* If this is your sport, join a naturist group through Departement Plein Air, Groupe Naturiste, Touring Club de France, 65 avenue de la Grande Armee, F-75782 Paris, France.
8. *Cap d'Agde.* A naturist city on the Mediterranean coast of France. There is a campground, Centre Heho Marin; an apartment village complex, Port Ambonne; a large luxury complex, Heliopolis, and the nearby Château de Maraval. For more information, write to Genevieve Oltra, Port Ambonne, F-34300 Cap d'Agde, France.
9. *Holland.* A recently completed naturist resort which can also accommodate wheelchairs can be reached easily from Amsterdam and is open all year round. Write to NNT-Sekretariaat, 't Kerkestuk 17, NL-2811 BC, Reeuwyk, the Netherlands.
10. Worldwide: *World Guide to Nude Beaches and Recreation,* by Lee Baxandall, describes free beaches from Alaska to Antarctica. For more information, write to Free Beaches Documentation Center, P.O. Box 132, Oshkosh, WI 54902.

12 Places for S&M Sex

Name	Telephone	Comments
1. Velvet's Dungeon	(212) 260-7411	Female domination
2. Mistress Marianne	(212) 794-0925	Black mistress
3. Dominatrix	(212) 260-0374	Offers real torture
4. The Castle	(212) 354-1870	Offers domination
5. Mistress Jezabelle	(212) 982-2671	All forms of torture
6. Rena	(212) 685-0086	Will be submissive
7. Mistress Mard	(212) 685-0086	Full torture equipment
8. Natasha	(212) 799-3492	Domination
9. Margot	(212) 570-9684	All fantasies, including enemas
10. Racquel	(212) 254-3700	All forms of domination

11. Belle Du Jour	(212) 243-1540	All forms of domination and submission including enemas. Five Mistresses and two slaves to choose from. Seven days a week. Noon to 10:00 P.M.
12. Ann Pierce	P. O. Box 26 Bellville, N.J. 07109	Creative dominance by appointment only. Unusually well equipped with several exciting dungeons to choose from. State interests in first letter. Include self-addressed stamped envelope.

4 Girls Who Will Talk Sexy on the Telephone (For a Fee)

There are some men who get their kicks out of talking sex to women on the phone. Whenever there is a demand, a supply will follow.

Here are four ladies who, for a fee of $35, will talk as sexy (or dirty) as the customer demands.

A MasterCard or Visa is necessary because the customer is charged via credit card before an off-color syllable is uttered. Then off you go.

1. Lisa—(213) 656-4042
2. Dolly—(213) 446-9456
3. Julie—(415) 931-3616
4. Laura—(212) 741-0216

Editor's note: Sorry, no guarantees on the phone numbers being in service after this book is published.

37 Abbreviations Used in Sex Ads

"If u cn rd ths, thn u cn gt a gd jb wth hi pa"

1. w/m—white male
2. w/f—white female
3. b/m—black male
4. b/f—black female
5. bi—bisexual
6. g—gay
7. s or str—straight
   1–7 also used in such combinations as:
 w/md/m—white married male
 s/j/f—straight Jewish female
 g/b/m—gay black male
 bi/b/f—bisexual black female
8. end—endowed (well-hung)
9. cut—circumcised
10. u/c—uncut (uncircumcised)
11. masc—masculine
12. fem—feminine
13. B & D—bondage and discipline
14. S & M—sadomasochism (sometimes qualified as *lt* or *hvy* or *lmts rspctd*— "light," "heavy," "limits respected")
15. w/s—water sports (urolagnia, or sexual excitement involving urine, the proper domain of "golden shower" lovers)
16. scat—scatology (coprophilia)
17. Fr—French (oral sex)
18. Fr a—French active
19. Fr p—French passive
20. Rear F—Rear French ("rimming")
21. Gr—Greek (anal sex)
22. Gr a—Greek active
23. Gr p—Greek passive
24. enem—enemas (given)
25. BB—bodybuilder
26. ff—finger fucking
27. FF—fist fucking
28. tpmn—top man (active partner or, sometimes, sadist or dominant leather man)
29. btmn—bottom man (passive partner or, sometimes, masochist)

30. vers—versatile (uninhibited, capable of playing both active and passive roles)
31. aggr—aggressive
32. j/o—jerk- [jack]-off artist (likes mutual masturbation)
33. tel j/o—phone freak (gets off on dirty phone calls)
34. aroma— "poppers" (amyl nitrate or butyl nitrite)
35. smoke—marijuana
36. TV—transvestite
37. str actg—straight acting (masculine, conservative gay)

Most gay ads end with the unforgettable phrase "No fems, fats, or phonies," which would make a great title for a novel.

—Prepared by Martin Greif especially for
The Book of Sex Lists

2 Sensuous Islands

There is something about climate that turns people on. Among people who have traveled widely, two places are mentioned frequently as the settings for the easiest seductions and the most sensuous sex.

1. *Jamaica, W.I.,* is an island of ravishing beauty. It has everything from miles of white beaches to lush green woods and miles of meadows to ice-capped mountains (where the world's number one coffee, Blue Mountain, is grown for export to Japan). Errol Flynn, Ian ("James Bond") Fleming, and Noël Coward are among the scores of famous visitors who fell in love with Jamaica and spent all their available time there. It is said that no woman can resist seduction under a full Jamaican moon.

   Jamaicans say, "Will you do me a rudeness?" —meaning, "Will you allow me to join my body to yours?"

2. *Cuba*, despite the drastic political changes and economic struggles of the past quarter century, was once "the Paris of the Americas," and for good reason. Its climate is similar to Jamaica's, and while it doesn't have the rich tropical beauty of that island, it does have those sensuous sea breezes, those tropical nights, and that languid make-love-to-me temperature. Although the Fidel Castro government has abolished the once-famed Cuban whorehouses and B-bars, Cubans have not become prudes. If you meet someone of the opposite sex (gay is still frowned upon, but no longer prosecuted) and would like to spend an hour with him or her, there are special hotels which rent for one, two, or three hours for purposes of bedding down.

16

Here are some of the history and some of the myths.

8 Strange Sexual Customs
Throughout the Ages

1. *Greece.* Tremendous emphasis was placed on the female breasts, frequently referred to in ancient Greek literature as the "apples of the bosom." Frank and easy acceptance of incest was based upon the story of Zeus, Father of the Gods, who married his sister, Hera. Pederasty was an acceptable practice.

2. *Rome.* Adultery was common. Chastity was a mockery. Ovid said, "The only woman who is chaste has no wooers." The common practice was for the wife to go home immediately after the marriage ceremony and sit on the phallus of Mutunus Tatunus. Thus, she sacrificed her virginity to the god of sex and fertility.

3. *India.* In the fourth century A.D., for many decades, everything imaginable was OK. Orgies were common, widespread, and condoned by religious authorities. This was the time of the *Kama Sutra.*

4. *Bali.* Until quite recently, trial marriage (the *gendak*) was encouraged in Bali. Promiscuity was considered acceptable. The only sexual taboos were sex with idiots, lepers, albinos, the sick, and the deformed.

5. *The Arctic Eskimos.* At one time chastity was rare among Eskimos. People of both sexes slept together in wide sleeping bags. Celibacy was regarded as harmful to the health of those who practiced it. Girls were purchased for marriage. A year of trial marriage was common. Wives were loaned to any visitor as a matter of hospitality or, in fact, to any young man having trouble finding a woman. Sex was not permissible for a woman during pregnancy, so wives frequently borrowed a woman from a neighboring couple, who came as her neighborly duty. Wife-swapping was common and acceptable.

6. *England.* Until the last century, women were advertised for sale in newspapers. Thus the London *Times* on July 22, 1797, reported: "By an oversight in the report of Smithfield Market, we are not in the position to quote this week on the price of women. An increasing value of the fairer sex is considered by various celebrated writers to be a sure sign of increasing civilization. At this market the price of women has lately risen from half a guinea to three guineas and a half...."

Also in England, auctions were held where women were sold to the highest bidder. Valuations were interesting. A farmer's horse ran away and the farmer offered a reward of five guineas for the return of his horse. A few days later his wife disappeared and he advertised a reward of four guineas for her return.

7. *Balearic Isles, West Indies, Cyprus.* These and other places sanctioned the custom of couvade. When a man's wife began to go into labor, the man went to bed and feigned all of the symptoms of labor pains. He did not get up until she completed birth.

8. *England, France, Scotland, and other places.* During the medieval period, the *jus primae noctis* or *droit du seigneur* (in France, *jus cunni*) prevailed. This is the right of the lord to take the bride of his subjects on the first night of the marriage. This feudal custom was widespread in England, France, and Scotland for almost a century. In India, certain tribes had a similar custom in which the right was given to the head priest.

146

Sexual Behavior of Former Nuns
and Priests
(Before, During and After Orders)

It is exceedingly difficult to get any information about the sex lives of nuns and priests. Obviously, they are not supposed to have any. In a precedent-shattering study, two researchers of Baylor College of Medicine have come up with some interesting answers.

Sex Activity of Former Nuns and Priests

Sex Activity	Percentage engaging in activity before entering orders:	While in orders:	After leaving orders:
Masturbation	47%	57%	85%
Intercourse	11%	15%	82%
Oral-Genital	9%	5%	75%
Homosexual	11%	21%	16%
Celibate	46%	32%	10%

The percentages given refer to those who replied. In many cases the individual engaged in more than one activity; therefore, the columns are not intended to add to 100%.

Fifty-three percent of the men and fifty percent of the women reported being less satisfied sexually after relinquishing orders than they would have liked. The next question was, What reason did they have for this decreased sexual satisfaction?

Reasons Most Frequently Cited for Decreased Satisfaction

Reasons	Times Cited
1. Lack of partners	57
2. Religious/moral reasons	44
3. Feelings of not being desirable	35
4. Communication problems	20
5. Orgasmic dysfunction (women only)	20

—From "A Sexual Intimacy Survey of Former Nuns and Priests," by Margaret H. Halstead, M.S. and Lauro S. Halstead, M.D., in The Journal of Sex and Marital Therapy, summer 1978. Reprinted (with minor changes) with permission.

13 Rules for Swingers

1. Always show respect for the personal attitudes, feelings, and "hang-ups" of others and maintain a continuing desire to better understand them.
2. Exude human emotion and warmth, but understand the type of emotional involvement which is properly reserved for a spouse.
3. Never attempt to divide a home.
4. Help newcomers locate themselves within a relaxed social environment wherein a satisfying personal life may be achieved.
5. Always keep dates unless you give ample notice of changing circumstances.
6. Always keep the first meeting on a "no strings attached" basis, but be prepared to swing if it is mutually agreeable or to give an honest answer to your intended partner if something doesn't click.
7. If married, continue at every juncture to discuss openly your problems and views with your spouse.
8. Never, under any circumstances, exert pressure on a partner to swing.
9. Never disparage another's religious convictions.
10. Restrict discussions of swinging in public places to known swingers and interested persons seeking information.
11. Protect the anonymity of others by refraining from unauthorized "name dropping."
12. Always maintain the highest of standards in personal cleanliness and appearance.
13. Do not engage in any unlawful activity that would bring discredit upon swingers as a group.

—from *A Swinger's Creed*

The 12 New Myths of Sex

For centuries there were myths that were widely accepted without criticism or examination. For example, it was believed that if a man masturbated enough, he would be subject to all kinds of diseases and eventually his penis would fall off. And, of course, it was believed that women never masturbated.

We know a lot more about these subjects today. Now Dr. Wardell B. Pomeroy points out that a whole new crop of myths have sprung up.

Summarizing Dr. Pomeroy, these are:

1. "Sexual problems can be cured very easily." Comment: This is not true. It takes a gradual learning process under a skilled therapist.

2. "Liberated women are causing increasing sexual problems for men." Comment: The truly liberated women do not cause problems for men. It is some of the up-tight women who are not truly liberated who give men a lot of problems.

3. "Masturbation is more satisfying than sexual intercourse." Comment: Absolutely not. It may be more intense on a physiological measuring instrument, but nothing equals a good relationship between people which includes sexual intercourse.

4. "Women's orgasms should all be earth-shaking." Comment: Some women expect stars to explode and bells to ring and whistles to blow when they have an orgasm. Not so. It just isn't all that "earth-shaking."

5. "Technique is more important than relationship: after all, sex is only for pleasure." Comment: While sexual techniques may be important, it should be remembered that sexual intercourse is the deepest form of communication between two people, and that is the most important thing.

6. "There is no difference between a vaginal orgasm and a clitoral orgasm." Comment: Wrong. Actually, it is only the vagina and vaginal organs which contract about once every second during an orgasm and which constitutes an orgasm. Stimulation of the clitoris unquestionably helps, but the orgasm is in the vaginal area.

7. "Penis size is irrelevant to sexual satisfaction." Comment: Not so. Within normal limits, it is the enlarged circumference of the penis, not the length, that is significant because it is this which gives the woman the feeling of fullness in the vagina.

Actually, if the enlargment of the penis is too great, it can cause pain in many women. It should also be recognized that in precoital play, some women will react to a larger penis the way some men react to larger breasts. However, this is not frequent.

8. "Sex is good for your health." Comment: It is more accurate to say, "Good health is better for sex." Sex acts relieve tension and are good for those suffering from insomnia, but sex has no direct effect upon health.

9. "There's something wrong with people who confine their sex experience to within marriage." Comment: Absolutely wrong. It's entirely a matter of preference. Those who have the desire to confine their sex experience and enjoy it that way are perfectly all right.

10. "Simultaneous orgasms are best for a couple." Comment: The effort to achieve simultaneous orgasms may spoil the sex act for one or both partners. Sequential orgasms, especially for the woman, may well be better.

11. "Young people today have gone wild sexually." Comment: There is no real evidence of this. Every generation for decades has been critical of the next generation and its sex life. Actually, by and large, the youth of today, considering the enlargement of knowledge of the subject, are no more absorbed in sex than were earlier generations.

12. "Older people are as interested in sex as younger people." Comment: Older people are frequently interested in sex, and should be, but certainly not to the degree they were when they were younger.

—For additional comments, see *McCalls*, October 1977, page 102.

10 Jewish Sex Laws and Customs

Jewish sexual life is carefully prescribed and circumscribed. Almost every aspect of sex has a rule. The rules come from the Torah (the five Books of Moses) and the Talmud (Code of Laws), the Mishnah, and the commentary on that code (the Gemara). In addition, over the years, rabbis (teachers) have suggested revisions, many of which have been accepted.

In most cases, the rules today are primarily of historical interest. However, from the Hassidim of New York City and Israel to the small number of Jews in Yemen who refused to leave (for religious reasons) to go to Israel, there are Jews who still observe the rules as they were observed thousands of years ago. These are:

1. *General Sexual Conduct:* Practically all forms of sex outside of marriage are prohibited. This includes any form of promiscuity, prostitution, and adultery and any form of lewd behavior.

2. *Transvestism:* The rule of the Bible is that "a woman shall not wear that which pertains to a man, neither shall a man put on a woman's garment." Orthodox Jewish women today cannot wear slacks. Conservative rabbis permit slacks if they are obviously tailored for a woman—if, for example, they have buttons or a zipper on the side—but women are still prohibited from wearing a fly in front.

3. *Abortion:* This is permitted in Jewish law only to save the life of the mother. However, modern Reform rabbis are more lenient and approve abortions where there is a pregnancy resulting from rape, evidence that the child is deformed, or other objective reasons. There is still no general approval of abortion among Conservative or Orthodox Jews.

4. *Birth Control:* Because the Bible prohibits the wasting of the seed, the Orthodox reject any form of contraception. Modern Conservative and Reform rabbis condone the use of contraceptives. Many Orthodox rabbis have approved the use of the Pill because, technically, the "seed" is not spilled on the ground.

5. *Homosexuality:* The Old Testament says that it is "an abomination" and punishes the act by death. Jewish tradition prohibited two men from sleeping together even when no sexual activity took place.

6. *Nudism:* Absolutely prohibited. In addition, Orthodox Jewish women do not wear short skirts, low necklines, or even sleeveless dresses. The Reform movement has moved away from this rigid position.

151

7. *Pornography:* Technically prohibited. The rabbinic authorities even ruled that it was illegal for a man to stare at any woman except his wife. However, there is good evidence that the rabbis and scholars who spent their days discussing and analyzing Jewish religion, laws, and customs frequently told sexy and scatological jokes. They just never put them down on paper.

8. *Prohibitions of Sexual Intercourse:* Many. There are 36 sins for which the punishment is death. A large number of these are sexual, as for example: Sexual intercourse with one's mother, with one's father's wife, with a daughter-in-law, with any other male, with an animal, between a woman and an animal, a woman and her daughter, with a married woman, with one's sister, with one's father's sister or one's mother's sister, with one's wife's sister (while the wife is living), with one's brother's wife or one's father's brother's wife, with a woman while she is menstruating. Also, violating the rules relating to circumcision.

   Although not punishable by death, there are many other taboos relating to sexual intercourse. For example, it is illegal to have sex when any light is burning. It is illegal to have sex during Yom Kippur or any other fast day. It is illegal for a man to approach his wife sexually while he is drunk or while they're having an argument.

   The prohibition of sex during the menstrual period was not simply while the wife was menstruating. Actually, no matter how many days the woman menstruated, the Bible said that the menstrual period was seven days. Therefore, the man had to refrain for a week following the first stain; then, to make sure, the Talmud added five more days. Thus, in the Jewish tradition, there are twelve days in which woman is in dry dock.

9. *Compulsory Sexual Intercourse:* The ancient Jews took seriously the biblical injunction to "be fruitful and multiply." Therefore, it became the duty of a man to have sex whenever permissible. There is some dispute as to when a man had fulfilled his duty. Some said that a man had to have two sons and others argued for a son and a daughter.

   It is a special blessing to have sex on a Friday night, because this makes the Sabbath complete. If a man marries a woman and lives with her ten years and she bears him no child, it is thought he should divorce her and try another wife. She is encouraged to try another man because the rabbis know that a woman might conceive children by one man after being barren with another, as modern medicine has proven.

There is some dispute as to whether a man has a right to refrain from intercourse with his wife for more than a week, but certainly not more than two weeks, for she too has sexual rights.

Actually, for the ordinary man, the rule is that he is to have intercourse every day when legally permissible. If he is a laborer and that is a burden, he complies by engaging twice a week. (Donkey drivers who go out among the villages to cart grain get home only twice a week, so that number suffices for them.)

A camel driver must service his wife once every thirty days. Sailors have the longest statute of limitations—six months! And if a man who has an occupation which gives his wife the right to sex every night wants to go into another occupation which will cut this frequency, the wife has a right to prevent it! Except if he decides to become a scholar, the wife can't object.

10. *Divorce:* The Jewish laws on divorce could fill a three-volume textbook. Here are some highlights:

    Technically, only a man can get a divorce. A wife can do this if her husband contracts boils (this was later enlarged and interpreted to include any loathsome disease including VD or leprosy).

    A man who becomes a dog-shit collector can be forced to divorce his wife. (This substance was used in tanning leather.) The man who became a coppersmith or tanner could be compelled to get a divorce, as the rabbis said, for "olfactory reasons."

    If a man marries and on consummation discovers his wife is not a virgin, he is duty-bound to divorce her, but the religious courts made proof so difficult that divorce on this ground was discouraged.

    A man who marries a virgin receives a seven-day honeymoon by law, but a man who marries a widow gets only three days.

Virgins have to be married on Wednesdays because the court sat on Thursdays so if the betrayed groom wanted to lodge a nonvirginity divorce action he had Thursday morning court to go to.

Widows should be married on Thursdays because they had no such problem.

9 Sexual Customs and Practices of Islam

The followers of the religion founded by the Arabian prophet Muhammad (570–632), preferably called Islam, live ambivalent and frequently paradoxical sexual lives. On the one hand they are directed by the Koran to lead ascetic lives, eschewing sex outside of marriage. However, the Hadith, the original oral religious traditions of the pre-Islamic Arabs (which Muhammad is said to have followed), makes regular and frequent sex important and almost prescribed. Hence the seeming contradiction in the following:

1. According to the Koran, illegal or unsanctioned sexual intercourse is a crime. Men were rarely punished while women were consigned to life imprisonment for adultery or fornication. This was later modified to a hundred lashes and banishment for a year. However, married women are still stoned to death for engaging in adultery.

2. Female slaves who do not have a good education get half the

punishment: fifty lashes and banishment for half a year. If married, they shall not be stoned to death, because stoning is not divisible by two.

3. Husbands are permitted to beat their wives, "but not in a dangerous manner."

4. A man can divorce his wife (twice!) by simply saying three times, "I have divorced you," or words to that effect.

5. Arab women will discuss sexual matters among themselves freely and without inhibition, even in the presence of children.

6. In orthodox Islamic countries the following directive of the Koran is followed: "If a man or a woman steal, cut off their hands...." And by the same injunction, if a man commits a sexual offense with a married woman, the punishment is to cut off the "short arm."

7. Recognizing that men are sexual animals, the Koran permits men to have up to four wives, but none of them sisters. It is also illegal to marry a married woman unless she is a married slave. Custom further permits the man who can afford it to bring in concubines or slaves for sexual purposes. Also, the man can partake of prostitutes. The fact is that a man may screw any woman who is not under another man's protection.

8. Women are on earth only to produce male children. Anything that interferes with that purpose is to be punished. To help this cause, Arabs practice female circumcision to eliminate a girl's desire for premarital sex by a clitoridectomy, or to make it impossible by infibulation.

   Customs like these were practiced until quite recently (and may still continue) in parts of Jordan, Mecca and southern Saudi Arabia, parts of Iraq and Iran, and the Sudan.

9. It is assumed that any time a man and woman are alone they will inevitably engage in sexual intercourse. Therefore, "pure" women are not permitted to work around men (to maintain their purity); they cannot drive cars (they would drive to assignations); they must dress to conceal their attractiveness (to avoid being raped).

   To sum up, the Islamic attitude is that women belong at home in the kitchen or bedroom and should stay where they belong.

21 Gay Facts About Ancient Rome

1. The male brothels of ancient Rome were advertised by large phalluses, and their inmates consisted of *pueri* (young boys who were, as today's classifieds would put it, "Greek passive") and *exoleti* (hairy adults who were their opposite).

2. Roman physicians prescribed the following to gays for a long-lasting erection: "a donkey's right testicle and a vulture's right lung tied together with strips of stork meat."

3. The favorite sexual sport in Rome consisted of breaking the ring of an actor or athlete who had been infibulated (had a ring placed through the prepuce to prevent intercourse), since the infibulated were reputed to be tireless lovers.

4. The Vetti brothers, male prostitutes in ancient Pompeii, advertised their trade with an unusual sign: a young man weighing his penis with a bag of gold in a pair of scales.

5. The poet Martial: "Oh, to have a young slave whose skin is soft, not with pumice but with sweet youth—to tempt me away from any female."

6. Because of his affair with King Nicomedes II of Bithynia, the young Julius Caesar was mocked as "the queen of Bithynia."

7. So famous was Rome for the joys of buggery that one poet created an elaborate pun on the name of the Eternal City: "Roma, which delighted in making love from behind,/Spelled AMOR—love—by inverting its own name."

8. The emperor Nero didn't really fiddle while Rome burned, but he did one better by inventing a sexual game in which he dressed in the skins of wild animals and attacked the genitals of men tied to stakes.

9. The male prostitutes of ancient Rome advertised their services by scratching their heads with their middle fingers, a practice that explains why for centuries no respectable person wore a ring on "the finger of infamy."

10. The statesman Azulus Hirtius, who once took the young Octavius (Caesar Augustus) to bed for three thousand pieces

of gold, was allegedly murdered by the future emperor to prevent him from ever telling the tale (43 B.C.).

11. The poet Catullus, who, loving Juventius, "the flower of indolent and lascivious youth," is said to have died "of exhaustion" at the age of thirty-four.

12. The emperor Caligula was murdered by a palace guard named Chaerea, his passive partner in buggery, who had been regularly forced to kiss the emperor's middle finger in public.

13. The emperor Augustus was once wildly applauded at a play when an actor innocently spoke the line, "See how that queen's finger governs the world!"

14. The emperor Hadrian's youthful lover Antinous committed suicide by drowning himself in the Nile at the age of twenty-one, possibly because he preferred to die at the height of his beauty rather than face the oncoming ravages of "age."

15. The emperor Tiberius trained very young children (his "minnows") to stay between his legs while he was swimming so that they could lick and nibble him until he became excited, and he used unweaned infants to excite him on dry land.

16. The emperor Commodus called his exceptionally well-endowed cupbearer "my donkey" and was eventually strangled by a wrestler named Narcissus.

17. Julius Caesar was so well-rounded that he was called "a husband to all wives and a wife to all husbands."

18. The emperor Claudius murdered his son-in-law Pompey for daring to bed his favorite slave boy.

19. As a senator, the future emperor Nerva engaged (for cold cash) the stud service of a young hustler named Titus Flavius Domitianus, who grew up to be Domitian, his predecessor as Roman emperor.

20. The emperor Nero, who was simultaneously married to the eunuch Sporus (his "wife") and the freeman Doryphorus (his "husband"), used to introduce his "wife" as his "empress" and was fond of being "deflowered" in public by his "husband."

21. The emperor Domitian so loved the handsome pantomimist Paris that he divorced his wife to be with him.

20 Gay Facts About Ancient Greece
(or, The Greeks Had a Word for It)

1. The poet Pindar, who, according to ancient sources, was "by nature as randy as a goat," died at the ripe old age of eighty in a most serene manner—in a gymnasium, with his head in the lap of a young, muscular athlete.

2. The ancient Spartans often had their wives' hair shorn and dressed them as young boys to arouse them enough to be capable of sleeping with them (and then *only* in the dark).

3. Classical Greeks delighted in the tiny organs of boys and found adult members monstrously ugly—hence Strato's mournful lament that "Agaton's little lizard was a rosy little finger; now [a summer later] it is more like an arm."

4. Addaeus of Macedonia (ca. 300 B.C.): "When you meet a boy who pleases you, take action at once. Don't be polite—just grab him by the balls and strike while the iron is hot!"

5. To Agathon, Greek dramatist and musician (ca. 450 B.C.), belongs the dubious distinction of being the first documented homosexual in history.

6. The youth Bathyllus was so delicately beautiful that Polycrates, tyrant of Samos, defied all convention by erecting a statue in his honor in the temple of Hera, goddess of women.

7. According to ancient Greek law, old men were forbidden to enter gymnasiums because a lover over forty was considered indecent. But the dramatist Euripides spoke (at seventy-two) of his love for Agathon (then forty): "A fine autumn is a beautiful thing indeed."

8. Greek democracy was born in 514 B.C. when male lovers Harmondius and Aristogeiton rebelled against the tyrant Hipparchus and his jealous attempt to break up their love affair.

9. Athenian orator Demosthenes cured his stuttering by declaiming with his mouth stuffed with pebbles until he met his young lovers Cnosion, Aristarchus, and Epicrates—and gave up pebbles for rocks.

10. An annual boys' kissing contest, held each spring, honored the Athenian exile Diocles who had died while defending a young friend.

11. The philosopher Aristippus: "The art of life lies in taking pleasures as they pass, and the keenest pleasures aren't intellectual, nor are they always moral."

12. The Theban general Pelopidas organized the Sacred Band, an elite military corps composed entirely of gay lovers.

13. That Zeno, founder of Stoicism, was gay was so well known that Stoicism at first was popularly associated with homosexuality.

14. Alexander the Great once passionately kissed his friend Bagaos in public to delighted applause and cries of "encore" from the crowd. He also ordered the satrap Orsines killed for snubbing Bagaos and saying he would not talk to a man who prostituted himself like a woman.

15. Strato of Sardis compiled an anthology of gay verse (*Musa Pueriis*), including several of his own compositions: "Animals, being mindless, only couple with females, whereas men, having the advantage of intelligence, do it differently."

16. Superpatriots, who may dimly know that "The Star-Spangled Banner" is set to the music of an early American populist tune, "Anacreon in Heaven," probably don't know that Anacreon was a gay Greek poet noted for his love affairs with the youths Smerdis, Leukaspis, Simalus, Euralus, and Bathyllus—to name but a few.

17. The poet Artemon left behind fragments of a love poem to a "graceful boy" ("Echedemus...was peeking through the doorway. I got him by surprise and kissed his lips.")

18. The philosopher Xenophon, despite his advocacy of the virtues of asceticism and his contempt for pleasure, nonetheless salivated over the well-formed physiques of young athletes.

19. The Macedonian king and general Demetrius I was so enamored of a youth named Damocles that he pursued him to a bathhouse, where the boy leaped to his death into a cauldron

of boiling water. (Another more sophisticated youth named Cleanetus simply asked Demetrius for money.)

20. Gossip about a cloak stolen from the great dramatist Sophocles by a male whore was spread about Athens by the playwright's rival Euripides who had enjoyed the same whore for free.

25 Countries Where Sexual Slavery Still Exists

Chattel slavery has, in theory, been outlawed in every nation of the world. However, in practice, slavery continues to exist and even flourish in many countries.

Experience has shown that a chattel slave is helpless against being used sexually by a master or mistress. In many instances, the slaves are purchased explicitly for sexual use. In others there is the pretense that this isn't why they're acquired.

The Anti-Slavery Society for the Protection of Human Rights is a London-based group organized to fight slavery throughout the world. In 1981, Alan Whitaker, an official of that society, said, "It is inaccurate to believe that even old-fashioned chattel slavery is finished."

An insight to reality is provided by the United Nations. In 1956, the UN adopted a Convention against slavery in any form. Twenty-five years later, only eighty-five of the UN's one hundred and fifty-four members have ratified it.

Here is a list of those countries that still permit slavery to exist and where slaves are known to have been used sexually:

1. *Afghanistan*—In remote areas, following an ancient Moslem form of serfdom, the poorest members of the tribe are subjects of the chief (a religious figure) and must obey his orders. They are literally slaves.

2. *Algeria*—When the poor sell their children into slavery for as little as fifty dollars the practice is ignored because the people

who do the buying have considerable political and economic clout.

3. *Chad*—Old-fashioned slavery is widespread, and the government claims to be too weak to stamp it out.

4. *Colombia*—Slavery here takes the form of debt bondage, which debts are inherited. A deeply indebted father is forced to leave his children in debt bondage. In 1972, the Anti-Slavery Society bought up and freed the Andoke Indian tribe. The entire tribe was in bondage to one rubber plantation owner.

5. *El Salvador*—Permits legal debt bondage similar to Colombia.

6. *Ethiopia*—Old-fashioned slavery has never been totally wiped out here.

7. *Guatemala*—Debt bondage.

8. *Guinea*—Slavery may be found in several forms.

9. *Haiti*—Poverty continues to produce slavery. It exists in rural areas and is frequently related to Voodoo rites.

10. *Honduras*—Debt bondage.

11. *India*—In 1981, Ashwini Sardin, a reporter for the Indian *Express* (the largest circulation daily newspaper in the country), wrote a series of reports on the purchase of slaves in India. One article began: "Yesterday I bought a short-statured skinny woman . . . for 2,300 rupees." The price was equal to about $300 and, as the Sardin pointed out, was about half of what a buffalo would cost in the same area. On August 11, 1981, in discussing this subject, *The New York Times* described the widespread trade in women in India "with some sold as servants and others as prostitutes." A reporter for the Hindustan *Times* recently commented, "The shameful fact is that in our country there is such abysmal poverty that human flesh sells for only a little more than mutton."

12. *Ivory Coast*—Many incidents of old-fashioned "white slavery" have been reported. An attractive white woman dare not travel this country alone.

13. *Lebanon*—Children are frequently sold into domestic servitude for a period of years. In theory these children are learning

to be domestic servants, but the wealthy purchasers often use the more attractive boys and girls as sexual toys.

14. *Libya*—The outlawing of slavery took place recently. However, in this nation the wealthy and powerful are above the law and so they continue to own slaves.

15. *Mali*—Old-fashioned African slavery continues.

16. *Mauritania*—In areas outside the cities slavery still exists. In October of 1980, Mohammed I.O. Haitola, Chief of the Republic of Mauritania, commented: "Slavery is the most primitive, hateful form of exploitation of man by man. We know it exists in our country . . . It will take a long time before we are finally rid of this hateful practice."

17. *Morocco*—See *Libya*. Similar situation.

18. *Niger*—Standard African slavery.

19. *Pakistan*—Poverty-related slavery. (See *India*.)

20. *Peru*—Slavery through serfdom.

21. *Philippines*—On the island of Mindanao, the Moslem Filipinos have had an unbroken tradition of owning slaves since the 16th century.

22. *Sri Lanka*—A few years ago the government denied there was any slavery in this country. Whereupon, a reporter for the London *Times* bought an eight-year-old boy for five dollars to prove its existence.

23. *Saudi Arabia*—Slave-owning was outlawed in 1962. At that time some 250,000 slaves were known to be in bondage. Although the government denies it, there a black market still exists in females sold for sex purposes to wealthy men. At last report an attractive girl went for $500.

24. *Syria*—Has the same conditions as Lebanon.

25. *Thailand*—One of the worst situations of all. Thousands of Thai children (especially female) ages 10 to 14 are sold to factories, brothels, massage parlors and wealthy individuals. There are professional buyers who know where and when the worst poverty will be found. For example, in the northeast,

during the dry season. Recently parents began to take their children to the Bangkok railroad station, where buyers congregate. The normal price is $50 to $100, although an especially pretty girl, guaranteed to be a virgin, can fetch (with much negotiating) as much as $500. Theoretically, the sale is a six-month lease, but if the parent can locate the buyer after six months, he usually says, "I'm sorry. She ran away."

163

17

Here is a potpourri, and we think the next item will drive you ape....

**2 Female Chimpanzees
Who Experienced Orgasms**

1. Nanette
2. Shu Shu

While some primates may be prelates, not all primates are people. Of those primates who are people, many human females have problems reaching orgasm during intercourse.

Dr. Dolores Elaine Keller, a biologist and full professor at Pace University in New York City, is also a psychologist and psychotherapist. Dr. Keller, who specializes in sexual disorders and marital therapy, wondered whether orgasmic difficulty was a generalized female primate condition.

She reasoned that if human females had less difficulty in reaching orgasm with clitoral stimulation, nonhuman primates should be tested to see if this was also true for them. Watching primates mate led her to conclude that intravaginal thrusting time is brief. This suggested why orgasm during intercourse might be difficult to attain for the female primate.

From prelates on down into the evolutionary past, predating

humans, apparently male primates insert penis, thrust and then ejaculate within ten seconds. Certainly by today's standards of proper primate sexual performance, premature ejaculation is a rampant primate problem.

Most female partners of such primates have trouble having orgasms during intercourse—even though the potential is there.

Keller investigated noncoital orgasm in *Pan troglodytes* chimpanzees at the Laboratory for Experimental Medicine and Surgery in Primates, a division of New York University's Medical Center.

Sure enough, two chimpanzees did experience orgasm with digital clitoral stimulation, and one, Nanette, also climaxed with the use of an electric vibrator on her clitoris, a sexual first for Pans and for Nanette.

Shu Shu was afraid of the vibrator (a modified Prelude 2 frequently used in sexual therapy for nonorgasmic human females), but did evidence thrusting pelvic contractions as well as vaginal contractions.

Vocalizations also occurred when Nanette had an orgasm—a series of throaty "hoo-hoo-hoos."

7 Men and Women Who Adopted a Different Sex

1. *Chevalier d'Eau de Beaumal* (1728–1810), the director of the king's residence in France, took a trip for reconnaissance purposes disguised as a woman. He enjoyed it so much that thereafter he lived as a woman. He created so much doubt that there were frequent bets on his true sex, with many efforts made to check the point.

2. *Abbé de Choisy* (1644–1724) decided at an early age that he wanted to live as a woman. He even pierced his ears and wore fancy earrings.

3. *Victoria Tasman* was arrested in Chicago in 1923 and, when deprived of a razor, sprouted a beard. She became known as the Smiling Bandit Queen of Chicago.

4. *Christiana Davies*, an Irish woman of Dublin, got married in 1667. Shortly thereafter, her husband disappeared and then she learned that he had joined the Army. To follow him she joined

the Army, trained and soldiered. She fought in a battle in Holland, was wounded and then taken prisoner. Released and discharged, she regained her health and then joined the Dragoons to fight in Italy. She was wounded in the Battle of Donawet, found her husband while recuperating, and they continued to soldier together for years, keeping her gender a secret. It was discovered several years later and both were discharged. They returned to Dublin where they lived for years.

5. *Loretta J. Velásquez* joined the Confederate Army in 1860 as Harry T. Buford. Her gender was discovered by accident, whereupon she was discharged. She enjoyed the Army so much that she rejoined the 21st Louisiana Regiment under another name. Wounded in battle, she was again discovered by the treating physicians and discharged.

6. *Dr. James Barry* (true name and origin unknown) enrolled at the University of Edinburgh at age 16 to study medicine. After practicing medicine for a short time, she joined the Army as a surgeon. She served with the British Army all over the world and rose to the rank of Inspector-General of All Army Hospitals. The fact that she was a woman was not discovered until 1865, when she died, and the attending physician performed an autopsy.

7. *Kuo Chun Ching* was a young woman (age 16) when she joined the Communist Party, then headed by Mao Tse-tung. In 1934 Mao led the Chinese Red Army on the famed "Long March" (6,000 miles) from Kiangsi to Yenan. Kuo wanted to go along as a fighting soldier. Some women were allowed to go along but only to perform rear echelon duties. So Kuo cut her hair and disguised herself as a man. She turned out to be one of Mao's best fighters. She was wounded twice and later received the highest decoration awarded by the Army.

Kinsey's 5 Basic Coital Positions

From the studies made by Dr. Alfred Kinsey and associates at the Institute for Sex Research, Bloomington, Indiana, it was concluded that there are five basic coital positions for heterosexual penis-vagina intercourse. All other positions are variations of these five.

1. Lying down
2. Kneeling/supine position
3. Sideways
4. Sitting
5. Standing

8 Facts to Prove That
Sex Business Is Big Business

1. More than 100,000 people are employed in the legal parts of the sex industry. This includes publishing sex books and magazines and manufacturing sex items such as vibrators, contraceptives, and sex-enhancement aids.

2. Another 100,000 to 200,000 people work in the illegal or semilegal portions of the sex business. This includes massage parlors, brothels (outside of Nevada), etc.

3. There are 20,000 adult book stores in the U.S. with an average gross per store of $200,000 a year.

4. The ten leading monthly sex magazines, including *Playboy, Playgirl, Penthouse, Hustler,* and *Oui,* sell more than 16 million copies each month.

5. The rapidly increasing video-cassette market consists of more than fifty percent porno video tapes. There are 800 full-time sex-movie houses in the United States. Attendance consists of between two and three million patrons each week spending approximately $10 million each week.

6. There are now an estimated 100 stores in the United States selling sex enhancement products. This industry is reaching a figure of close to $10 million per year.

167

Frequency of Male Heterosexual Intercourse

Age	Under 20	20 to 30	30 to 40	40 to 50	50 to 60	Over 60
Not once	9%	3%	2%	6%	7%	10%
A few times	11%	4%	5%	7%	16%	34%
Once or twice a month	12%	5%	6%	9%	46%	24%
Once or twice a week	36%	33%	30%	44%	18%	22%
3 or 4 times a week	18%	27%	33%	21%	10%	10%
5 times a week	10%	22%	18%	11%	2%	0%
Daily or oftener	4%	6%	3%	2%	1%	0%

7. The sex business has reached the point where it has its own newsletter, published by Dennis Sobin in Washington, D.C., entitled *The Adult Business Report*. A one-year subscription to all reports is $150. The address for subscriptions is: R.P.E. Publications, 36 N Street, S.E., Washington, DC 20003.

8. The amount of business done in sex by the underground economy is difficult to measure. For example, *The New York Times* recently estimated that a New York prostitute earns between $20 and $40 per trick and makes $1,000 to $1,500 tax-free each week.

3 Cases of Men Being Raped by Women

1. In Vinnitsa, a city in the Soviet Union, a group of young women raped a young man in a dormitory of an armament factory. They

Frequency of Female Heterosexual Intercourse

Age	Under 20	20 to 30	30 to 40	40 to 50	50 to 60	Over 60
Not once	13%	5%	2%	7%	12%	·28%
A few times	12%	7%	6%	9%	28%	43%
Once or twice a month	16%	18%	12%	34%	30%	12%
Once or twice a week	28%	20%	23%	22%	11%	9%
3 or 4 times a week	20%	32%	34%	16%	10%	5%
5 times a week	8%	12%	19%	12%	9%	3%
Daily or oftener	3%	5%	4%	0%	0%	0%

tied a form of tourniquet around the base of his penis to keep him from losing his erection and then took turns.

2. In the Kurile Islands, the captains of fishing boats are afraid to let their men go ashore. There are thousands of women working in the canneries there who may go for years without being with a man. The rape of a strange male is not infrequent. Any sailor who sets foot on the island does so at the risk of his life.

—Sex in the U.S.S.R. by Mikhail Stern
and August Stern

3. In England, a gentleman who was going out with a Spanish girl enrolled in night school and learned Spanish. He became friendly with another woman attending the class, and they got into a discussion of rape and the man said, "I don't believe a woman can be raped without her cooperation." Some time later the woman to whom he had made the remark invited him to go on a picnic. Some other girls joined them and it was suggested

that they go sunbathing. They got him to take all his clothing off except his shorts. Suddenly the girls all grabbed him and holding him down, they shoved a vibrator up his rectum. Much to his surprise, he got an erection quickly and had an orgasm. He had never believed this was possible.

—Report of the Committee on the Operation of the [British] Sexual Containment Act

Frequency of Sexual Activity of Homosexuals

1. Once or a few times	4%
2. Every other month	3%
3. Once a month	8%
4. 2–3 times a month	15%
5. Once a week	20%
6. 2–3 times a week	30%
7. 4–6 times a week	11%
8. 7 times a week or more	7%
9. Never	2%

—from *Homosexualities* by Alan P. Bell and Martin S. Weinberg

6 Factors That Suggest That the Peak Seasons for Sexual Activity Are Late Summer and Early Autumn

Everyone remembers Alfred Lord Tennyson's famous dictum, "In the spring a young man's fancy lightly turns to thoughts of love." If love means sex, the statisticians have proven that Tennyson had the wrong season. Here's the evidence:

1. A study of birth records shows a very high percentage of babies are conceived in July, August, and September.
2. Rape statistics show a peak in the months of July and August.
3. Public health statistics show that gonorrhea peaks in August.
4. New cases of syphilis (the disease takes six to eight weeks to show) peak in November and December
5. Sales of condoms peak in late July and early August.
6. Testosterone in the human body peaks in September.

Rachel Copelan's 7 Steps to Sexual Fulfillment (Complete Orgasm) in Women

Rachel Copelan is a sex therapist, marriage counselor, author, and lecturer. She is the author of The Sexually Fulfilled Woman and The Sexually Fulfilled Man. Copelan is also the hostess of her own syndicated television program in which she provides a fascinating and provocative exploration into modern life styles.

1. *Self-Awareness:* Accept the fact that you are normal and need sex.
2. *Self-Suggestion:* Talk to yourself during intercourse (silently!).
3. *Body Relaxation:* Release inhibitions with mental persuasion.
4. *Sexual Breathing:* Increase energy by focusing air through the vagina.
5. *Sharing a Fantasy:* Open up mentally and physically about everything.
6. *Muscle Squeezing:* Awaken your hidden nerve endings inside the vagina.
7. *Expanding Orgasm:* Turn up your sensory awareness—sight, sound, taste, and touch.

—Exclusive for The Book of Sex Lists

3 Aids to Perk Up a Sexually Dull Marriage

All too frequently an otherwise excellent marriage begins to come apart because the sex aspects start to become dull, stale and even boring. Here are some suggestions for outside help.

1. A marriage encounter group. These are usually held over a weekend and can be helpful. Although often sponsored by a religious organization, the religious aspect is not stressed. The following are national organizations. To get information about a local encounter near you, write to one of these.

> Episcopal Expression
> 6 Commonwealth Boulevard
> Bellerose, New York 11426

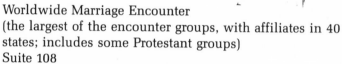

> Jewish Marriage Experience
> 199 Boston Avenue
> Massapequa, New York 11758

> National Marriage Encounter
> 5305 West Foster Avenue
> Chicago, Illinois 60630

> Worldwide Marriage Encounter
> (the largest of the encounter groups, with affiliates in 40 states; includes some Protestant groups)
> Suite 108
> 10059 Manchester Road
> Warson Woods, Missouri 63122

2. Marriage enrichment programs. These may or may not include encounter groups, but frequently have direct counselling, advisory functions and other methods to help a marriage. The emphasis here is on preventative measures, so try here early. The following is a center for these organizations:

> Association for Marriage Enrichment
> 459 S. Church Street
> P. O. Box 10, 596
> Winston-Salem, N.C. 27013
> President Couple: David and Sarah Catron

3. Psychodrama—a "role-reversal" technique to help in any psychological problem and particularly good for marriage and sex problems. For local psychodramatists and programs write to:

> Moreno Institute
> 259 Wolcott Avenue
> Beacon, N.Y. 12508

18

The expression "far-out" is not limited to California.
Here are some other far-outs.

11 Far-out Letters
Received by the Project

The Project is a not-for-profit theatre and research group which studies sexual variety and presents weekly discussions and theatrical productions of erotic fantasies.

The Project's files comprise more than 1,500 personal sex histories, proclivities, fantasies and lifestyles.

Headquarters are on the top floor of a loft building in SoHo, in lower Manhattan. However, mail should be addressed to The Project, 2211 Broadway, New York, N.Y. 10024. The phone number is (212) 787-2111.

The following are actual extracts from the thousands of letters that have been received by The Project during the past few years.

1. "I am a helpless piece of fruit being tossed with apple and orange slices and bananas by a beautiful woman. I have a huge tub and a giant Haitian fork and spoon in my basement, and I always ask my girlfriends to put me in and toss me."

2. "Whenever we are going to have sex, my wife and I put a raw fish in bed with us. I was brought up in a fish store and whenever I was feeling insecure, I would hide under my mother's skirts and breathe the smell of fish on her body."

3. "I am a queen in a pleasure palace with a whole harem of men. My husband is kept hanging in a cage at the side of my bed, and he is forced to watch while I make it with all my servants."

4. "I pay prostitutes to put tail feathers in their ani (plural of anus) and walk around me while I lie on the bed and play with myself."

5. "I am very proud of my one inverted tit. I am in a glass elevator with ten young studs. As the elevator goes up the side of the building, they strip off my clothes and admire and start licking and caressing my inverted tit."

6. "I dream of Dracula coming through the window, biting my neck, and carrying me off to screw in his coffin."

7. "My first experience with a woman was my mother taking me to the live poultry market. I felt jealous sitting in my little baby buggy while the chickens were getting all the attention. Now, whenever I have sex, I fantasize being one of those chickens."

8. "He drapes my nude body with clusters of tiny silver and golden bells which are attached by gossamer threads to several huge sticks. He begins to poke and taunt me with the sticks, and a haunting melody arises from the shimmering bells."

9. "I fantasize a whole sorority of girls tying one of their sisters down and tickling her underarms, ribs, and feet."

10. "I get turned on by the thought of a woman silencing me by pressing the palm of her hand over my mouth."

11. "This great goddess in the sky with a giant Afro sends down a ladder for me. As I climb up, my clothes shed like a snake's skin and my organ is growing to meet the size of my goddess.

As we make hair-raising sex, our love juices fall on the earth below, and the people are so happy that they prepare hamburgers and hotdogs and declare a holiday."

—Prepared by The Project especially for
The Book of Sex Lists

7 Prevalent Women's Sexual Fantasies

Quotations are phrases that repeatedly appear in letters or are used in typical situations.

1. *No Way Out*
   "He made me do it."
   "I had to submit."
   "The policeman tells me I must take off all my clothes and do as he says or I will be locked up."

2. *Making It in an Exotic Place*
   "In the john on the airplane."
   "On the beach as the waves flowed over us."
   "On the Ferris wheel at Coney Island."
   "In my parents' bed."

3. *Threat of Discovery*
   "My God, look what they're doing!"
   "My brother and his wife are about to come home."
   "My roommate is sleeping in the next room."

4. *Seducing a Young Boy*
   "One of my students."
   "My little cousin."
   "I knew it was his first time."
   "I taught him how to do it."

5. *Erotic Activities*
   "He uses a vibrator on me."
   "He paints my body with bright colors and rubs the paint in with his hands."
   "He inspects my privates with a flashlight."
   "We take a shower together."

175

6. *Threesomes and Moresomes*
   "He brought his best friend in."
   "My girlfriend and I worked him over."
   "It is just me and a whole platoon of men."

7. *The Father Figure*
   "Daddy tells me I'm a naughty little girl and fondles me to orgasm."
   "He squeezes my breasts and tells me little girls should be seen, not heard."

   —Prepared by The Project especially for
   The Book of Sex Lists

7 Popular Men's Fantasies and Some Recurring Phrases and Situations

1. *The Voracious Vixen*
   "She knows exactly what she wants—and gets it."
   "She peels off her clothes and then starts to loosen my tie."
   "She's all animal."

2. *Double Your Fun*
   "Especially two sisters."
   "I want a black and a white girl at the same time."
   "I've always wanted a pair of identical twins in bed so I don't know which one I'm screwing."

3. *The Best Parts*
   "Give me a gal with magnificent mammaries."
   "I always used to masturbate to the story of Rapunzel. I wanted to wrap my body in her long silken hair."
   "Why isn't there more interest in the most beautiful part of a woman's body—her soft, pink, ticklish feet?"
   "I love the smell of their underarms, like burnt leaves in the fall."

176

4. *The Watcher*

"I want to see two women make it with each other."

"I want to watch her with my best friend."

"I love to see two women wrestling, tearing at each other's bathing suits and falling out all over."

"I dream of a woman making it with a dog and I'm just watching."

5. *The Adventurer*

"I take on a whole island of Polynesian women."

"I'm the only man on this whole planet of women."

6. *The Pain Lovers*

"She puts me across her knee and paddles my bottom good.

"She puts her cigarette out in my pubic hair and singes it."

"She puts clamps on my nipples."

7. *Exotic Costumes*

"She straddles me in nothing but her garter belt and black stockings."

"There's nothing like a chick in high stepping boots."

—Compiled by The Project especially for
The Book of Sex Lists

J. Aphrodite's 10 Favorite Sex Fantasies

In 1975 a book was published by a respectable publishing house. It was titled *To Turn You On: 39 Sex Fantasies for Women.* Its author was identified as "J. Aphrodite."

This was the first "hard core" porn book for women. It was designed to do for women what porn did for many men: to free them from their inhibitions and to free them from guilt about sexual images and fantasies that seemed offbeat.

To Turn You On was a fun book. Its author appeared on several television shows wearing a Lone Ranger–type mask to conceal her identity.

Actually, people in publishing knew that Carole Livingston was "J. Aphrodite." The mask was a sure attention-getter to people twisting their TV dials from station to station.

To Turn You On was too strong for the women's magazines and book clubs but the Playboy Book Club bought 12,000 copies of it and sections of the book appeared in *Playgirl*.

Bantam Books bought mass market paperback rights.

To Turn You On was a breakthrough book. It was female sex fantasy without the pretense that it was a serious sociological study or the protection of an introduction by a serious psychologist—several of whom volunteered to write such an introduction.

Carole Livingston has since written two very successful books: *Why Was I Adopted?* and *I'll Never Be Fat Again!*

Here she summarizes with some humor the plots of ten of the thirty-nine fantasies in *To Turn You On*.

1. *Visit to the Gynecologist*—A routine checkup develops into considerably more. Handsome doctor, patient who has a crush on him and he starts to check her "sexual responses." His fingers probe unexplored territory and bring delightful results. Monthly checkups are encouraged to make sure sexual responses keep on responding.

2. *The Masseuse*—Unwinding at the health spa with Ingrid, a formidable German girl. Although Ingrid speaks no English, words become unnecessary as her expertise in body manipulation leads to the best massage the spa never advertised.

3. *Domination*—Here is the ageless "I'm the boss around here" theme. In this variation the man of the house brings in not just a man to have his woman make love to, but another woman as well. The lady has to admit that although her man runs the show, she does indeed enjoy the domination.

4. *A Dog Day*—Rover (here called King) is not merely man's best friend; he becomes woman's too. Enough said?

5. *Tutor and Student*—Here the tutor is the older woman who deals with young Henry, the boy who has yearnings for more than piano lessons. He is a quick study on all counts.

6. *Free Afternoon*—Some housewives are quite inventive in passing time while waiting for their husbands to come home from work. These two ladies find there's at least as much fun to be had in a bed as on a tennis court.

7. *Nude on the Therapist's Knee*—An invitation to get in touch with "feeling free" leads this woman out of her clothes and into a new form of therapy. This doctor takes an active role in the welfare of his patients.

8. *The Delivery Boy*—If you believe older women lose their sex drive, here's a fantasy to prove you wrong. In this case our heroine is a widow who persuades the young delivery boy to put down his packages and stay awhile.

9. *The Schoolgirls*—These youngsters are caught in unusual locker room activity by the dean of their school. Punishment is ordered but first a replay of the "crime" must be enacted—in front of the dean. Afterwards a spanking is administered by the overexcited dean.

10. *Pay for Play*—If you've ever wondered how to kill time while waiting for a date to show up, here's something different than shopping. This woman standing in a hotel lobby is mistaken for a lady of the evening. Impulsively she decides to accept the offer and forty minutes later she's back in the lobby, still on time for her date and a few dollars richer.

—Prepared by Carole Livingston especially for *The Book of Sex Lists*

27 Sex Taboos Enjoyed by Some Men

The following fascinations for some men are sometimes considered sex offenses and are legally punishable in some parts of the world. The American Psychiatric Association now calls them *paraphilias*, variations of and deviations from "normal" sexual activity. The condition exists when the person (rarely female) is obsessively dependent on these situations in order to have erotic arousal and to facilitate and achieve orgasm.

In *Love and Lovesickness*, Dr. John Money discusses the twenty-seven paraphilias on this list.

1. *Acrotomophilia* (fantasizing that one's partner is an amputee)
2. *Apotemnophilia* (fantasizing oneself as an amputee and sometimes actually scheming to have one or more limbs amputated)

179

3. *Asphyxiophilia* (choking oneself to obtain arousal)
4. *Autoassassinatophilia* (staging or imagining one's own murder)
5. *Coprophilia* (an obsession with feces, varied in expression; it may involve the sight and sound of a person defecating). The porno film *Pink Flamingos* features the transvestite Divine, a 300-pound "sex symbol," eating a dog's feces. In 1981 Divine starred with Tab Hunter in a film called *Polyester* in which a scratch-and-smell card was given to each member of the audience. Some of the odors were quite repulsive.
6. *Ephebophilia* (the condition in which an adult has real or imagined activity with an adolescent)
7. *Exhibitionism* (being responsive to the shock or outcry of a stranger upon showing one's sexual organ)
8. *Fetishism* (being aroused by a non-sexual object such as the heel of a shoe)
9. *Frotteurism* (the need to rub against a stranger, especially in a tightly packed crowd)
10. *Gerontophilia* (the need for a partner much older than oneself)
11. *Kleptophilia* (the condition in which a person must steal or imagine stealing)
12. *Klismaphilia* (a dependency on being given an enema)
13. *Homicidophilia* (the rare condition in which one must sadistically murder one's partner or fantasize the murder in order to obtain sexual satisfaction)
14. *Masochism* (the need to be punished or hurt)
15. *Mysophilia* (a dependency on something soiled or filthy, such as sweaty underwear or used menstrual pads)
16. *Narratophilia* (being responsive to reading or listening to erotic narratives)
17. *Necrophilia* (the need to have sexual activity with a corpse)
18. *Pedophilia* (a dependency on the imagery or actuality of sexual activity with a boy or girl in early puberty)
19. *Pictophilia* (a dependency on erotic pictures)
20. *Rapophilia* (a dependency on the terrified resistance of a non-consenting stranger)
21. *Sadism* (the need to punish or humiliate one's sexual partner)
22. *Scoptophilia* (a dependency on looking at sexual organs and watching sexual activity openly. It is not surreptitious as in voyeurism.)

23. *Somnophilia* (the need to fondle a stranger who is asleep)
24. *Troilism* (the need to be the third member of a sexual partnership; typically, a husband arranges for his wife to have another male partner so he can fantasize her in the role of a prostitute)
25. *Urophilia* (being dependently responsive to the smell or taste of urine or the sight and sound of someone urinating)
26. *Voyeurism* (being dependently responsive to the risk of being caught while illicitly peering at another person or couple undressing or engaged in sexual activity; a voyeur is also known as a peeping Tom)
27. *Zoophilia* (a dependency on sexual activity with an animal; sexual contact, oral or genital, may occur sporadically in the course of human development without leading to long-term zoophilia)

19

*If this were a movie, the next section
would call for parental discretion.
It is definitely not for prudes or sourpusses.*

11 Inside Stories About the Making of the Film
Caligula

1. The screen test, *Caligula*-style: More than 300 women auditioned for parts in *Caligula* by performing in sexual screen tests so that director Tinto Brass could see "Not just whether, but *how*. Are they good at it? Do they fuck cheerfully or not?"

2. One extra did indeed have two penises—not all the grotesqueries were made up.

3. Director Brass had oral sex with a Penthouse Pet on the set before the entire crew to show an actor how he wanted it done. His wife described his behavior as "just his usual extroverted self."

4. The extra playing a Roman guard who had his penis tied and was forced to drink wine until bloated, then was stabbed by Tiberius (Peter O'Toole) in a display of imperial cruelty, was *actually* stabbed by accident and had to be hospitalized.

5. Question: How do you prevent an eel from biting a woman while inside her?

   Answer: If you were the first assistant of *Caligula* and faced that problem for the Harem Monsters scene, you had the brainstorm of putting a condom over its head and holding it on with Scotch tape. That, unfortunately, didn't solve the problem—it killed the eel before it could perform. If you were the woman matched with the eel, you used your imagination—and put it in tail first.

6. The fake cock for the castration scene was made out of pork sausage.

7. A Penthouse Pet pissing on an actor on camera did it three times. On the third take, she wasn't supposed to piss but she did. Director Brass screamed at her, "For chrissakes, you want to be an actress but you can't even take a 'don't piss' direction!"

8. It is against Italian law to have minors on a movie set where sexual activity occurs. The filmmakers got around this one by hiring especially young-looking eighteen-year-old women and shaving their pubic areas.

9. The bed built for Caligula, his wife, his sister, a dozen women slaves and his horse was modelled after the main altar in Saint Peter's Basilica.

10. *Penthouse* wanted *Caligula* to be a soft-core soft-focus copy of the magazine. Tinto Brass wanted to make a kind of anarchist "Busby Berkeley Goes to Rome" —a big-budget, hardcore slapstick comedy. He almost accomplished his goal. Only after the film was completed did *Penthouse* realize what he'd done. It then took three years and three different film editors to undo the "damage."

11. The climactic (pardon the pun) orgy scene on the ship was a real orgy. It was another example of director Brass's obsession with recreating actual pagan sex. It lasted two days and included more than 300 people.

> —From the book *Ultimate Porno*, by PierNico Solinas. This list was prepared especially for *The Book of Sex Lists* by Louis Rossetto

24 Ladies' Tank Tops Offered in the Pages of *Easyriders*

Easyriders is a magazine published for adult bikers (motorcycle enthusiasts). The subscription price is $23 a year, and the Circulation Department address is Box 711, Burbank, CA 91503.

1. HONKY-TONK STUFF
2. THE LEFT ONE IS A BEAUT!
3. SCREW HOUSEWORK
4. I LOVE TO BOOGIE
5. IF IT SMELLS GOOD, EAT IT!
6. STUFF
7. HEAD GIVER
8. LOOKING FOR TEN POUNDS OF SWINGING MEAT
9. MY BODY IS AN OUTLAW; IT'S WANTED ALL OVER TOWN
10. SHOW YOUR MEAT
11. LUNCH HERE
12. I'M AN EASYRIDER
13. DO IT TO IT
14. HOT AND JUICY
15. SHOW ME YOUR DICK
16. MUSTANG RANCH TRAINEE
17. LIQUOR UP FRONT
    POKER IN THE REAR
18. MOTORCYCLE MAMA
19. NO PUTT
    NO BUTT
20. I'M HIS 'CAUSE HE GIVES GOOD FACE
21. SIT ON A HAPPY FACE
22. SMILE IF YOU'RE HORNY
23. YOU CAN'T BEAT MY MEAT
24. BEAT ME, BITE ME, WHIP ME, FUCK ME LIKE THE DIRTY PIG THAT I AM. CUM ALL OVER MY TITS AND TELL ME THAT YOU LOVE ME. THEN GET THE FUCK OUT.

8 Types of Men (from a Virility Viewpoint)

1. *The No-Nonsense Pragmatist*
   Coat of arms: $2 + 2 = 4$

2. *The Reluctant Civilized Brute*
   Coat of Arms: A tethered bull rampant.
3. *The Thinker*
   Coat of Arms: A phallus contemplatively couchant, wearing a monocle, reading a scroll.
4. *The Rogue*
   Coat of Arms: A phallus rampant, piercing a "keep out" sign.
5. *The Operator-Manipulator*
   Coat of Arms: A solid gold phallus on a field of dollar green.
6. *The Satyr*
   Coat of Arms: A phallus rampant, piercing a dog-eared address book.
7. *The Romantic Outcast*
   Coat of Arms: A lone figure on a mountaintop, silhouetted against a sunset.
8. *The Mild Male*
   Coat of Arms: None. And if he did have one, he wouldn't display it.

—Source: Max Gunther, *Virility 8*

Gary Null's 5 Reasons to Be Celibate

Celibacy has usually been reserved for people with strong religious convictions. However, the celibacy Gary Null advocates is not based on religious dogma, guilt, or self-denial, but rather on an understanding of what he characterizes as "compulsive behavior."

Here are five of the reasons he suggests one should be celibate by choice—if only for a month or two at a time.

1. Sex requires a substantial amount of time and energy. Thus, by eliminating sex from the agenda, a person can devote energy to productive and creative non-sexual pursuits.
2. Sex demands contriving and manipulating to achieve sexual conquest. On the other hand, if a person knows you enjoy their company without the relationship requiring sex, they are put at

ease, drop their defenses, and a meaningful friendship can develop.
3. Too often we have sex for the wrong reasons and with the wrong partners.
4. One can broaden one's perspective by putting aside sex just as one should occasionally banish radio, television, phone calls, work, partying, and even reading. This forces a person to seek his or her own inner resources and one learns to really know one's self.
5. After a period of one or two months of deliberate celibacy, introspection will help one to be in touch with one's true feelings. If the decision is made to have sex again for a while, the sexual experience will be heightened by its freshness.

10 Men's T-Shirts Offered in *Easyriders*

1. I COULD MAKE LINDA LOVELACE GAG
2. LOVE ME, LOVE MY TOOL
3. HARLEY FUCKIN' DAVIDSON
4. GET OFF MY ASS!
5. PAYBACKS ARE A BITCH
6. HARLEY RIDERS EAT MORE PUSSY
7. SHOW ME YOUR TITS
8. I'M A PERVERT
   (IN CASE OF EMERGENCY, GIMME HEAD)
9. BORN ON A MOUNTAIN
   RAISED IN A CAVE
   BIKING AND FUCKIN'
   IS ALL I CRAVE
10. SHOW YOUR PUSSY

21 Pseudonyms Used by Contemporary Writers of Pornography

1. P.H. Alice
2. Ophelia Bawls

186

3. Willie B. Commings
4. Ben Dover
5. Will U. Goedown
6. Dick M. Harder
7. B. Hott
8. Mike Hunt
9. Dick Hurdy
10. Dick Hyman
11. Pussy Katz
12. Peter Large
13. Wanda Layer
14. I.M. Licken
15. Melinda Lovitt
16. Peter Peckerman
17. John Peters
18. Lucy N. Ready
19. Dick Rudd
20. Clyde Torris
21. Walter Wang

9 Popular Places for Masturbation

For men:

1. In the bathroom
2. In bed under the sheets
3. In bed on top of the covers
4. In a closet
5. In any locked room

For women:

1. In the bathtub
2. In bed with a vibrator
3. In bed without a vibrator
4. In a plane in the washroom

187

Hansen's 10 Sexiest Cakes

Hansen's specializes in custom cakes, as well as cakes for weddings and bar mitzvahs. They can reproduce anything or put any idea in sculptured cake form.

(Hansen's is located in Los Angeles and Beverly Hills, California.)

1. The *Flying Penis* cake—an erect penis winging its way through the air.

2. *48 Double D* cake—bigger-than-life breasts out of which came two buxom women. The opening Hansen's made on top of each boob wasn't wide enough to let the ladies, who happened to have 48 double D's themselves, out of the cake. The bakery was called back during the party to cut a wider opening for the girls. (Hansen's reports that they now always request exact measurements.)

3. *Surprise Party* cake—18 gorgeous nude women jumped out of it for a movie studio executive.

4. *Shot from Behind* cake—male buttocks with testicles hanging from the center.

5. *What-a-Way-to-Go* cake—for a fiftieth wedding anniversary, Hansen's sculptured a man and a woman copulating (Greek style).

6. The *Last Days of Pompeii* cake—a mosaic cake which depicted the morally loose people of Pompeii, including sexual orgies, homosexuality, and masochism.

7. The *Jerk* cake—a male figure lying down masturbating with his larger-than-life penis.

8. *Female Torso* cake—the nude female from the neck to the thighs.

9. *Sexy Secretary* cake—a wonderfully proportioned secretary bending over at the water cooler.

10. Self-Portrait cake—occasionally Hansen's receives a request from a young actress who wants a nude sculpture done of her, to be sent to an agent or a producer.

—Exclusive for *The Book of Sex Lists*

8 Classified Ads From
the Pages of *Easyriders*

Here is a sampling of ads that appeared in the classified section of America's number one motorcycle magazine. We have omitted the names and addresses of the advertisers.

I need some sweet-smellin' female mail.

Crazy, kinky, can't spell, but try like hell. Need letters and photos to pass the time, so come on, drop me a line.

Two down and lonely tramps need letters from serious ladies 20–35. Letters w/pictures answered first.

That sweet young thing on page 35 in February, 1981 issue, the one sitting on the chopper. I think you're about the foxiest thing I've ever seen. If you're not all hitched up and involved, take a chance—I did.

Train: I love your caboose, and that powerful engine of yours. Can't hardly wait for June to come, so you can run over my tracks! Love ya.

California youngster (21) desires perfumed correspondence with foxy photos to end the blues.

Have problems at home? Ex-biker family seeks single female or unwed mother 16–30 years old, for self-sufficient homestead. Permanent home for right people. Hassle-free environment.

White male, 26, looking for an ol' lady to putt with this summer. No game players, please! Must be into sex, drugs, and rock and roll. Will answer all replies. Send photo. Chicagoland area.

17 Factors Which Predispose to Incest
Between Fathers and Daughters

1. Disorganization of the family

With Respect to the Adult Partner:
2. Socially and emotionally disturbed relationship with spouse
3. Unsatisfying sexual partnership
4. Detectable psychopathological personality
5. Violent and quick temper
6. Reduced self-control as a result of heavy drinking
7. Jealous attitude toward daughter or stepdaughter
8. Hypersexuality or sexual passion

With Respect to the Female Victim:

9. Dependence on authority of father or stepfather
10. Unsatisfactory relationship with mother or stepmother
11. Uncritical attitude; not gifted with normal intelligence
12. Extreme sexual curiosity
13. Strong Oedipal connection to father or stepfather
14. Low intelligence
15. Feelings of neglect
16. Social isolation
17. Previous heterosexual experience (coitus)

—Adapted from *Incest*, by Herbert Maisch

38 Most Common Factors Helping to Sustain Incestuous Relationships Between Fathers and Daughters

With respect to the victim:

1. Feeling of shame or guilt toward mother or stepmother
2. Fear of men
3. Passive behavior (not resistant)
4. Lack of knowledge concerning rights
5. General feelings of shame
6. Fear of judicial punishment or being placed in a home
7. Fear of family breaking up
8. Fear of loss of father or stepfather
9. Encouraging and provoking behavior
10. Sexual motives
11. Silence because of material advantages
12. Silence out of gratitude to man if he is caring and protective
13. Apathy, indifference
14. Emotional attraction to partner
15. Belief that incest is father's right
16. Confession, disbelief by mother and resultant disillusionment

With respect to the male:

17. Disturbed emotional relationship with wife; warning child to say nothing
18. Disturbed sex life with wife
19. Threats and intimidation toward victim
20. Situation where man is at home while wife is at work
21. Male tyrant in family
22. Caring and protective attitude toward victim
23. Payments in money and other gifts
24. Victim falsely advised of possibility of prison, etc.
25. Development of alcoholism
26. Favorable opportunity because of unemployment
27. Social isolation of victim
28. Emotionally colored attraction for partner
29. "Magic rituals"
30. Development of a perversion
31. Use of force

With respect to the wife or mother:

32. Rejection or refusal of marital intercourse
33. Neglect of husband and wife
34. Illness or death of wife
35. Wife's knowledgeable toleration of incestuous relationship
36. Sexual promiscuity
37. Rejection of daughter's confession
38. Collusion

—Adapted from *Incest*, by Herbert Maisch

191

20

Jackie Gleason used to say, "What fun it is!"
Here are some people having fun....

Henny Youngman's 5 Favorite
Sex One-Liners

1. Is it proper to have sex before marriage?
   Not if it delays the ceremony.
2. Do you talk to your wife during sex?
   If I'm near a telephone.
3. Do you smoke during sex?
   I never noticed.
4. A guy says to his wife, "How come you never tell me when
   you're having an orgasm?"
   "Because you're never around."
5. One guy says to another guy, "My wife cut me down to sex once
   a week."
   The other guy replies, "You're lucky. I know two guys she cut
   out altogether."

—Prepared by Henny Youngman especially for *The Book of Sex Lists*

William M. Gaines

Bill Gaines's 10 Foods
That Are Better Than Sex

William M. Gaines is the founder and publisher of *Mad* magazine. He is also a rather substantial eater. This section was made with loving care and with the assistance of Bill's live-in co-eater, Anne Griffiths.

 1. White truffles
 2. Fresh caviar from Caspian sturgeon
 3. Pennsylvania Dutch smoked sausage
 4. Tortellini alla panna with freshly grated Parmigiano Reggiano
 5. Fresh foie gras des Landes
 6. Prosciutto crudo di Langhirano
 7. Smoked Scotch salmon
 8. Peeled Royal Riviera pears with very heavy cream
 9. Raspberries with *crème fraîche*
10. White Castle hamburgers

19 Graffiti Inscriptions Copied from Bathroom Walls in 1981

1. Sign up now for the P.T.A. trip to Plato's Retreat
2. If you are high enough to read this line then you're probably pissing on the man in the next booth!
3. Miss Piggy gives great head
4. I trade orgasms
5. I won't go until you come
6. If you see it moving, please fondle it!
7. Save water. Do your fucking in an unfilled tub.
8. Don't stand close to the urinal, the crabs here are jumpers
9. When I see Jeanne's jugs jiggle, I reach for my dick
   I know it sounds awful but they're things I want to lick
10. The French they are a funny bunch
    What we call pussy, they call lunch
11. Phil Atio loves Connie Lingus
12. I'd rather fuck the Burger King and eat the waitress
13. I give no-cal cum
14. Tampax is not the best thing in the world but it's next to the best
15. Stop the gay revolution—wear baggy trousers
16. Minnie Mouse is a lesbian
17. Free love is never free
    underneath:
    Save your coupons and you'll see
18. Women's Lib? Put 'em behind bras!
19. Eve got a bum rap
    underneath:
    Balls. She gave Adam crabs
    underneath:
    Adam had 'em

21 Cities in the United States with Erotic-sounding Names

1. Blue Ball (Arizona)
2. Love Hollow (Arizona)

3. Balls Ferry (California)
4. Lick Observatory (California)
5. Lovelock (California)
6. Nut Tree (California)
7. Relief Hot Springs (California)
8. Twin Peaks (California)
9. Middlesex (New Jersey
10. Balls Mills (Pennsylvania)
11. Beaver (Pennsylvania)
12. Bird-in-Hand (Pennsylvania)
13. Black Gap (Pennsylvania)
14. Black Lick (Pennsylvania)
15. Blue Ball (Pennsylvania)
16. Honeyhole (Pennsylvania)
17. Honey Pot (Pennsylvania)
18. Hookers (Pennsylvania)
19. Intercourse (Pennsylvania)
20. Keisters (Pennsylvania)
21. Little Gap (Pennsylvania)
...which must indicate *something* about Pennsylvania.

7 Sexy Wines

Jules I. Epstein is a prominent insurance broker who is a member of numerous gastronomic societies. He is a restaurant reviewer and food and wine critic. Presently, he is head of the

New York chapter of the Confrérie de la Chaîne des Rôtisseurs, largest of the wine tasting gastronomic societies.

Jules Epstein's extensive wine cellar contains more than three thousand bottles of wine. Here are his comments and his list:

"I say unequivocally that there is no wine better than sex. However here are wines I have consumed that come close."

1. 1931 Quinta de Noval Vintage Port
2. 1953 Schloss Eltz Trockenbeerenauslese
3. 1945 Château Lafite-Rothschild
4. 1949 Musigny Comte Georges de Vogue
5. 1928 Château Latour
6. 1959 Château Corton Grancey Louis Latour
7. 1955 Château Petrus

—Exclusive for *The Book of Sex Lists*

11 Erotic Chocolate Candies

Your sex fantasy in chocolate? Yes, if you're in the New York or New Jersey area. Or, you can order by mail. Prices range from $2.99 and up.

The source for the first ten listed below is Candyland. Two of Candyland's four addresses are 15 Grand Avenue, Palisades Park, NJ 07650, and 130 Rockland Plaza, Nanuet, NY 10954. Item eleven, the chocolate penis, is available from Andras Confections Ltd., 250 W. 35th St., New York NY, 10001.

1. Willie's wonka
2. Bosom buddies
3. Pandora's box
4. Dolly pops
5. Peter pops
6. Bare essential
7. Fickle finger of fate
8. Ball pops
9. Living end
10. Hubba bubba
11. Chocolate penis

10 Sexy Tennis Shots

Tennis is a sexy game, but orgasm is rarely achieved except with the topmost two shots. That is, unless the opposition is particularly antagonistic. In any case, all of the following shots can bring the involved player deep sensuous satisfaction.

1. Overhead smash
2. Service ace
3. Backhand crosscourt
4. Backhand down the line
5. Service winner
6. Service return at server's feet
7. Service return at server's groin
8. Put away volley at the net
9. Baseline drop shot
10. Topspin lob

Prepared by Nick Meglin especially for *The Book of Sex Lists*

21

This section could be labeled "For Women Only."
But if you fellows want to take a peek permission is granted.

3 Exercises to Help Women Become Better Sex Partners

1. While urinating, stop the flow by contracting the muscles of the vagina and hold the contraction for three or four seconds. Do this about fifteen times each day. If you urinate five times each day, then do it three times during each urination. Do it regularly. (The reason for this is that the muscles involved in controlling your urine flow are the same as those involved in your sex activity. By strengthening these muscles, you will find that you enjoy sex activity more and you can be a better sex partner.)
2. Dilate the vagina. This is especially important for women who find they have pain during coitus (generally called dyspareunia). It involves dilating the vagina with either a lubricated object or the fingers. Be sure to use a sterile lubricating jelly such as Vaseline.
3. While flat on your back, either on the floor or in bed, with your feet stretched out straight, lift your feet together about four inches from the floor or mattress. In the beginning hold for just

a few seconds. As you get more strength, try to hold for five to ten seconds. This helps strengthen the entire abdominal area.

7 Ways to Select Your Baby's Gender

1. If you have intercourse when the north wind is blowing, you will have a boy. If you have intercourse when the south wind is blowing, you will have a girl. The authority for this is Aristotle (384–322 B.C.), a Greek philosopher and one of the greatest thinkers of all time. Although in many fields of learning Aristotle's theories are still valid, this one has not been capable of replication in modern times.

2. Use a thermometer and have intercourse at the preovulatory drop, that is, *before* ovulation. This will give you a boy. (See Landrum Shettles, *Choose Your Baby's Sex*, 1977.)

3. Use a thermometer, watch for the postovulatory drop, and have intercourse within two days following ovulation. This will give you a boy. (Susan Harlop, *New England Journal of Medicine*, June 28, 1979.)

   [If this confuses you, don't worry, it confuses us too. But seriously: Don't wait too long after ovulation because "overripe eggs have been associated with chromosomal abnormalities and birth defects." *Science News*, July 14, 1979, p. 24.]

4. If you really seriously and desperately want a boy, our research indicates you have to use artificial insemination. The male's sperm is put into a special solution that is difficult to swim in. The little sperm that carry the Y chromosome that makes boys are the better swimmers, so they have a better survival rate. Thus, with this method you should have a ninety-percent chance of having a boy.

5. Another suggested method to create a boy: Abstain from intercourse until shortly after ovulation. (Get doctor's approval for next step.) Before intercourse, the woman douches with a solution of two tablespoons of baking soda in a quart of water.

Next comes intercourse, with the man penetrating as deeply as possible. If the woman reaches an orgasm, this further neutralizes the acid in the vagina.

6. By the same authority, to have a girl: Continue intercourse until two days before scheduled ovulation, then abstain. (Get doctor's approval for next step.) Just before intercourse, the woman douches with solution of two tablespoons of vinegar in a quart of water. Male penetration during intercourse should be shallow. Woman should not have an orgasm in order to preserve acidity in the vagina. (Reference for methods 5 and 6: *Sex, A User's Manual*, Putnam's, 1981.)

7. A Canadian experiment indicates a possibility that the food a woman eats can determine the sex of the child conceived. X sperm have been found to like an environment rich in calcium and magnesium; Y sperm like potassium. So, for a boy, the woman should eat salty foods, sausages, hams, tea, coffee; for a girl, eggs and milk.

6 Things to Do When You Get an Obscene Phone Call

1. Hang up promptly. Under no circumstances should you engage in conversation.
2. Report it promptly to the phone company. Phone companies have special units to handle this sort of thing.
3. If it's repeated, unless there is a good reason to the contrary, change your phone number and get an unlisted number.
4. Never give out information about yourself or your telephone to people or organizations you know nothing about. If you get called in a survey (which may or may not be legitimate) you may cooperate if you desire, but do not give out information about your phone number, your address, or anything personal.
5. Answer the phone in as professional and unemotional a manner as possible. For example, "Smith residence." If there is no

prompt reply, or if there is any heavy breathing or anything out of the ordinary, hang up promptly.

6. Under no circumstances should you hide and let the phone ring. Don't run out of the apartment or house and don't give up. This frequently gives the caller his kicks.

5 Replies of Girls Who Work in Massage Parlors on Why There Is a Need for Massage Parlors

1. They satisfy sexual needs—5%
2. They contribute to relaxation and physical health—26.7%
3. They provide men with affection and relieve loneliness—20%
4. They reduce sex crimes and abuse in the streets—20%
5. There is really no need for massage parlors—3.3%

—From Frank H. Farley and Sandy A. Davis, "Masseuses, Men and Massage Parlors: An Exploratory Descriptive Study," *Journal of Sex and Marital Therapy,* vol. 4, no. 3.

14 Rules for the Care and Feeding of the Female Breast

The United States has been frequently called the "breast-culture country." More than fifty percent of all display advertising features a female breast. Motion pictures, television, and magazines focus on the female breasts as the center of attraction.

One would believe that with all this attention, a great deal would be known about the breast. However, more myths and misconceptions exist about the female breast than any other portions of the human anatomy. The following information is the result of long and careful research on the subject:

1. Should all women throw away their bras? Answer: Stand in front of a mirror, and view yourself from the waist up. Put your arms at your sides. Your nipples should line up with the point on your arm that is midway between your shoulder and your elbow. Higher is okay. If your nipple is lower, you ought to wear a bra to prevent further sagging. Large-breasted women almost always need bras because the heavy breast definitely tugs downward (a matter of gravity) and needs support. Women should definitely wear bras while engaging in vigorous sports. The bouncing of the breasts lengthens the skin and ligaments, so a well-fitted bra will help. If you do not wear a bra when you need one, the ligaments of the breasts will lose their elasticity, and your breasts will become pendulous.

2. If you decide to wear a bra, be certain to wear one that fits properly. A too-tight bra will weaken the muscles and inhibit breathing. If it's too loose, it serves no purpose. Take time to be sure your bra fits properly.

3. Is there any exercise to firm the breast? You probably cannot increase the firmness of the breast, but you can firm up other muscles which have the same effect. (The exercises to do are given in the separate list which follows this one.)

4. Is there any way to tell whether you need exercise in the breast area? Yes. Lift up your breast and put a pencil underneath. If it does not fall down, you need exercise. This also indicates that you probably need a good bra.

5. Is there any relationship between breast health and food? Yes. There are five items which seem to affect the breast adversely: coffee, tea, cola, chocolate, and cocoa. These beverages contain methyl-xanthine and tend to create breast problems, including breast tumors or cysts (nonmalignant).

6. What can exercise do for the breast? Directly, nothing. The female breast is about 80% glandular tissue and 20% fat. It has no muscle. Although exercise cannot affect the breast itself, it can do a great deal to make the breast look firmer and fuller. This is because underneath your breast, like a cushion, is the

supporting pectoral muscle, which can be strengthened and toned and can give the breast the lift it needs.

7. Wash and soap the breast regularly, but do not use soap on the breast when you are pregnant or nursing. Use a lotion in the winter to keep the skin soft and smooth.

8. If you're using an estrogen-based birth-control pill, you need extra B-complex vitamins, folic acid, selenium, vitamin E, vitamin C, and iodine. (See the article by Carlton Fredericks in *Harper's Bazaar*, September 1979.)

9. "Shall I breast-feed my baby?" Yes, if you can. Breast-feeding offers many advantages to the health of both the mother and the child that substitutes can't supply.

10. "Will breast-feeding ruin the shape of my breasts?" No. Obviously, during pregnancy and lactation, the breasts will increase in size and change in form. But actually, breast-feeding facilitates the return of your body to its earlier shape. Nursing activates the release of a hormone called oxytocin which helps provoke uterine contractions, with the result that a breast-feeding mother will go back to normal shape more rapidly than one who doesn't.

11. Is jogging harmful to the breast? Although there is some contrary opinion on the subject among medical authorities, the weight of opinion is in the direction of saying no. That is, if you use a good supportive bra. The best sports bra has a wide, stretchable, preferably cotton underband to prevent riding up and will distribute the pressure over as wide an area as possible. Avoid one with too much elastic—they often "give" too much to provide reliable support. Your bra should have a wide backband and ample shoulder straps.

12. Should you massage your breasts? Yes, or have your companion do it. Gentle massaging enhances skin tone and stimulates circulation. Any time you bring more blood to any part of the body, it generally helps that part of the body, and the breasts are no exception. Incidentally, gentle massage has been found to help relieve the feeling of congestion and soreness which sometimes precedes menstruation. In massage, use the fingertips or palms of the hands with good moisture creams or lotions for lubrication. Use a circular motion.

Beauty hint: After your shower, pat some powder blusher into your cleavage if you're going to wear a dress with low décolletage. Use a dusty rose or a peach color blusher if your skin is pale and wine or russet if your skin is deeper in tone.

13. How often should you examine your breasts? You should check your breasts ten to fourteen days after the start of your period. Make your examination in the shower or when bathing because the wet, soapy skin makes the finding of any lump easier. Then examine your breasts in the mirror. Check for any changes in the shape or contour, any unusual swelling, or any dimpling of the skin.

    Finally, examine each breast while lying down by putting a pillow under the shoulder on the side of the breast you are examining. Put that hand behind your head and use the opposite hand to feel the entire breast area. At this point, squeeze the nipple gently to see if there is any discharge. Know what's normal for you. For many women, benign lumps appear in the breast from time to time. For more information on this subject, ask for literature from the American Cancer Society at 777 Third Avenue, New York, NY 10017 or the Office of Cancer Communications at the National Cancer Institute, Bethesda, MD 20205. (Ask for publication 80-2000.)

14. Breasts too small? Believe it or not, Dr. Richard Willard of the Cameron Memorial Hospital in Indianapolis has been using hypnosis to enlarge breasts. He has succeeded in increasing the bust measurement between two and four inches. He claims that hypnosis and subsequent self-hypnosis can increase the size of the blood vessels to bring more oxygen and nutrients to the area, with the result that over a period of time was to cause the bust to get larger. (See "Use of Hypnosis to Enlarge the Breasts" in *Harper's Bazaar*, May 1978.)

    —Compiled by The Association for Research, Inc.

6 Exercises for the Female Breasts

1. Put your hands out in front of you and grasp your wrists with each hand. Now push up as though you were pushing up your

sleeve, but hold tight enough so that your hands do not do any slipping. This is an isometric exercise which is a classic for the pectorals. To do it properly, you should even feel a movement in the breast area. Do a slow count to three and repeat ten times.

2. Hold an unopened soup can (any brand) in each hand. Extend your arms straight forward, then swing them in large circles, first forward then backwards. Do this ten times.

3. Hold a towel over your head. Swing it back and forth over your head, keeping your arms straight and the towel taut. Repeat, gradually increasing to ten times.

4. Sit in the lotus position (if possible) or any comfortable position on the floor. Put your hands behind your head and lean forward slowly. Try to touch the floor with your forehead, but do it gently and slowly. Repeat ten times, but don't strain.

5. When you are in a physical condition to do so (get a doctor's OK) push-ups are excellent for the muscles that support and surround the breast.

6. Swimming (almost any stroke) is an excellent toner for the breast. Most women swimmers have firm well-formed breasts.

18 Women Who Demonstrated That the Term "the Weaker Sex" Is Nonsense

1. *Babe Didrikson Zaharias* (United States; 1914–1956). Some call her the greatest athlete (male or female) in the history of the world to date. In twenty years of competition she earned more medals, set more records, and won more tournaments in more sports than any athlete, male or female, in all times. She was outstanding in basketball, almost every event in track and field, life saving, figure skating, billiards, football place kicking, baseball, diving and lacrosse.

In the 1932 Summer Olympics she took three gold medals and set three world records (breaking her own) for the javelin throw, the eighty-meter hurdles and the high jump. Later in that same year she entered the National Women's Track and Field Championship as an individual and earned a total of 30 points for first place. The Illinois Track Team with twenty-two members came in with 28 points and took second place!

From 1940 to 1950 she won every available golf title, including the U.S. National and World Opens. She gave exhibitions to demonstrate uncanny precision in field place kicking of a football and throwing a baseball with accuracy over 300 feet! With it all, she was unquestionably a *woman* who won first place for her designs of dresses at a Texas fair.

2. *Jacqueline Smith* (Great Britain; born 1951) won the world championship and set a new world record with ten consecutive dead center parachute jumps in the world championships held at Zagreb, Yugoslavia, on September 1, 1978.

3. *Marjorie Gestring* (United States; born 1922) was the youngest individual (male or female) ever to win an Olympic event. At the Olympic Games in Berlin in 1936, she took the springboard diving title at the age of 13 years, 268 days.

4. *Gertrude Ederle* (United States; born 1906) was the youngest person, male or female, to break a world record. She was 12 years and 298 days old when she broke the women's 880-yard free-style swimming world's record with a time of 13 minutes, 19 seconds. This took place at Indianapolis, Indiana, on August 17, 1919.

In 1925 she became the first woman to swim the English Channel, twenty-one miles from Cape Gris Nez, France, to Dover, England, and she set a new world record of 14 hours and 31 minutes, better than any man had ever done before that time.

5. *Olga Korbet* (U.S.S.R.) at the 1972 Olympic games became the first person (male or female) to do a backward somersault on the uneven parallel bars. In 1973 she was named Absolute Champion of the U.S.S.R.

6. *Nadia Comaneci* (Rumania; born 1947). During the Olympics in Montreal in 1976 she astounded spectators and judges by doing seven perfect gymnastic routines (four on the uneven bars and three on the beam). She became the first athlete in the history of the Olympics ever to achieve a ten score in any event. Until then, it was considered by the experts to be unattainable. In 1977 the Associated Press named her the Athlete of the Year.

7. *Vera Caskavska* (Czechoslovakia) holds the world record for individual gold medals for Olympic gymnastic events. She won three at the 1964 games and four in 1968. The male record for gold medals in gymnastics is six.

8. *Cathy Rigby* (United States) became the first U.S. gymnast to win any medals at the world gymnastic championship. She performed on the balance beam.

9. *Andrea Mead Lawrence* (United States) in 1950 took two gold medals in skiing and was the first U.S. skier (male or female) to take a gold medal in any ski competition. No American male has ever taken a first in *any* Olympic ski event!

10. *Margot Oberg* (United States; born 1962) won her first surfing title at the age of 12 in a contest (The Menehuse), in 1976 at La Jolla, California, beating out fifty boys in her division to come in first.

11. *Heather McKay* (Australia; born 1941) won her first squash championship in 1960 and has never lost a tournament match since that time. She has won every available championship and holds some sixty titles.

12. *Billie Jean King* (United States) took a record of twenty titles at

Wimbledon, setting a record. She won the singles six times, women's doubles ten times and four mixed doubles.

13. *Helen Wills Moody* (United States) is the only person (male or female) to win Wimbledon singles eight times. The male record is seven.

14. *Charlotte Dodd* (British; born 1881) was the youngest champion to win at Wimbledon. She was three months short of her sixteenth birthday when she won in 1897. (The youngest male singles champion to win the Wimbledon title was Wilfred Baddley, who won in 1891 at almost twenty years of age.)

15. *Chris Evert* (United States) in 1976 became the best woman tennis player in the world and, according to *Sports Illustrated,* "dominated her game as no other man or woman did in any sport." She was named "Sportsman [sic] of the year" by that magazine, the first woman so honored.

16. *Robyn Smith* (United States) in 1972 finished seventh in International Jockey standings with ninety-eight mounts and a twenty-percent winning percentage. Since the first six jockeys were all Europeans, the best *United States* jockey in 1972 was a woman!

17. *Kittie O'Neil* (United States), deaf from birth, contracted spinal meningitis, and the prognosis of the physicians was that she would be paralyzed for life. By will and determination, she beat the prognosis to become the fastest woman water skier and in 1976 she broke the world women's land speed record, driving an automobile 612 miles per hour. At that time, the record set by a man was 627 miles per hour but Kittie's backers would not support her efforts to beat the male record.

18. *Amanda McKerow* (United States; born 1957), a 17-year-old ballerina, became on June 20, 1981, the first American (male or female) to win a gold medal in the prestigious Moscow International Ballet competition. (Her win was in the Junior Women's Division.)

22

Places to go and people who will help
when you need advice and information.

69 National Organizations
on Sex and Sex-related Subjects

General

1. American Association of Sex Educators, Counselors, and Therapists, 5010 Wisconsin Avenue, N.W., Washington, DC 20016
2. National Sex Forum, 1523 Franklin St., San Francisco, CA 94109

Gays

3. Association for Gay Psychologists, 463 West Street, A627, New York, NY 10014
4. Gay Academic Union, P.O. Box 927, Hollywood, CA 90028
5. Gay Activists Alliance, P.O. Box 2, Village Station, New York, NY 10014
6. Gay Caucus of Membership of the American Psychiatric Association, c/o Frank L. Rundelle, M.D., President, 44 West 62nd Street, Apt. 28-C, New York, NY 10023

7. Homophile Effort for Legal Protection, P.O. Box 3416, Hollywood, CA 90028
8. Homosexual Information Center, 6715 Hollywood Blvd. North, Hollywood, CA 90028
9. National Coalition of Black Gays, P.O. Box 57236, West End Station, Washington, DC 20037
10. National Gay Task Force, 8 Fifth Avenue, New York, NY 10011
11. One, Inc., 2256 Venice Blvd., Los Angeles, CA 90006
12. Parents of Gays, 21 West 13th Street, New York, NY 10011
13. Tangent Group, 6715 Hollywood Blvd., North Hollywood, CA 90028

Gay—Religious

14. Dignity, Inc., 1500 Massachusetts Avenue N.W., Suite 11, Washington, DC 20005
15. Evangelicals Concerned, c/o Ralph Blair, President, 30 East 60th Street, Suite 803, New York, NY 10022
16. Universal Fellowship of Metropolitan Community Churches, 5300 Santa Monica Blvd., Suite 34, Los Angeles, CA 90029

Lesbians

17. Lesbian Feminist Liberation, 243 West 20th Street, New York, NY 10011
18. Lesbian Mothers National Defense Fund, P.O. Box 21567, Seattle, WA 98111
19. Lesbian Resource Center, c/o University YMCA, 4224 University Way N.E., Seattle, WA 98105
20. United Sisters, P.O. Box 41, Garwood, NJ 07027

Anti-abortion

21. Alternatives to Abortion International-Hillcrest Hotel, Suite 511, 16th & Madison Streets, Toledo, OH 43699
22. Americans Against Abortion, 655 South Lewis Street, Tulsa, OK 74102
23. Baptists for Life, 2113 Alamo National Bldg., San Antonio, TX 78205
24. Catholics for a Free Choice, 1411 K Street N.W., Washington, DC 20005
25. National Committee for Human Life Amendment, 1707 L Street, N.W., Suite 400, Washington, DC 20036

Pro-abortion

26. National Abortion Federation, 110 East 59th Street, New York, NY 10022
27. National Abortion Rights Action League, 825 15th Street, N.W., Washington, DC 20005
28. National Family Planning Council, 7060 Hollywood Blvd., Suite 414, Los Angeles, CA 90028
29. Religious Coalition for Abortion Rights, 100 Maryland Avenue, N.E., Washington, DC 20002
30. Reproductive Freedom League, c/o ACLU, 22 East 40th Street, New York, NY 10017

Fertility study and problems

31. American Fertility Society, 1608 13th Avenue South, Suite 101, Birmingham, AL 35205
32. Baren Foundation, 6 East Monroe Street, Chicago, IL 60603
33. National Research Foundation for Fertility, c/o Alfred Koener, Executive Secretary, 53 E. 96th Street, New York, NY 10028
34. New York Fertility Research Foundation, 1430 Second Avenue, New York, NY 10021
35. Resolved, Inc., P.O. Box 472, Belmont, MA 02178

Family Planning

36. Academy of Psychologists in Marital Sex and Family Therapy, C.W. Post Center, Long Island University, Greenvale, NY 11548
37. Alan Guttmacher Institute, 515 Madison Avenue, New York, NY 10022
38. Association of Planned Parenthood Physicians, 810 Seventh Avenue, New York, NY 10019
39. Couple to Couple League, P.O. Box 11084, Cincinnati, OH 45211
40. Family Life and Population Program, 475 Riverside Drive, Room 621, New York, NY 10027
41. Family Planning International Assistants, 810 Seventh Avenue, New York, NY 10019
42. Human Life and Natural Family Planning Foundation, 1511 K Street, N.W., Washington, DC 20005
43. International Planned Parenthood Federation, Western Hemisphere Region, 105 Madison Avenue, New York, NY 10016

44. Planned Parenthood Federation of America, 810 Seventh Avenue, New York, NY 10019
45. Program for the Introduction and Adoption of Contraceptive Technology, 4000 N.E. 41st Street, Seattle, WA 98105

Sexual Liberty and Information

46. Alliance Against Sexual Coercion, P.O. Box 1, Cambridge, MA 12139
47. Coalition on Sexuality and Disability, c/o Anne Berkmann, 122 East 23rd Street, New York, NY 10010
48. Council for Sex Information and Education, Box 23088, Washington, DC 20024
49. International Society of Reproductive Medicine, 2960 West 8th Street, Los Angeles, CA 90005
50. National Center for Reproductive and Sexual Help, 424 East 62nd Street, New York, NY 10021
51. National Committee for Sexual Civil Liberties, 18 Ober Road, Princeton, NJ 08540
52. Sex Information and Education Council of the U.S. (SIECUS), 84 Fifth Avenue, Suite 407, New York, NY 10011
53. Sexual Freedom League, P.O. Box 0105, College Grove Station, San Diego, CA 92115
54. Society for the Scientific Study of Sex, 310 East 46th Street, Suite 12H, New York, NY 10017

Sex Information Relating to Children

55. Childhood Sensuality Circle, P.O. Box 5164, San Diego, CA. 92105
56. Rene Guyon Society, 265 South Robertson Blvd., Beverly Hills, CA 90211

Anti-Censorship

57. Media Coalition Group, 425 Park Avenue, New York, NY 10022
58. National Coalition Against Censorship, 132 West 43rd Street, New York, NY 10036

Rational-Emotive Therapy (Dr. Albert Ellis Group)

59. Institute for Rational-Emotive Therapy, 45 East 65th Street, New York, NY 10021

Religious Counseling

60. National Association of Christian Marriage Counselors, 11611 Webbs Chapel Road, Dallas, TX 75229
61. Rabbinic Center for Research and Counseling, 128 East Dudley Avenue, Westfield, NJ 07090

Divorce Problems

62. Adam & Eve, 1008 White Oak, Arlington Heights, IL 60005
63. America's Society of Divorced Men, 575 Keep Street, Elgin, IL 60120
64. Committe for Fair Divorce and Alimony Laws, P.O. Box 641, Lenox Hill Station, New York, NY 10021
65. Free Men, P.O. Box 920, Columbus, OH 21044
66. Institute for the Study of Matrimonial Laws, c/o Sidney Siller, 370 Lexington Avenue, New York, NY 10017
67. Men's Rights Association, P.O. Box 189, Forest Lake, MN 55025
68. National Association for Divorced Women, c/o Lynch, Jones & Rayan, 20 Exchange Place, New York, NY 10005

Adult Movies

69. Adult Film Association of America, 1654 Cordova Street, Los Angeles, CA 90007

5 Organizations Against Sexual Freedom

1. Morality in Media
   Suite 239
   475 Riverside Drive
   New York, NY 10115

2. Citizens for Decency through Law
   2331 West Royal Palm Road
   Phoenix, AR 85021

3. Women against Pornography
   358 West 47th Street
   New York, NY 10036

4. The National Viewers and Listeners Association
   Arleigh, Colchester
   Essex Co 7 7RH
   England.

5. Society for Protection of Community Standards, Inc.
   3/48 Bauchop Road
   Lower Hutt
   New Zealand.

Diana "of Versailles," (Louvre).
Copy of Alexandrine Greek work.

23

In today's liberated society,
many are happy and some are gay.
Here is a section for bisexuals
and people who used to be tagged
homosexuals.

32 Great Achievers Who Were Bisexual

1. *Alexander the Great* (356–323 B.C.). Conqueror of most of Asia and acknowledged as one of the greatest leaders and generals of all time.

2. *Horatio Alger* (1834–1899). American author of a new genre of stories which influenced a complete generation of youth to adopt a new life and work ethic in order to go "from rags to riches."

3. *Hans Christian Andersen* (1805–1875). Danish poet, novelist and writer of some of the world's most famous fairy tales.

4. *Aristotle* (394–322 B.C.). One of the greatest thinkers of all time. He systemized the science of logic. His work *Organism* (six essays on logic) is still the starting point for a student of the subject. His biological observations were astonishingly accurate.

5. *Francis Bacon* (1561–1626). A brilliant British statesman, essayist, and philosopher. He formulated and introduced the modern scientific method of inductive reasoning and method.

6. *Ludwig van Beethoven* (1770–1827). Regarded by many as the greatest classical composer of all time, he composed some of his greatest symphonies while totally deaf.

7. *Sandro Botticelli* (1441–1510). One of the greatest of the Renaissance painters. His paintings are in every great museum. Some of the most renowned are "Adoration of the Magi" (once hung in Leningrad, now in the National Gallery, Washington, D.C.) and "Nativity" (National Gallery, London).

8. *George Gordon Noel Lord Byron* (1788–1824). One of England's greatest poets, he created the "Byronic hero," a figure in literature. His "Don Juan," an epic satire, is one of the world's literary masterpieces.

9. *Julius Caesar* (102–44 B.C.). A great controversial figure in history. Either a defender of the rights of the people or an ambitious demagogue. But unquestionably he excelled in war, politics, statesmanship, oratory, and the social graces. He gave the world the Julian calendar which we still use. His *Commentaries* is considered by many to be a literary masterpiece and is still used in schools and colleges throughout the world for the study of Latin.

10. *Caius Valerius Catullus* (87–54 B.C.). Regarded as one of the greatest lyric poets of all times. Some of his poems are still, two thousand years later, read, quoted, and loved, especially the poem which ends *"frater ave atque vale"* ("hail, brother, and farewell") and "On the Death of Lesbia's Sparrows."

11. *Benvenuto Cellini* (1500–1571). The greatest goldsmith of all time. Also wrote one of the most remarkable autobiographies ever published.

12. *Johann Wolfgang von Goethe* (1749–1832). German poet, dramatist, novelist, and scientist. Napoleon met him in 1808 and said, "There is a great man!" He was very prolific, his collected works encompassing 150 volumes. Regarded by many as Germany's greatest writer.

13. *John Maynard Keynes* (1883–1964). One of the greatest economists of all time. His 1936 work, the *General Theory of*

Employment, Interest and Money, influenced governments, presidents, and prime ministers throughout the world. Keynesian economics (not followed by President Reagan) are still a significant theory accepted by many leading economists.

14. *Billie Jean King* (born 1943). Regarded by many as one of the greatest women tennis players. She won twenty world tennis championships from 1961 to 1979. She participated in setting a record for the greatest crowd at a tennis match when 30,472 fans came to watch her beat Bobby Riggs (former U.S. and Wimbledon champion) in straight sets on September 20, 1973. It was called "the tennis match of the century."

15. *Christopher Marlowe* (1564–1593). English dramatist, second only to Shakespeare. Many authorities see his work in *Titus Andronicus* and *King Henry VI.*

16. *William Somerset Maugham* (1874–1965). One of the most popular English writers of this century. His books have been read, reread, loved, and made into movies such as *Of Human Bondage, The Moon and Sixpence,* and *The Razor's Edge.*

17. *Michelangelo Buonarroti* (1475–1564). Great Italian painter, architect, sculptor, and poet. His painting of the ceiling of the Sistine Chapel stands as one of the artistic masterpieces of the world.

18. *John Milton* (1608–1674). Great English poet, author of *Paradise Lost,* considered by some to be the most important epic poem in the English language.

19. *Vaslav Nijinsky* (1890–1950). Ranks among the great male ballet dancers. He was premier danseur with Diaghilev's Russian Ballet and introduced many great ballets, including *The Afternoon of a Faun.*

20. *Pindar* (518–438 B.C.). Greek lyric poet. Formulated and developed the ode, still frequently called the "Pindaric ode," later used by Dryden, Pope, and Swift.

21. *Plato* (427–347 B.C.). Greek philosopher and writer. His writings have had great influence on the human race.

22. *Marcel Proust* (1871–1922). Outstanding novelist whose works contain a penetrating psychoanalysis of his generation.

23. *William Shakespeare* (1564–1616). Considered by many the greatest dramatist the world has ever known. The majority of his sonnets are addressed with affection to a noble young man.

24. *Gertrude Stein* (1874–1946). American author who exercised great influence on the development of realism in American letters. Her "A rose is a rose is a rose" will live forever alongside "a rose by any other name. . . ."

25. *Socrates* (469–399 B.C.). Greek philosopher and teacher. Although he wrote nothing, his disciple, Plato, recorded his teachings. Wrongly condemned to death. His martyrdom remains one of the greatest spiritual triumphs of the human race. Originator of the Socratic method of teaching.

26. *Peter Ilyich Tchaikovsky* (1840–1893). One of Russia's greatest musicians and composers. His ballets (*Swan Lake, Sleeping Beauty,* and *The Nutcracker*) are even more popular today than when composed almost a century ago.

27. *William Tatem Tilden, Jr.* (1893–1953), considered by many as the greatest male tennis player of all time. He won many championships throughout the world. He had the fastest service ever measured—163.6 mph—and won the U.S. tennis championship seven times (the record).

28. *Nicholas Udall* (1505–1556). English schoolmaster and playwright. He became a headmaster at Eaton and later wrote *Ralph Roister Doister,* regarded as the first English comedy.

29. *Leonardo da Vinci* (1452–1519). Enormously talented as a painter, sculptor, architect, engineer, and scientist.

30. *Walt Whitman* (1819–1892). Noted American poet. His poetry influenced most of the civilized world, inspiring experimentation in verse and subject matter.

31. *Oscar Fingall O'Flahertie Wills Wilde* (1854–1900). Brilliant and versatile English writer, he authored plays (*The Importance of Being Earnest, Lady Windermere's Fan,* and others) that are still presented almost a century later, and a novel (*The Picture of Dorian Gray*) that is a classic.

32. *Thomas Lanier "Tennessee" Williams* (born 1914). One of America's great playwrights. His *A Streetcar Named Desire* and *Cat on a Hot Tin Roof* are particularly widely known.

The Religious Preferences of Homosexuals

1. Protestant—36%
2. Roman Catholic—21%
3. Jewish—5%
4. Other—5%
5. Agnostic or Atheist—33%

—*Homosexualities* by Alan P. Bell and
Martin S. Weinberg

The Number of Partners Homosexuals Say They Have Had

Number	Percent
3–4	1%
5–9	3%
10–14	4%
15–24	5%
25–49	8%
50–99	12%
100–249	20%
250–499	13%
500–999	14%
1000 or more	20%

86 World-famous Homosexual Lovers and Their Bedmates

1. Colette and Missy (the Marquise de Belboeuf)
2. Noël Coward and his secretary, Cole Lesley
3. American painter Marsden Hartley and a German soldier half his age.
4. Novelist E.M. Forster and George Merrill
5. Athlete and adventurer Richard Halliburton and silent-film star Rod La Rocque

6. French dramatist Molière and actor Michel Baron
7. German writers Elisabeth Bettina von Arnim and Karoline von Gunderode
8. Poet W.H. Auden and Chester Kallman
9. W. Somerset Maugham and his secretary, Gerald Haxton
10. Writer Natalie Clifford Barney and painter Romaine Brooks
11. Poet Amy Lowell and Ada Russell
12. Actress Charlotte Cushman and sculptor Emma Stebbins
13. Artist J.C. Leyendecker and Charles Beach (his model for the Arrow Collar Man)
14. Walt Whitman and trolley-car conductor Peter Doyle
15. Poets Arthur Rimbaud and Paul Verlaine
16. American President James Buchanan and his vice president, William Rufus DeVane King
17. Playwright and novelist Thornton Wilder and writer Samuel M. Steward
18. John Wojtowicz (the real-life hero of *Dog Day Afternoon*) and transsexual Ernest Aaron
19. Lyricist Lorenz Hart and actor Tyrone Power
20. Eleanor Butler and Sarah Ponsonby (known as "the Ladies of Llangollen")
21. Novelist Ivy Compton-Burnett and scholar Margaret Jourdain
22. Natalie Clifford Barney and Oscar Wilde's niece, Dolly
23. Cole Porter and John Vernon ("Black Jack") Bouvier III (Jackie's father)
24. Journalist Dorothy Thompson and Christa Winsloe (author of *Mädchen in Uniform*)
25. Jean Cocteau and the adolescent poet Raymond Radiguet ("Monsieur Bébé")
26. Errol Flynn and Tyrone Power (Truman Capote and Howard Hughes also shared Flynn's bed)
27. Composer Benjamin Britten and tenor Peter Pears
28. Queen Christina of Sweden and opera singer Angelica Georgini
29. Poet Frank O'Mara and painter Larry Rivers
30. Composers Stephen Foster ("Old Folks at Home") and George Cooper ("Sweet Genevieve")
31. Poet Sara Teasdale and Margaret Conklin
32. John Henry Cardinal Newman and Ambrose St. John
33. Playwright Federico García Lorca and painter Salvador Dali
34. Writer Christopher Isherwood and artist Don Bachardy

Errol Flynn

35. American composer Daniel Gregory Mason and pianist John Powell
36. Maurice Chevalier and his secretary, Felix Paquet
37. German scientist Alexander von Humboldt and his valet, Seifert
38. Marie Antoinette and the Duchesse de Polignac
39. Russian artist Pavel Tchelitchew and American writer Charles Henri Ford
40. Writer Katherine Mansfield and her "slave," Ida Baker
41. Composer and pianist Ferruccio Busoni and futurist painter Umberto Boccioni
42. Revolutionary patriots Alexander Hamilton and John Laurens
43. Poet Hart Crane and Emil Opffer
44. André Gide and film producer Marc Allegret
45. Writer Jean Genêt and French resistance fighter Jean Descarnin
46. Artist Jean Cocteau and actor Jean Marais

47. Edith Emma Cooper and Katherine Harris Bradley, who together wrote books as "Michael Field"
48. King Richard II of England and Piers Gaveston
49. Composer Francis Poulenc and singer Pierre Bernac
50. German emperor Rudolph II and his chamberlain, the appropriately named Wolfgang von Rumpf
51. Composer Franz Schubert and painter Moritz von Schwind
52. Peter Ilyich Tchaikovsky and his valet, Aleksei Sofronov
53. Peter Ilyich Tchaikovsky and his student, Vladimir Shilovsky
54. Gertrude Stein and Alice B. Toklas
55. Feminists Susan B. Anthony and Anna Dickinson
56. Writer Jane Bowles and her Algerian lover, Shirifa
57. English writer and socialist Edward Carpenter and his working-class lover, George Merrill
58. Lytton Strachey and painter Duncan Grant
59. Economist John Maynard Keynes and painter Duncan Grant
60. Lord Ronald Gower (the model for Lord Henry in The Picture of Dorian Gray) and his valet, Alfonso Cassietti
61. Composers Maurice Ravel and Manuel de Falla
62. Writers Vita Sackville-West and Virginia Woolf
63. Poets Allen Ginsberg and Peter Orlovsky
64. English novelist Hugh Walpole and Danish opera star Lauritz Melchior
65. Oscar Wilde and Lord Alfred Douglas
66. Novelist I.A.R. Wylie and Dr. S. Josephine Baker (who tracked down "Typhoid Mary")
67. Frederick the Great and Lieutenant Hans von Katte
68. Edward Fitzgerald (translator of Omar Khayyam) and William Kenworthy Brown
69. Russian impresario Serge Diaghilev and dancer Vaslav Nijinsky
70. Russian impresario Serge Diaghilev and dancer Serge Lifar
71. Russian impresario Serge Diaghilev and dancer Leonide Massine
72. Poet Stefan George and his "boy-god," Maximilan Kronberger
73. English artists Charles Shannon and Charles Ricketts
74. Billie Jean King and her former secretary, Marilyn Barnett
75. Ralph Waldo Emerson and the splendidly named Martin Gay
76. Marcel Proust and his chauffeur, Alfred Agostinelli
77. Marcel Proust and pianist Reynaldo Hahn
78. Yves St. Laurent and Pierre Berg

79. Radclyffe Hall (*The Well of Loneliness*) and Mabel Veronica Batten
80. Classicist Edith Hamilton and Doris Fielding Reid
81. English writer Gerald Heard and painter Christopher Wood
82. T.E. Lawrence (Lawrence of Arabia) and the Arab boy, Dahoum
83. Occultist Aleister Crowley and female impersonator Herbert Pillitt
84. Mad King Ludwig II and his handsome equerry, Richard Hornig
85. Novelist Winifred Ellerman (known as "Bryher") and poet H.D. (Hilda Doolittle)
86. Blues singer Bessie Smith and male impersonator Gladys Fergusson

14 Marriage Vows Made by a Homosexual Couple

Jack McConnel and Michael Baker were lovers. They wanted a legal marriage. Jack legally changed his name to Pat Lyn McConnel.

Michael went alone (permitted in Minnesota) to the license bureau and obtained a marriage license for Jack and "Pat" to be married. On September 3, 1971, in a friend's apartment, a Methodist minister solemnized their marriage as they said to each other:

"Touch me," said McConnel, in his vows to his 29-year-old lover. "I am your lover, brother, sister and friend."
Said Baker, "Hold me. I hold your spirit, emotion, reason and flesh."
McConnel: "Keep me. I hold you in joy, health, sickness, poverty and wealth."
Baker: "I, Jack, take you, Michael."
McConnel: "I, Michael, take you, Jack."
Baker: "To be my wedded spouse."
McConnel: "To be my wedded spouse."
Baker: "To touch."
McConnel: "To hold."
Baker: "To keep."

McConnel: "Today."
Baker: "Tomorrow."
McConnel: "And yesterdays till death."
And later: "As a sign of my love, with this ring, I marry you," the lovers repeated to each other.

This may be the only same-sex couple to have accomplished a legal marriage in the United States.

—Source: *The Gay Crusaders*, by Kay Tobin and Randy Wicker

5 Men's Gay Bars in New York City

1. The Spike—120 11th Avenue, New York, N. Y. 10011
2. The Eagle's Nest—142 11th Avenue, New York, N. Y. 10011
3. The Anvil—500 West 14th Street, New York, N. Y. 10011
4. Keller's—384 West Street, New York, N. Y. 10014
5. Sneakers—392 West Street, New York, N. Y. 10014

2 Women's Gay Bars in Manhattan

1. Duchess—Christopher Street and Seventh Avenue
2. Déja Vu—Waverly Place and Sixth Avenue

8 Gay Beaches

1. Will Rogers State Park Beach, Los Angeles
2. Queen's Surf, Honolulu
3. Russian River, San Francisco

4. Riis Park, Far Rockaway, New York
5. Jones Beach (Section 6) New York
6. Fire Island Pines, New York
7. Provincetown, Massachusetts
8. Condado Beach, Puerto Rico

4 Gay Drugs

1. Flagyl
2. MDA
3. Amyl Nitrate (Butyl Nitrite if Amyl not available)
4. Ethyl Chloride

4 Gay Diseases

1. Amebiasis
2. Anal gonorrhea
3. Giardiasis
4. Kaposi's sarcoma

145 Gay Writers, Poets and Playwrights

1. At 33, E. M. Forster was awakened to his true nature when
   George Merrill, Edward Carpenter's lover, "touched [his]
   backside—gently and just above the buttocks."

2. At 32, *Horatio Alger* fled the town of Brewster, Massachusetts, after being accused of "unnatural familiarity with the boys."

3. Novelist *Yukio Mishima* took every page he ever wrote to his mother for approval; after his suicide his mother said: "My lover has come back to me."

4. *Sir Francis Bacon*, who, like his brother, Anthony, was gay, was constantly in trouble with his mother who railed against the steady stream of servants and envoys who were the "bloody bed-companions of my son."

5. Drama critic *Alexander Woollcott* loved to dress in drag and once cried on Anita Loos's shoulder because he'd never be able to become a mother.

6. Injected with cells from sheep fetuses, 80-year-old *W. Somerset Maugham* would demonstrate to embarrassed guests his ability to achieve an erection.

7. As a young woman, *Sidonie-Gabrielle Colette* wore a bracelet engraved "I belong to Missy" (her lover, the Marquise de Belboeuf).

8. E. E. Cummings believed that novelist *John Dos Passos* was gay. Dos Passos (who had a slight speech impediment) was asked by Cummings (who believed in the sexual meanings of dreams) what he had dreamed of the night before. The reply: "Why, I dweamed I had a bunch of aspawagus and I was twying to give it to you."

9. *Jean Genêt* wrote *Funeral Rites* after learning of the death of his lover, French resistance fighter Jean Descarnin: "I felt that I could only reply to the rigidness of his corpse with the rigidness of my penis."

10. *Christopher Marlowe* supposedly penned the epigram, "All they that loved not tobacco and boys were fools."

11. Biographer *Lytton Strachey* spent most of his youth in battle with economist John Maynard Keynes (Keynes had made off with several of Strachey's lovers, including the artist Duncan Grant).

12. No list would be complete without the anonymous author of

Alcibiades in School (1632), a work in which St. Paul returns to earth to investigate reports of sodomy within the church and is driven away by the pope and his prelates who consider him a killjoy and a loony.

13. In his early years in Greenwich Village, film critic *Parker Tyler* (who wore his hair long and had penciled eyebrows and mascaraed eyelashes) was known as "the beautiful Parker Tyler."

14. Married to gay writer/statesman *Harold Nicolson*, writer *Vita Sackville-West* carried on love affairs with *Violet Trefusis* and *Virginia Woolf*, to name just two.

15. *Allen Ginsberg* and his lover *Peter Orlovsky* claim to have slept with both Jack Kerouac and Neal Cassady, Kerouac's "Dean Moriarty" in *On the Road*.

16. Novelist/hustler/bodybuilder *John Rechy* was once told by an irate transvestite, "Your muscles are as gay as my drag."

17. *Lionel Johnson*, the British poet who introduced "Bosie" Douglas to Oscar Wilde, died of a fractured skull at 35, after falling off a barstool.

18. When *A Streetcar Named Desire* was criticized by the owlish Thornton Wilder, *Tennessee Williams* remarked, "This guy has never had a good lay."

19. The life of gay *Hans Christian Andersen* ended even more strangely than a fairy tale; he died falling out of bed.

20. *John Wilmot*, Earl of Rochester, whose Restoration poems speak of the delights of buggering his page ("There's a sweet soft Page of mine/Does the trick worth Forty Wenches"), was banished from court for destroying the king's clocks when they refused to answer his drunken question, "Dost thou fuck?"

21. Versifier *Rod McKuen* was quoted in a popular magazine as having said, "I have had sex with men; does that make me gay?"

22. In *Leaves of Grass*, poet *Walt Whitman* uses the erect, spiky calamus plant as a suitable phallic symbol for the large body of poems dealing with the love of men for men.

23. *Beau Brummell* was so much the dandy that he once complained that he had caught cold from sitting in a room with a damp stranger.

24. *Carl Van Vechten* once doctored Keats's famous poetic line to read, "A thing of beauty is a boy forever."

25. Poet *Hart Crane* regularly shared the shore leaves of an American sailor with Wagnerian heldentenor *Lauritz Melchior.*

26. *Herman Melville's* unrequited love for the heterosexual Nathaniel Hawthorne is evident in a line from his review of one of Hawthorne's books: "He expends and deepens down ...and further shoots his strong New England Roots into the hot soil in my Southern soul."

27. Poet *W. H. Auden,* according to *Christopher Isherwood,* suffered from a painful anal fissure.

28. In a fashionable restaurant, French journalist *Jean Lorraine* once shouted at the top of his lungs the following couplet: "I spent the night between two fellows from the docks/Who took turns and cured me of the hots."

29. *Mary Renault,* author of *The Persian Boy,* claims that in childhood she was "an honorary boy."

30. English poet *A. E. Housman,* far from being the scholarly Cambridge don usually portrayed in textbooks, made merry with a string of Venetian gondoliers supplied by his friend Horatio Brown and was a regular patron of the male brothels in Paris.

31. A. E. Housman's brother, playwright *Laurence Housman (Victoria Regina),* was also gay, as was his sister Clemence.

32. After the death of his beloved William Kenworthy Browne, *Edward Fitzgerald,* the translator of Omar Khayyam, cruised the Suffolk docks looking for "some fellow to accost me and fill a very vacant place in my heart."

33. Novelist *Violette Leduc* so despised being a woman that she fantasized about dressing herself in a tight body stocking with a false penis attached so that she could attract the attention of gay writer Jean Genêt.

34. German poet *August von Platen* immortalized his handsome student Hofmann as "Cardenio" in a series of beautiful love sonnets.

35. German poet *Stefan George* so worshipped the boy Maximilian Kronberger, whom he called "Maximin," that he dressed him in a blue tunic and placed violets in his hair.

36. The spirit of *Constantin Cavafy's* gay poetry has been perfectly captured in the exquisite illustrations to the works by English artist *David Hockney*, also gay.

37. Although his many love affairs with women became the raw material of his novels, French writer *Henri de Montherlant* never wrote about his even more intense affairs with men.

38. *Bram Stoker*, the author of *Dracula*, wrote passionate letters to Walt Whitman declaring his love.

39. Poet *May Sarton's* verses reflect her lesbianism, but her novel, *Mrs. Stevens Hears the Mermaids Singing*, is probably the best piece of fiction on the subject yet written.

40. His strange life as a closet case gives new meaning to the most famous line in *James M. Barrie's* Peter Pan: "Do you believe in fairies? . . . If you believe, clap your hands!"

41. Seventeenth-century French poet *Claude de Chauvigny* was noted for his blasphemer's prayer: "All I ask of Thee, Lord/ Is to be a drinker and a fornicator,/ An unbeliever and a sodomite,/ And then to die."

42. *George Baxt* wrote the first mystery novel to feature a gay detective, *A Queer Kind of Death*.

43. *Edward Barnfield* wrote "The Affectionate Shepherd," probably the most explicitly homosexual poem of the English Renaissance: "If it be a sin to love a lovely lad,/ Oh, then sin I."

44. Lovers *Margaret Anderson* and *Jane Heap* founded *The Little Review*, one of the most influential literary magazines of the 1920s.

45. Irish novelist *Forrest Reid* correctly surmised *Henry James's* homosexuality and dedicated his mildly gay novel, *The*

Garden God, to the American writer, only to have James condemn the book for its "artless portrayal of sinister matters."

46. Novelist *George Sand* (Aurore Dudevant) was so well known as a lesbian that, upon her death, Turgenev wrote to Flaubert: "What a good man she was, and what a kind woman."

47. Using as a pretext for mischief the *"privilege du cape"* — which allowed a Frenchman who could not find a convenient pissoir to approach a cop and ask him to extend one arm (holding the cape) so that he could take a leak behind it—*Jean Cocteau* used to amuse himself by choosing only the handsomest young cops and pretending that he was drunk.

48. In *Contemporary American Authors*, poet *Peter Orlovsky* calls himself "secretary for *Allen Ginsberg*," to whom he was "married, Chrismiss [*sic*] 1954."

49. At 27, gothic novelist *Matthew Gregory "Monk" Lewis* was deeply in love with 14-year-old William Kelly.

50. *Marcel Proust's* greatest love was Alfred Agostinelli, his Italian chauffeur.

51. Mystery writer Raymond Chandler once uttered the ambiguously classic line, "In the artistic society of London one man in three is homosexual, which is very bad on the ladies but not at all bad on me."

52. Poet *Robert Graves* deleted from his autobiography any mention of his homosexual youth.

53. *Gertrude Stein's* early novel *Fernhurst* deals with the real-life affair between Bryn Mawr's president Cary Thomas and one of her teachers, Mary Gwinn.

54. *T. E. Lawrence*, who dedicated *Seven Pillars of Wisdom* to his beloved Arab boy, Dahoum, used to have himself regularly flogged by a young man named Bruce.

55. As a lover of rough trade, poet/reformer *Paul Goodman* was once called the "pipe–smoking Socrates of the bars and docks."

56. *Gore Vidal* wickedly points out that the work of *Truman Capote* has been analyzed by a Professor Nance and boasts that *his* output has been studied by a Professor Dick.

57. Writer *J. R. Ackerley* summed up upper-class British homo-sexuality by writing of his brief affairs with "several hundred young men, mostly of the lower orders and often clad in uniforms of one sort or another."

58. Poet *Vachel Lindsay*, like composer Edvard Grieg, lost his heart to Australian composer and pianist Percy Grainger.

59. In a letter to a friend, poet *Edmund John* gives us a very good idea of the "tone" of late-Victorian homosexuality: "I have received your adorable illustrated letter this morning and love it so much that I immediately made an altar before it, lit by amber candles in copper candle-sticks, burnt incense before it and kissed its extreme beautifulness."

60. *Norman Douglas*, who left his wife to settle in Capri to enjoy the gay life, once compiled an anthology of graffiti collected in several languages from the walls of men's rooms throughout Europe.

61. Philosopher *George Santayana* spent his life in love with an unresponsive heterosexual who couldn't even remember his name.

62. *Dorothy L. Sayers*, eminent medievalist and creator of the famous Lord Peter Wimsey mystery novels, wrote (and pub-lished) lesbian poetry on the side.

63. In breaking off her ten-year love affair with Oscar Wilde's niece, poet *Natalie Clifford Barney* bought Dolly Wilde a one-way plane ticket to London and then devoured an entire chocolate cake to console herself.

64. The homosexuality of *George Kelly*, Princess Grace's uncle, is undetectable in his plays, but thanks to Rosalind Russell and Joan Crawford, his Harriet Craig *(Craig's Wife)* has become the camp symbol of domestic overfastidiousness.

65. Writer-dandy *Ronald Firbank*, who is reputed to have dined exclusively on champagne, fruit, and flowers, died under-nourished at forty.

66. Feeling guilty, *Lord Byron* insisted that his young Greek friend, Nicolo Giraud, visit an English doctor to cure his relaxed anal sphincter.

67. Sixteenth-century French essayist *Michel de Montaigne* was

said to be gay; his writings contain one of the earliest references to lesbianism (a masculine woman hanged for using a dildo on her partner).

68. Asked what he'd do if a Hun were raping his sister, pacifist *Lytton Strachey* suggested that he'd be man enough to take her place.

69. *Truman Capote:* "I was a beautiful little boy . . . and everyone had me—men, women, dogs, and fire hydrants. I did it with everybody. I didn't slow down until I was nineteen, and then I became very circumspect."

70. Upon his release from Reading Gaol, *Oscar Wilde* had his sexual "reformation" tested by heterosexual friends who took him to a local whorehouse, where he is said to have remarked after the visit, "It was just like cold mutton."

71. English poet *Charles Churchill:* "Women are kept for nothing but the breed;/ For pleasure we must have a Ganymede./ A fine, fresh Hylas, a delicious boy./ To serve our purposes of beastly joy."

72. *André Gide's* doubts about the gay life vanished after he came five times in a single night with Mohammed, a boy procured by Oscar Wilde ("that perfect little body, so wild, so ardent, so somberly lascivious.")

73. Journalist and railroad buff *Lucius Beebe* was known to invite luscious young things to his private railroad car for what one was described as "whisky and sofa."

74. The biographer of *T. E. White* suggests that the author of *The Once and Future King* was himself a queen.

and....

75. Mercedes de Acosta
76. Edward Albee
77. Gavin Arthur
78. James Baldwin
79. William Beckford
80. Eric Bentley
81. William Blake
82. Elizabeth Bowen
83. Jane Bowles

84. Paul Bowles
85. Malcolm Boyd
86. John Horne Burns
87. Hall Caine
88. Thomas Carlyle
89. Willa Cather
90. Lonnie Coleman
91. Marie Corelli
92. Aleister Crowley

93. Hilda Doolittle ("H.D.")
94. Emily Dickinson
95. Charles Henri Ford
96. Janet Flanner
97. Thomas Gray
98. Julian Green
99. Thomas Gunn
100. Radclyffe Hall
101. Richard Hall
102. Richard Halliburton
103. Edith Hamilton
104. Gerald Heard
105. Gerard Manley Hopkins
106. Richard Howard

107. J.K. Hysmans
108. William Inge
109. Max Jacob
110. Henry James
111. Jill Johnston
112. Jonathan Katz
113. Dolores Klaich
114. Vernon Lee
115. Pierre Loti
116. Federico García Lorca
117. Terrence McNally
118. Robert McAlmon
119. Robin Maugham
120. Charlotte Mew
121. Merle Miller
122. Kate Millett
123. John Milton
124. Molière
125. Robin Morgan
126. John Cardinal Newman

127. Rose O'Neill
128. Walter Pater
129. Robert Patrick
130. Roger Peyrefitte
131. Felice Picano
132. William Plomer
133. James Whitcomb Riley
134. Rainer Maria Rilke
135. A. L. Rowse
136. Jane Rule
137. Hubert Selby, Jr.
138. Sir Philip Sidney
139. Stephen Spender
140. Samuel M. Steward
141. Sara Teasdale
142. Dorothy Thompson
143. Horace Walpole
144. Hugh Walpole
145. Edmund White

—Prepared by Martin Greif Especially
for *The Book of Sex Lists*

Note: The source for much of the above material is *The Gay Engagement Calendar*. Copies of the calendar are available from The Main Street Press, William Case House, Pittstown, NJ 08867 for $6.95.

8 Pieces of Gay Clothing

1. Levi 501's
2. Adidas
3. Bandanas
4. Tank tops
5. Construction boots
6. Jock straps
7. Bomber jackets
8. Any black leather

182 Gay Local Information Telephones

The following telephone numbers are a source of local information about what's happening in the particular gay community.

Alabama
1. (205) 251-0682
2. (205) 539-3424

Alaska
3. (907) 276-3909

Arizona
4. (602) 263-8196
5. (602) 257-0350
6. (602) 277-0479
7. (602) 623-5268

Arkansas
8. (501) 376-7397

California
9. (213) 399-9813
10. (213) 464-7400
11. (213) 578-9359
12. (408) 293-4525
13. (408) 295-1340
14. (415) 431-1411
15. (415) 548-8283

16. (415) 756-7954
17. (415) 861-5019
18. (415) 863-9000
19. (415) 864-2174
20. (714) 232-7528
21. (714) 623-9958
22. (714) 534-3280
23. (714) 746-5660
24. (714) 824-7618

25. (805) 544-8210
26. (805) 963-3636
27. (916) 265-5808
28. (916) 441-2075
29. (916) 447-1171
30. (916) 448-3777
31. (916) 451-5552

Colorado
32. (303) 443-3680
33. (303) 447-9670
34. (303) 491-7232
35. (303) 492-8567
36. (303) 741-4429
37. (303) 837-1598

Connecticut
38. (203) 436-8945
39. (203) 522-5575
40. (203) 624-5510

Delaware
41. (302) 738-8066

Florida
42. (305) 294-5239
43. (305) 294-6284
44. (305) 462-2004
45. (305) 833-6282
46. (305) 876-2600
47. (305) 638-4085
48. (305) 667-6969
49. (305) 832-9118
50. (813) 366-5838
51. (813) 974-4297
52. (904) 355-0771

Georgia
53. (404) 523-7786
54. (404) 592-0661

Hawaii
55. (808) 524-4700
56. (808) 537-9478
57. (808) 923-9556

Illinois
58. (217) 384-8040

59. (309) 323-3333
60. (312) 236-7575
61. (312) 337-2424
62. (312) 492-3227
63. (312) 929-4357
64. (618) 453-5714

Indiana
65. (317) 283-6977
66. (317) 926-9600
67. (812) 238-1454
68. (812) 336-4299

Iowa
69. (319) 234-1981
70. (515) 292-7000
71. (319) 353-6265
72. (319) 353-7162
73. (319) 365-9044
74. (515) 288-0330

Kansas
75. (316) 267-1852
76. (913) 864-3091

Louisiana
77. (318) 226-1308
78. (504) 387-8537
79. (504) 947-4297
80. (504) 948-4310

Maine
81. (207) 646-9735
82. (207) 780-4085

Maryland
83. (301) 235-4357
84. (301) 235-8593
85. (301) 366-1415

Massachusetts
86. (413) 545-0145
87. (413) 545-3438
88. (617) 267-9150
89. (617) 426-9371
90. (617) 426-4469
91. (617) 487-0387
92. (617) 487-2313

93. (617) 752-8993
94. (313) 963-1568
95. (617) 756-0730
Michigan
96. (313) 463-3563
97. (313) 577-3450
98. (313) 622-1977
99. (517) 482-4577
100. (616) 857-4269
Minnesota
101. (612) 222-9621
102. (612) 376-2722
103. (612) 827-2821
104. (612) 871-2601
105. (612) 874-9235
Mississippi
106. (601) 373-3592
Missouri
107. (314) 361-7284
108. (816) 921-4419
Montana
109. (406) 243-4153
110. (406) 373-5906
111. (406) 452-0412
112. (406) 587-5831
113. (406) 728-8758
Nebraska
114. (402) 475-5710
Nevada
115. (702) 452-3776
New Mexico
116. (505) 268-2937
New York
117. (212) 741-2710
118. (212) 777-1800
119. (315) 423-3599
120. (315) 475-6857
121. (518) 462-6138
122. (607) 256-6482
123. (607) 273-5146
124. (607) 722-3629

125. (607) 797-3453
126. (716) 244-8640
127. (716) 244-8970
128. (716) 836-8970
129. (716) 881-5335
130. (914) 948-4922
North Carolina
131. (919) 763-3695
Ohio
132. (216) 621-3380
133. (216) 733-5612
134. (216) 775-8131
135. (419) 243-9351
136. (513) 228-4875
137. (513) 241-0001
138. (614) 422-9212
Oklahoma
139. (918) 587-4669
Oregon
140. (503) 248-1990
141. (503) 399-8763
142. (503) 485-1075
Pennsylvania
143. (215) 928-1919
144. (215) 563-8599
145. (215) 868-8133
146. (412) 441-0857
147. (412) 521-4560
148. (717) 234-0328
149. (814) 868-0588
Rhode Island
150. (401) 751-3322
South Carolina
151. (803) 448-4638
152. (803) 626-3427
Tennessee
153. (615) 573-4209
154. (901) 228-4105
Texas
155. (214) 748-6790
156. (512) 477-6699

157. (512) 477-7747
158. (512) 478-8653
159. (512) 733-7300
160. (512) 733-7742
161. (804) 625-1130
162. (713) 529-7014
163. (806) 763-6111

Utah
164. (801) 466-3477
165. (801) 531-0833

Vermont
166. (802) 254-8176
167. (802) 656-4173

Virginia
168. (804) 233-3430

Washington
169. (206) 322-2000

170. (206) 329-8707
171. (206) 329-8737
172. (206) 525-0999
173. (206) 632-4747
174. (206) 682-6044
175. (206) 866-6162
176. (206) 866-6544

West Virginia
177. (304) 432-1323

Wisconsin
178. (414) 552-7331
179. (414) 963-6555

Wyoming
180. (307) 237-8798
181. (307) 266-6091
182. (307) 632-9102

3 Gay Sex Gadgets

1. Cock rings
2. Tit clamps
3. Crisco

7 Gay Cult Stars

1. Judy Garland
2. Marilyn Monroe
3. Bette Midler
4. James Dean
5. Dolly Parton
6. Divine
7. Maria Callas

24

Women (and men) who play for pay are widely available. Here are some names they are called and some numbers with which to call them.

52 Labels for Prostitutes

1. Alley cat
2. Ass peddler
3. Baggage
4. Bimbo
5. Blister
6. Bucket broad
7. Butt peddler
8. Chippy
9. Cash bag
10. Cab moll
11. Cash escort
12. Delilah
13. Daughter of joy
14. Fancy quiff
15. Floosey
16. Flooze
17. Grisette (French)
18. Human mattress
19. Hotsy
20. Hustler
21. Gash
22. Hooker
23. Burlap sister
24. Crack saleslady
25. Hot piece
26. Harlot

27. Demimondaine
28. Fille de joie (French)
29. Jade
30. Jezebel
31. Lady of the evening
32. Nookie
33. Pay for play girl
34. Popsy
35. Pro-lady
36. Pross
37. Prossy
38. Minx
39. Sin sister
40. Sadie Thompson
41. Strumpet
42. Sportin' woman
43. Pickup for dough
44. Trull
45. Trucker's delight
46. Pavement pounder
47. Painted Lady
48. Puta (Spanish)
49. Putana (Italian)
50. Tart
51. Tail peddler
52. Working girl

The 1 U.S. City to Adopt Laws
That Regulated Prostitutes

On July 5, 1870, the city council of St. Louis, acting under provisions of the city charter, which authorized the city to "regulate or suppress" prostitution, passed the Social Evil Ordinance.

The provisions of this ordinance followed the lines of those in Berlin. Six physicians were appointed by the Board of Health to inspect registered prostitutes in the six districts of the city. Women found to be suffering from venereal diseases were committed to a special "Social Evil Hospital" until they received a certificate saying they were cured.

This ordinance remained in effect until 1874, when it was nullified by action of the Missouri state legislature. An interesting provision of the ordinance was that prostitutes were divided into three classes: inmates of brothels, free-lance prostitutes, and "kept women," i.e., mistresses.

The law was repealed because, through the efforts of churches, more than 10,000 people signed a petition which was brought to the state legislature by a large number of young girls wearing spotless white gowns.

> —From John C. Burnham, *Medical Inspection of Prostitutes in America in the 19th Century: The St. Louis Experiment* and *Bulletin of the History of Medicine*, XLV (1971).

21 Telephone Numbers That Will Bring a Call Girl to Your Home or Hotel Room

There are enterprises that, for a substantial fee, will provide a woman who will arrive at your hotel room (or apartment)— usually from a little to a lot late—and will render unto you almost any desired sexual service. Prices vary from about $35 to $150. You can get most information over the phone.

The best telephone approach is your diffidence. If you come on too strong they suspect the police. The best line is: "I got your number from a friend of mine who said you treated him nicely." If asked, his name is "Joe Denver" or "Pete Camden."

Name	Telephone	Comment
1. Brooklyn Escorts	(212) 332-2046	Service somewhat erratic
2. Peyton Place	(212) 934-9113	24-hour service
3. Bel Aire	(212) 683-5715	24-hour service
4. N.Y. Outcall	(212) 691-7734	2:00 a.m. to 2:00 p.m.; will supply girls for parties, etc.

5. La Boutique	(212) 244-5620	Expensive
6. Diana	(212) 734-3087	Hotels only
7. First Class	(212) 580-5001	Minimum—$125
8. Candie	(212) 768-8426	Black—Mon. to Fri., $35 minimum
9. Bette's Escorts	(212) 864-1269	24 hours, hotel or office
10. Laura	(212) 686-2609	
11. Eye Catchers	(212) 568-8006	
12. Flash	(212) 864-1344	
13. Sherri	(212) 532-7472	Specializes in two for $70
14. Charlie's Angels	(212) 732-6105	Can have three girls
15. Music Box	(212) 777-8291	Individual calls, parties, etc.
16. Eurasian	(212) 719-5309	Said to specialize in girls from the Orient
17. N.Y. Escorts	(212) 750-1108	Minimum $80 per hour
18. Mrs. Rodriguez	(212) 532-1395	Puerto Rican girls
19. Lucky Lady	(201) 332-5410	Covers large area of New York and New Jersey
20. Cachet	(212) 242-0338	
21. Connoisseur	(212) 877-3860	Manhattan only

11 Places That Offer Gay Males for a Price

This list is chancy, since gay males who work for money move about a lot and may be gone before you call. Some may be single men working alone (the women are generally part of a stable). Prices are very negotiable.

Name	Telephone	Comment
1. Venus Escorts	(212) 946-4017	Purports to stock pre-op transsexuals
2. Cowboys	(212) 683-1386	Offers some dominance
3. Steff or Karles	(212) 677-1738	
4. Bob	(212) 243-5466	$55 no S & M
5. Kenny	(212) 683-3657	$65
6. Rafael	(212) 772-2287	Athletes; call after 5:00 P.M.
7. Jason	(212) 675-8998	A muscle man
8. William	(212) 772-7645	$65
9. Mark	(212) 246-5825	Young; $75
10. Model	(212) 598-9687	Handsome, muscular; includes domination
11. Stud	(212) 685-7617	

1 Civilization Which Required Every Female to Become a Prostitute

In Babylonia (then generally called Chaldea), in the tenth century B.C., every female was required by law, before marriage, to enter the Temple of Mylitta.

It was then her duty to offer herself as a prostitute to any man who would pay a fee for her sexual services. It was a violation of law for her to leave until her act of prostitution was completed and (possibly most important) the fee paid by her customer was deposited on the altar of the goddess Mylitta (Venus) for the use of the priests.

The beautiful and voluptuous remained only a few minutes. The plain and wealthy made "arrangements" and did not remain long. The poor and homely remained a long time—some as long as three years!

—Source: William W. Sanger, *The History of Prostitution*

5 Legal Whorehouses in Nevada and How to Get to Them

Whorehouses are legal in those counties of Nevada that do not outlaw them. They're illegal in the counties containing Reno and Las Vegas.

Lincoln County, which borders on Las Vegas, was an "open county" and housed many brothels. However recently its citizens reversed themselves and outlawed prostitution, and the houses had to move.

Some present prominent legal bordellos are:

1. *Sheri's Crystal Palace.* Long a Lincoln County legend, it recently moved to Lathrop Wells. Go north on Las Vegas Boulevard, make a left on Bonanza Road (Route 95), and follow it north (about 90 miles) to the town of Lathrop Wells. Make a left on Route 373; Sheri's is about 10 miles south.

2. *The Chicken Ranch.* Operated by Walter Plankinton, the self-proclaimed King of the Brothels. In July 1981 the bordello was incorrectly listed in the new Las Vegas telephone directory as being located at 125 Las Vegas Boulevard. Between 200 and 300 women work as Centel telephone operators at that address.

   Walter Plankinton declared that the mistake was "deliberate" because "someone at the phone company had a sense of humor." Plankinton added, "I didn't think it was very funny."

   The error actually was made because Plankinton wanted a listing in the Las Vegas directory which is serviced by Centel. But the Chicken Ranch is in Pahrump, in Nye County, which is serviced by Nevada Bell Telephone Company. Nevada Bell bills the Chicken Ranch which, in turn, pays Centel for actually providing the service. Thus the confusion.

   (The Chicken Ranch name was taken from the famous whorehouse in Texas that inspired the musical, *The Best Little Whorehouse in Texas.*)

   Take Interstate south to Exit 33. (Route 14 is the main highway west of the Strip.) Stay on the exit road to Homestead Road, and then make a left and continue for about seven miles. This house accepts Visa or MasterCard.

3. *Cherry Patch Ranch.* A new one that is particularly proud of its swimming pool. Take Interstate 15 north to U.S. 95 to Mercury. Exit and take State Route 16 south five miles to Arch Meadows. Then turn right to the Cherry Patch.

4. *Shamrock Ranch.* Near Lathrop Wells. See 1 above.

5. *Bobbie's Buckeye.* In Tonopah, Nevada. Located in Nye County.

6 Telephone Numbers That
Will Bring a Call Girl to
Your Hotel Room in Las Vegas

Your lady will come direct to you for a fee. Your fantasy will be fulfilled. And you can pay for most of the services with a credit card.

These numbers were accurate at press time. Some may change with the passing of time.

	Name	Telephone	Comment
1.	Showgirls of Las Vegas	(702) 735-5011	Doubles, couples, fetishes. All major credit cards.
2.	Dreamgirls	(702) 871-4553 or (702) 873-6260	Domination, two for one, showers and massages. Major credit cards.
3.	Pussycats	(702) 362-0075	24 hours. Visa and MasterCard
4.	Call Girls	(702) 876-3336	24 hours, 7 days. Major credit cards.
5.	Good Time Girls	(702) 734-6827	All the girls have health certificates. Major credit cards.
6.	Centerfolds	(702) 871-6300	Advertised as "the perfect way to climax your stay in Las Vegas." Male escorts also available.

1 Place That Had Legal
Schools for Prostitutes

In most of the city states in Greece (Athens, Sparta, etc.), houses of prostitution were legal, regulated and heavily taxed. The enterprises were highly competitive, so there was much price cutting.

At one time the price in some brothels was only an obol (about a penny and a half). There was a special public official who supervised and kept order.

Houses, to improve the quality of the "servicing" personnel, opened schools, attached to the brothels, where young women were taught to be efficient, competent, satisfying, and knowledgeable sexual partners.

26 Massage Parlors in 10 Cities

The massage parlor is a sexual phenomenon of the last two decades. In many places where the brothel is illegal the massage parlor is the substitute. What goes on in a massage parlor frequently depends on the current attitude of the police (permissive or prohibitive), the appearance of the customer ("he looks like a cop"), the familiarity of the customer with the masseuse, etc. This list carries with it no guarantees but for the travelling man it is a good starting point. (Sorry ladies, there are currently no massage parlors for women. There were some but they have closed. Apparently not enough demand.)

Chicago
1. Weird Harold's Massage Parlor, 541 S. Wabash Ave.

Denver
2. New Tokyo Massage, 2801 S. Broadway.
3. Bit Massage, 3153 Broadway.
4. Oriental Massage, 3154 W. Alameda.

Houston
5. Japanese Massage, 10109 Airline.

245

6. North Freeway Massage, 9655 N. Freeway.
7. Paradise Massage Parlor, 11088 Easter Freeway.

Indianapolis

8. Bee Bee Massage, 2514 W. 16th St.
9. Odyssey Massage & Therapy Salon, 1836 E. 38th St.

Miami

10. Marcie's Massage, 3321 NW 17th St.
11. Royal Massage Studio, 1150 SW 22nd St.
12. Modern Massage Clinic, 211 NE 97th St.
13. DeLeon Massage & Therapy, 712 W. 51st St.

Los Angeles

14. Estelle's Massage Studio, 536 Larchmont St.
15. Beverly Massage, 4107 Beverly Blvd.
16. Atlantis Massage, 930 Wilshire Blvd.
17. Sobador Mexicano Massage, 419 N. Evergreen Ave.

New Orleans

18. Abbe's Penthouse Massage, 330 Exchange Alley.

New York City

19. Delicate Touch, 140 W. 42nd St.
20. Silver Slipper, 121 W. 45th St.
21. Dating Room, 251 W. 42nd Street
22. Two-Hundred East, 200 E. 14th St.

San Diego

23. Pink Paradise Massage, 2616 University Ave.

Philadelphia

24. Carol Professional Massage, 1903 Pine St.
25. LaMonica Health Spa, 1607 Sansom St.
26. Health Therapy Massage, 211 S. 17th St.

25

Among other things, here are keys to the sexual significance of your handwriting, your lucky number, and your favorite Tarot card.

12 Sex Traits Revealed by Handwriting

1. When the writing slants forward, the individual is an extrovert in matters of sex. He shows his emotions.
2. When the writing contains thick strokes, it shows the writer to be a possessor of permanent emotions.
3. When the writing is straight up and down, and not slanted in either direction, it indicates that the writer is governed by intellect rather than emotion in matters of sex and love.
4. Thin strokes indicate a cautious person who will not rush into love or sex affairs.
5. The farther the slant is forward in the writing, the more impulsive will the individual be in matters of sex.
6. If the writer has letters with a little hook at the beginning of many of the letters, it indicates that the writer will be a tease and a deceiver.
7. If certain of the letters are left open, as for example, the a, the g, the c, the d, and the o, this will indicate that the writer will be a talkative lover.

8. When characteristics 5 and 6 are found in combination, you get someone who will be a liar in love.
9. One who places heavy cross bars on the *t*'s is subject to fits of temper.
10. One who has heavy slants off by themselves in order to dot the *i*'s and cross the *t*'s is domineering in sex and love.
11. One who leaves spaces between the middle lines of *d*'s and *t*'s will be lazy in sex and love.
12. One who writes straight up and down and ends the final letter of each word abruptly and without any follow-through will be selfish in matters of sex and love.

> —Adapted from *Sex and Love as It Is Written* by Frederick St. John, American Institute of Grapho Analysis (1937)

Your Number and Its Sexual Significance

To obtain your number, add together the day, month and year of your birth. This will always produce a four-digit number.

Thus, if you were born on August 11, 1922, you add

$$
\begin{array}{r}
8 \\
+\ 11 \\
+1922 \\
\hline
1941
\end{array}
$$

Add these four digits together:

$$
\begin{array}{r}
1 \\
+\ 9 \\
+\ 4 \\
+\ 1 \\
\hline
15
\end{array}
$$

If this results in a single-digit number, that's it. If the result is a two-digit number, add the two digits together like this:

$$
\begin{array}{r}
1 \\
+5 \\
\hline
6
\end{array}
$$

and the resultant single digit is your number for numerological purposes.

Example: Frank Sinatra was born 12/12/1915.

$$
\begin{array}{r}
12 \\
+\ 12 \\
+\ 1915 \\
\hline
1939
\end{array}
$$

$$
\begin{array}{r}
1 \\
+\ 9 \\
+\ 3 \\
+\ 9 \\
\hline
22
\end{array}
$$

$$
\begin{array}{r}
2 \\
+\ 2 \\
\hline
4
\end{array}
$$

So Frank Sinatra's number is 4.

Here is the sexual significance of your number according to some who claim to know.

1—Your sex life will be creative and original. On the other hand, some of your partners may find you overtalkative. You want to dominate your partner. Your mate requires warmth and patience. Affection is very necessary to your well-being.
ROBERT REDFORD and SALLY KELLERMAN

2—You are sensitive and modest to the point of fearful shyness. You go to extremes that result in strong, unreasoned likes and dislikes. You can't stand any hint of coarseness in your partner. You reach for permanent relationships. No one-night stands for you. Your mate must surround you with an orderly and beautiful environment in order to reap your rich rewards.
VALERIE PERRINE and TELLY SAVALAS

3—You can give great joy to your partner and express yourself with bubbling fun. However, you are moody and like to indulge in extravagant gossip, which could make you a "kiss and tell" partner. If your mate isn't wary of criticizing you, you become cold and unforgiving. You would reject a lover for a thoughtless word and mourn later for your hastiness.
ALAN ALDA and FAYE DUNAWAY

4—You are very serious and lacking imagination. Lovemaking is real and earnest, and the form of the act is more important than the act itself. The way into your bed is through patience and indirection. Whatever your mate wants to do, you are likely to want just the opposite.

ELTON JOHN and CATHERINE DENEUVE

5—You are as energetic and resourceful in your love life as in anything else in your life. You are also restless and fickle. Rather than a comparison shopper, you are more apt to be an impulsive rolling stone who jumps into bed without thought— and then moves out and on to new experiences. Your partner must beware of trying to hold on to you, because more than anything else you fear the loss of your freedom. The person who gets you for a mate needs open hands.

HENRY WINKLER and DORIS DAY

6—You are idealistic and home-loving. You are a nester. Unfortunately for you, flattery is irresistible to you and may affect your common sense in the selection of your mate. In bed you can be dominant or very giving. Contradiction is the key to your character and keeps your mate off balance most of the time.

JAMES CAAN and SANDY DUNCAN

7—Your approach to sex is analytical and perfectionistic. You are likely to avoid emotional commitments because you find it hard to give up an intellectual approach. Your partner is likely to find you silent and withdrawn. You need a mate with an equally intellectual approach to sex, and the missionary position will suffice most of the time. You may break out in a rare display of spontaneity in bed, but that is infrequent.

CANDICE BERGEN and GEORGE SEGAL

8—You place great demands on your mate. You enjoy watching the performance, but generally you are more concerned with your own satisfaction. You are quite willing to use sex as a weapon. You need love but are not so ready to show it to your partner.

CHEVY CHASE and KATE JACKSON

9—You love home and family and you make a faithful mate. You are also very possessive and can smother your partner with the intensity of your desires. You are a great romantic, easily disenchanted when the mate fails to remain on the pedestal you have created. If you play the field you can find no happiness. For you, contentment is your own fireside.

SHIRLEY MacLAINE and WARREN BEATTY

Sex and the Man's Eating Habits

Can a man's eating habits reveal much about the kind of lover he will be? An article in the magazine *Mademoiselle* says yes.

1. *The Exotic Eater.* The man who likes to start dinner with escargots and finish with a pomegranate is adventurous and experimental and probably will be so in his sex life.
2. *The Gourmet.* He's finicky about his food and sends back the vichyssoise because it's not cold enough and the sweetbreads because they are not hot enough. He will probably be just as finicky in his love-making and be interested in quality, surroundings, ambiance and the like. If you are interested in quantity, he may not be the man for you.
3. *The Meat and Potatoes Man.* He is likely to be solid and dependable as a lover, but be prepared, he may be a "Biff, bam, thank you, ma'am."
4. *The Health Food and Vitamin Freak.* He is careful about his health and his life. He probably studies the subject and will probably know enough about sex to lead a good, healthy sex life.
5. *The Hearty Eater (sometimes the Fat Man).* He may be a hearty and good lover. On the other hand, spending all that time eating and carrying around all that avoirdupois may make him sluggish in bed.

22 Major Sexual Cards of the Tarot

The Tarot is a deck of seventy-eight cards with symbolic pictures on them. By laying them out in various ways, some people believe that auguries of the future and pictures of the past and present are revealed to the knowledgeable reader.

The cards are customarily divided into two sets or groupings. The more important group of twenty-two cards is known as the Major Arcana. The remaining fifty-six cards are called the Minor Arcana and these cards, divided into four suits, are the ancestors of our modern deck.

Many interpretations exist for the cards. The following is a brief sexual interpretation of the Major Arcana. (For a more detailed description of this aspect of the cards, see *The Sexual Key to the Tarot*, by Theodore Laurence.)

I—*The Magician*. This represents the struggle to control one's sex life by any available means and, especially for a woman, the ability to create a warm atmosphere for one's partner.

II—*The High Priestess*. The sex symbol of one's dreams with all the promise and all the variety a woman uninhibited can offer her mate.

III—*The Empress*. An orgasmic card, promising fulfillment and inspired sexual pleasures.

IV—*The Emperor*. He is a sexual giant, lusty and powerful, a dream come true for those women who seek domination and sexual satisfaction.

V—*The Hierophant*. He is a masturbator who fears his own sexuality. He should look for a partner who is satisfied with oral-genital gratification. Sodomistic or lesbian practices are indicated.

VI—*The Lovers*. No traditionalists, these love sex and know no taboos. The relationship is not conventional.

VII—*The Chariot*. The Charioteer in his triumphant vehicle careens from conquest to conquest. No woman can hold him but all will enjoy his whirlwind courtship and quick possession.

VIII—*Strength*. Here is the lady who can stop the Charioteer if anyone can. She is filled with sexual energy, with power to sate any man she desires.

IX—*The Hermit*. He is a sexual gourmet who would never kiss and tell. Fortunate is the woman who finds him in her future, for she will know delicious satisfaction without fear of exposure.

X—*The Wheel of Fortune*. As the wheel of life turns, new sex partners replace old, moving from the animal to the sublime and back again, in endless rhythm.

XI—*Justice*. The man who finds this card in his spread is warned that his female companion is no pushover. She must be wooed and won, but the payoff is ecstasy, if not constancy.

XII—*The Hanged Man.* The questioner is advised that mastur-batory preference is not necessarily permanent. A care-fully chosen sex partner can be a sexual revelation.

XIII—*Death.* Where there is an end, there is also foretold a new beginning. A sexual adventure draws to an end; a new one comes your way.

XIV—*Temperance.* Sexual self-control is rewarded with height-ened gratification and rewarding, if varied, orgasm.

XV—*The Devil.* This is a lusty, animalistic card, speaking of nymphs and satyrs and destructive eroticism. If this card appears, beware!

XVI—*The Tower.* This universally understood phallic symbol, here struck down by a bolt of lightning, foretells the loss of sexual powers resulting from abuse and misuse by either sex.

XVII—*The Star.* The Star personality is erotic and virile. The card holds forth a promise of sexual bliss in every facet of the relationship.

XVIII—*The Moon.* The dark side of the moon hides sexual perversions and the uncontrolled excesses of the animal nature. The bright side reflects the possibility to calm and control the wildness and open the way to sexual security and satisfaction.

XIX—*The Sun.* Sexual union arises from love and produces mutual orgasmic satisfaction. The relationship with the mate transcends the physical.

XX—*Judgment.* When the call comes, the door to healthy and satisfying sexual activity opens. This is the chance to put aside abusive sex perversions and experience greater orgasmic pleasures.

XXI—*The World.* In a woman's reading, sensual fulfillment is offered. In a man's reading, he may expect erotic pleasures in large measure.

O—*The Fool.* You have journeyed through sexual life from the door first opened by the Magician. You have experienced all forms of sexuality. It is for you to choose. Or, as the number of the card implies, you stand at the beginning of life's journey. Adolescence is behind you, and sexual experience lies ahead.

The Sexual Symbolism of 14 Gemstones

1. Aquamarine—love and affection for the wearer
2. Beryl—hope for an encounter
3. Carnelian—friendship
4. Cat's-eye—protection from the evil eye
5. Chrysoprase—joy or gaiety
6. Diamond—fidelity and sincerity
7. Hematite—sexual impulse
8. Lapis lazuli—capacity for love
9. Loadstone—virility
10. Pearl—chastity
11. Ruby—passion
12. Sapphire—preservation of chastity
13. Topaz—affection
14. Turquoise—love

26

...and some of the history of people who have made headlines, and heroes and heroines who made headway.

18 Good Guys and Gals of Sex

Here are eighteen men and women who have contributed to modern sexual freedom. We list them with apologies to the hundreds of other men and women who also contributed so much to the sexual freedoms we enjoy today.

1. *Mary Steichen Calderone, M.D., MPH* (born 1904)
   This physician has been named one of the fifty most influential women in the United States. Going to work for the first time at age 50, as medical director of the Planned Parenthood Federation of America from 1953–1964, she set the family planning movement into high gear by enlisting the active acceptance and support of "family planning as responsible medical practice" by the American Medical Associations.

   In 1964 she left to co-found SIECUS (Sex Information and Education Council of the U.S.) of which she has been director and president ever since. In that capacity she has become one of the acknowledged leaders in what is now a world wide movement to understand, accept, and dignify human sexuality as an integral part of every person's health and personality structure from the moment of birth throughout life.

Dr. Calderone's book, *The Family Book about Sexuality* (written with Eric Johnson), embodies these principles and was designed to encourage parents and other heads of families to share information and positive attitudes about sex with children under their care.

2. *Robert Latou Dickinson, M.D.* (1861–1950)

with

3. *Lura Bean, M.D.*

This pair, now overshadowed by the Kinseys of the world, were two gynecologists who should not be forgotten. They worked over the strenuous objections of the American Medical Association to prepare the first medical study of human sexuality.

They tested more than a thousand patients over a thirty year period.

They also experimented with electric vibrators to bring allegedly frigid women to orgasm. Presaging today's research, the conclusion they reached was that sexuality in the female is as strong as it is in the male. They also declared that sexual satisfaction is a necessary ingredient in happiness and that most sexual frustration is caused by either guilt or ignorance.

4. *Albert Ellis, Ph.D.* (born 1913)

He established the school of Rational-Emotive Therapy (RET). His book *Sex Without Guilt*, published in 1958 by Lyle Stuart, helped to free millions of people from the shackles of guilt that had been imposed on them by parents, teachers, and the clergy, many of whom wallowed in hypocrisy and ignorance.

Esquire magazine refused an ad for *Sex Without Guilt*, claiming that it was "too pro-sex." Much of the sexual revolution since the 1960s stemmed from and was nourished by the works of Dr. Ellis. He has probably enabled more people to help themselves with their sexual problems than any other contemporary writer.

He has written more than forty books on sex, love and psychotherapy during the past twenty years including *The Art and Science of Love, Encyclopedia of Sexual Behavior, Sex and the Liberated Man,* and *The Intelligent Woman's Guide to Dating and Mating.*

Famed screenwriter Dalton Trumbo said in a letter to his son, Christopher, "Ellis is a man who will take his place in history as the greatest humanitarian since Mahatma Gandhi. I don't know if you will ever be able to understand the flood of savage joy which filled my heart on first reading *Sex Without Guilt*. I felt, with Keats, 'like some watcher of the skies when a new planet swims into his ken.'"

Dr. Albert Ellis

5. *Henry Havelock Ellis, M.D. (1859–1939)*
He studied medicine and psychology, and although he never practiced, this professional background gave his writings the credentials of authority. He then wrote the greatest study in the field at that time, *Studies in the Psychology of Sex*. This consisted of seven volumes, the first of which was published in 1897.

Ellis took some then extremely radical positions such as that there is nothing wrong with masturbation, that a female who enjoys sex is normal, that the repression of sexuality is harmful, and that people have tremendous variances in sexuality and sexual desires, and that practically all of these are within the range of the normal. His works were very influential and laid the foundation for others.

6. *Edward Bliss Foot, M.D.* (1829–1906)
Foot was a physician who took the public position that sex is normal and should be pleasurable and that indifference is the only sexual disease. In 1872, he published *Plain Talk About The Human System*. This sold more than a half million copies in spite of confiscations by the authorities and the enmity of Anthony Comstock, a crusader against (what he considered) obscene literature, who was an organizer and a special agent of the New York Society for the Suppression of Vice.

In his book, Dr. Foot described the latest in prophylactics, including a fish-bladder condom, and a "womb veil" (actually a diaphragm). In violation of federal law, he offered the devices by mail. He helped influence others who came later to reexamine outmoded moral attitudes.

7. *Benjamin Franklin* (1706–1790)
One of the greatest Americans of all time. He supported and fostered sexual tolerance with his wit and wisdom in "Poor Richard's Almanac," which he published from 1732 to 1757. His "Speech of Miss Polly Baker" probably was the first public attack on the double standard. He fathered a lovechild and gave him both his name and his loving attention. The child, William Franklin, grew up to become Governor of New Jersey.

8. *Dr. Sigmund Freud* (1856–1939)
The founder of psychoanalysis, a system which revealed the psychological problems rooted in childhood sexual incidents and traumas. He was one of the first physicians who listened carefully to the patient, insisting that what the patient said was important. This was especially true with respect to sexual matters.

Although the emphasis has shifted, much modern sexual psychology still uses Freud as its touchstone. His written works are contained in twenty-four volumes.

9. *Dr. Alfred Charles Kinsey* (1894–1956)
He put human sexuality on a firm quantitative foundation through the use of scientific statistical methods. He and his

associates produced *Sexual Behavior in the Human Male* in 1948 and, later, *Sexual Behavior in the Human Female* in 1953.

Dr. Kinsey proved that at most one percent of the women who claim to be frigid cannot attain orgasm, but that the problem for some is that orgasm comes from methods other than coitus, which, nevertheless, most women prefer.

He demonstrated that homosexual experiences and preferences are far more widespread than people had believed. Generally speaking, he showed that of most sexual acts the great proportion are "normal."

10. *Charles Knowlton, M.D.* (1800–1850)
This remarkable physician was almost wholly self-educated. In 1832 he published a book on birth control titled *The Fruits of Philosophy: or, The Private Companion of Young Married People.*

The first edition carried no author identification but one year later a second edition identified Knowlton as the writer.

Though the book offered a moderate point of view, it violated current feelings and Knowlton was arrested, fined one thousand dollars and jailed for three months in Cambridge, Massachusetts.

11. *Benjamin Barr Lindsey* (1869–1943)
An outspoken, courageous and brilliant American judge, he became the leading authority on juvenile courts in the United States. He wrote *The Companionate Marriage* in 1927, based on his experience. It advocated trial marriage and suggested that young people live together openly before deciding on marriage rather than engaging in sex furtively. In this respect Lindsey anticipated what young people advocate and do today. He further outraged the clergy and the bluenoses when he advocated that birth control devices be made freely available to all.

12. *William H. Masters, M.D., (1915)*
        and
13. *Virginia E. Johnson*
These sex researchers published *Human Sexual Response* in 1966 after a twelve-year study. For the first time they made available precise descriptions of responses of the human sexual organs as a result of the laboratory observations in volunteers of ten thousand male and female organs. They

developed much of modern professional sex therapy to deal with such problems as premature ejaculation, impotence, and the inability to achieve orgasm.

14. *John Money, Ph.D.*
Dr. Money, of the Johns Hopkins School of Medicine, is a psychologist who is a leading authority in the medical-surgical sex field. With Howard W. Johnson, he helped organize the first transsexual operation in the United States. He has developed and demonstrated new theories of the existence of male characteristics in females and vice versa, brought up to date the modern theories involving chromosomes and placed on a more scientific basis modern medical theories concerning the reasons for the existence of homosexuality.

15. *Wardell Pomeroy, Ph.D.*
He was Dr. Kinsey's director of field research, actually conducted the same number of interviews (8,500) as Kinsey, and was his senior co-author.

After leaving the Institute, he spent ten years as a sex therapist until he retired, moved to the West, and became the Academic Dean of the Institute for Advanced Study in Human Sexuality in San Francisco. His books, particularly *Boys and Sex* and *Girls and Sex* have had a profound influence in opening up the world of sexuality to young people so that they could look upon it, and consider their actions about it, in an orderly, informed and responsible fashion. He has distinguished himself in four areas: as researcher, therapist, educator and author.

16. *Bertrand Arthur William Russell* (1872–1970)
This champion of individual freedom did not limit his advocacy to words. He set examples through his own actions. He became identified with "free love"—a concept that included sex without marriage. This and his other ideas so infuriated some people that his appointment to teach philosophy at the College of the City of New York was cancelled as was a five-year contract to lecture for the Barnes Foundation.

He lectured at many colleges, wrote many books and left his mark in many fields. His books include *Marriage and Morals* (1929) and *Unpopular Essays* (1950).

17. *Margaret Sanger* (1882–1966)
Sanger founded the birth control movement in the United

States and was an international leader in the field. While a nurse on the Lower East Side of New York City she observed the close ties between poverty and uncontrolled fertility.

At one point she was jailed for thirty days for operating the first birth-control clinic in the United States.

In 1921 Mrs. Sanger founded the American Birth Control League which was later to become the Planned Parenthood Foundation of America. She launched the National Committee on Federal Legislation for Birth Control in 1929.

She wrote many books that were bold for their time, including *What Every Girl Should Know* (1916); *What Every Mother Should Know* (1917) and *My Fight for Birth Control* (1931).

Margaret Sanger showed great courage in fighting for the right of every woman to plan the size of her own family.

18. *Dr. Theodore Hendrik van de Velde (1873–1937).*

This Dutch gynecologist wrote the book *Ideal Marriage* in 1926. It was a new kind of marriage manual. For the first time a book said there was more than one way to have sexual intercourse and that the missionary position was not ordained by God. He also took the position that cunnilingus and fellatio aren't bad, although he believed they shouldn't result in orgasm. He gently and almost imperceptibly led the Western world from Victorianism to modern sexuality.

6 Wrong-Way Corrigans and Riegels
of Sex*

1. *Dr. Samuel Auguste Andre David Tissot (1728–1797).* His book *Onanism and Advice to the People in General with Regard to*

---

*Our older readers will, of course, recognize these references. However, for the benefit of our younger readers: On July 17, 1938, a flying Irishman by the name of Douglas Corrigan filed a flight plan to California. He took off from Floyd Bennett Airfield in Brooklyn in a small plane. The next day he arrived at Boldonnel Airport, Dublin, Ireland.

He claimed he had mistakenly flown "the wrong way."

Corrigan received many honors for the flight, including a life membership in the famed Liars Club.

In the 1929 Rose Bowl, Ray Riegel, playing for California, picked up a fumble near the Georgia Tech goal line and then ran the wrong way almost 100 yards until he was tackled by his own teammate, Benny Lom, on Cal's one-yard line.

In the next play Cal's punt was blocked and Georgia Tech scored a safety, giving them two points—or enough to win by a score of 8 to 7!

Their Health was published in 1765. It flatly stated that masturbation will cause acne, blindness, impotence, insanity and several other terrible ailments, possibly excepting leprosy. He warned also against wet dreams. Tissot took the position that each loss of semen through masturbation or wet dreams caused the body to lose approximately one ounce of very valuable fluid, the equivalent of forty ounces of blood! He took similar attitudes toward other aspects of sexuality. The book became standard reading in the medical profession, and it propagated erroneous knowledge for more than a century.

2. *Clyde François L'Allemand (1790–1833).* He wrote *Des Pertes Seminales* in three volumes, and these were published between 1836 and 1842. He built upon the works of Tissot, taking the position that having wet dreams was like a "foul disease" of a venereal nature like gonnorrhea. His other attitudes against sex were equally hysterical.

3. *William Acton (1813–1875).* He wrote *The Function and Disorders of the Reproductive Organs in Childhood, Youth, Adult Age and Advanced Life* in 1857. It supported the thesis espoused by the first two and underlined it. He taught that sex was the cause of many diseases of the reproductive organs and that the less one indulged the better.

4. *Richard von Krafft-Ebing (1840–1902).* A German physician and neurologist, he became a professor of psychiatry at Strasbourg and became the leading world authority on the psychological aspects of mental disorders, blaming most of them on some aspect of sex. His most famous work was *Psychopathia Sexualis* (1886), which took the position that in its various manifestations, sex was really a collection of loathsome diseases. He regarded most mental disorders as being caused by moral degeneracy and masturbation. He particularly attacked all forms of fetishism, homosexuality, sadism and masochism.

5. *Sir Alexander Cockburn. (1802–1880)* His written opinion in the case of *Regina v. Hicklin* (1868) probably had more to do with the flowering of censorship and the creation of a blackout of sex information throughout the English speaking world than the actions of any other individual. The case itself involved a Protestant pamphlet castigating the Catholic practice of the Confessional. The pamphlet pointed out that Catholic women

discuss such matters as fellatio and cunnilingus with the priest. It objected to this practice.

Chief Justice Cockburn, presiding over the Court of the Queen's Bench, found the pamphlets obscene under this rule:

"I think the best test of obscenity is this, whether the tendency of the matter charged as obscenity is to deprave and corrupt those whose minds are open to such immoral influences, and into whose hands a publication of this sort may fall." The rule was followed wherever English was spoken for nearly a century. Few decisions have caused so much harm over so long a period of time.

6. *Anthony Comstock*. (1844–1915) Comstock was a moral crusader. Serving in the Union Army during the Civil War, he was offended by the profanity, the sexual frankness of the soldiers, the sex with the prostitutes who followed the Army, and the racy pictures and pamphlets the men exchanged.

Returning to civilian life, he began a movement to rid the United States of sex in any form of portrayal—in literature and art, on the stage, in pamphlets of sex advice, in the dissemination of birth control measures, and in practically every other portrayal of sexual encounter except in the closed bedroom between two legally married people of opposite sexes. Anything else he considered taboo.

Almost singlehandedly, he lobbied through Congress the first major obscenity law which prohibited placing anything obscene (interpreted as sexy) in the mails. It suddenly became a felony to mail a pamphlet containing sex or birth-control advice. The first offense provided for a fine of five thousand dollars and imprisonment of up to five years. Subsequent offenses carried fines of up to ten thousand dollars and ten years in prison.

Comstock formed the infamous Society for the Suppression of Vice and got official sanction to become the enforcer of the law. During the first year of the Comstock Law, he and his society seized 200,000 pictures and photographs, more than 100,000 books, more than 60,000 rubber contraceptives, and 30,000 boxes of pills and powders with alleged aphrodisiac qualities.

The United States suffered under Comstock's restrictive view of the law until the middle of the following century when the

United States Supreme Court under the leadership of Chief Justice Earl Warren handed down a series of decisions which restricted the application of the Comstock Law to hard-core pornography. Though limited, the law is still alive and operating.

5 Hollywood Sex Scandals (Selected from Hundreds)

England has its royal family. In the United States, our royalty has been the Court of Hollywood. Film stars are something special, something above mere mortals. They live dream lives, earn dream salaries, and are recognized and catered to wherever they go.

Movie stars don't die. Like good soldiers, they just fade away. And long after their departure into obscurity or death, their faces and voices persist, communicating with us from the silver screen or from our more intimate television screens.

Because of our intense interest in the familiar faces of Hollywood, we retain a morbid curiosity about their sex lives, too. Events that would scarcely merit mention in the local newspapers for three consecutive days if they happened to local people are history and legend because they happened to our dream princes and princesses.

Here are five of the most notorious Hollywood sex scandals. We skip the obvious Errol Flynn, Lana Turner, Howard Hughes, and Mary Miles Minter stories to bring you just this sampling.

1. Marilyn Monroe's affair with Robert Kennedy and assignations with President John Kennedy surfaced to become public knowledge and gossip after her suicide. Her life became tragedy largely because of her lack of self-esteem. After signing a contract with 20th Century-Fox she remarked, "Well, that's the last cock I'll ever *have* to suck." And Henry Ephron, in his book *We Thought We Could Do Anything*, describes how Marilyn was summoned from the movie set by a Fox executive but

assured Henry and his wife, "I'll be right back. This is only a five-minute job."

2. Rudolph Valentino was a silent screen lover who made women swoon, but apparently he couldn't make them come. When his first wife, Natacha Rambova, divorced him, it was revealed that their marriage had never been consummated. He married his second wife, Jean Acker, before the divorce from Natacha was legal.

   There was no boy-makes-girl sex with Acker either. It was later revealed that both of Valentino's wives were aggressive lesbians. The slurs about Valentino's manhood are said to have contributed to his early death by destroying his will to live.

3. Clara Bow was labeled the "It" girl in the press releases and "the other woman" in a divorce action brought by the wife of mild-mannered, high-priced Hollywood physician Dr. William Earl Pearson. The "love balm" that he was rubbing her with and putting into her turned out to be his own sex organ. But this scandal went onto the back burner when Clara's secretary, Daisy DeVoe, sold her own diary about the men in Clara's life.

   It seems that Miss Bow took on football players in groups and film stars as if they were groupies. She put out for everyone from wide-eyed Eddie Cantor to close-mouthed Gary Cooper. Among those to whom she freely distributed her favors was Rex Bell, whom she later married. Bell and Bow left lotus land for Las Vegas land, and he became governor of Nevada, and little Clara became the governor's wife.

4. Marion Davies was one of three Irish sisters, all of whom managed to corral very wealthy, very powerful, very generous male companions and sponsors. In Marion's case, the fish she hooked was William Randolph Hearst, an influential newspaper and magazine publisher who didn't have to worry about where his next serving of coffee and cake was coming from, thanks to his inherited interest in the Homestake Mining Company, worth about one-third of a billion dollars.

   Hearst loved Marion, whom he had spotted as a chorus girl in a Broadway musical. He moved her in with him at San Simeon even while his wife, Millicent, mother of his four sons, was tending the milk fund in New York City.

   At the time, "W.R.," as he was called, owned more than twenty newspapers, including three in New York City alone (the *Daily Mirror*, the *Evening Journal*, and the *New York American*).

Hearst set up the first major vanity film company, Cosmopolitan Pictures, through which he planned to make Marion Davies a star. But to her, acting was a waste of time, and she couldn't have cared less. She did, however, care about Charles Chaplin, the demure comedian about whom his first wife wrote, "He was hung like a horse."

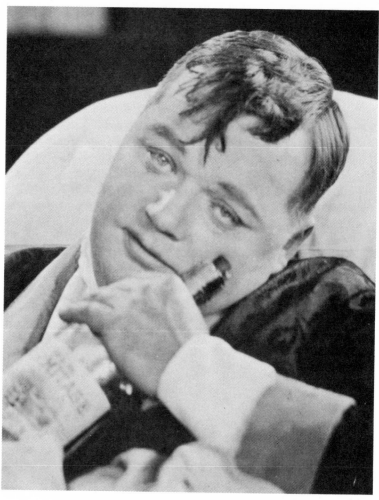

Fatty Arbuckle: a bottle got him in trouble

It was during one of the Chaplin-Davies sexual encounters on Hearst's own ship that the publisher encountered them, raced for his pistol while Marion stuttered "M-m-m-m-urder!" and what followed somehow resulted in the death of Tom Ince. Ince's body was quickly cremated, bullet and all, and the official story was that he'd died of indigestion. Chaplin? Poor Charlie was no longer welcome at the Hearst estate.

5. Coca-Cola received some unwanted publicity when rumor had it that it was a Coke bottle that Roscoe "Fatty" Arbuckle inserted into the vagina of starlet Virginia Rappe, causing her to hemorrhage and die.

Fatty, as he was called affectionately, was a five-thousand-dollar-a-week comedian. This would today, allowing for inflation, be the equivalent of fifty thousand dollars a week. His comedies were box-office blockbusters, and the adage that "nobody loves a fat man" was certainly not true with Roscoe, for everybody loved him.

Well, perhaps not everybody. Virginia Rappe, whose face was on the cover of the sheet music of the song "Let Me Call You Sweetheart," apparently didn't want Fatty to call her sweetheart that night. That night was the night Fatty threw a party to celebrate his new three-year, three-million-dollar contract with Paramount Pictures.

He had taken two cars full of film folk and pretty women to swinging San Francisco for a party. It was during the party at the St. Francis Hotel that he wandered into suite 1221, closed the door behind him, and destroyed Virginia Rappe and his film career in a matter of minutes.

After help arrived, Virginia Rappe was found half-nude, bleeding profusely, and shouting hysterically, "He hurt me. I'm dying." She died. He was tried for murder. A mistrial was declared when the jury couldn't decide after forty-four hours of deliberation. A second jury couldn't reach a verdict, though ten of the twelve jurors voted for conviction. At a third trial, the verdict was acquittal. The jury said there was no evidence to connect him with any crime, and that "a grave injustice has been done him."

But, as Dr. Albert Ellis will tell you, there is no justice. Cleared though he was by the courts, his career as a comic was ended. He died alone and almost forgotten in New York City on June 28, 1933, at the age of forty-six. But the Arbuckle-Rappe scandal lives on, nearly half a century later.

6 Political Sex Scandals of the Last Decade

1. *Congressman Wilbur D. Mills* (D. Ark.). On October 7, 1974, the Washington park police stopped a speeding car that lacked lights. Two of the occupants, both drunk, turned out to be Congressman Mills and Fanne Fox, a local stripper who was also known as the "Argentine bombshell." (After the incident she billed herself as the "Tidal Basin Bomb.") Mills finally confessed to being an alcoholic and engaging in exhibitionism and antics unbecoming a Congressman. He resigned from Congress and took the cure. Recently he attempted a political comeback.

2. *Congressman Wayne L. Hayes* (D. Ohio). In 1976 Elizabeth Ray charged that he had placed her on his payroll as a clerk-typist when in truth she was hired to provide the Congressman with sex. The clincher: Elizabeth couldn't type!

3. *Representative John Young* (D. Texas). In 1976, he was accused by Colleen Gardner of hiring her as a sex companion while putting her on the government payroll. Her new job paid $25,800—a nice rise from her original $8,500 salary. The Justice Department cleared Young of any crime.

4. *Representative Allan Howe* (D. Utah). Howe was arrested in 1976 in Salt Lake City and charged with soliciting a woman for sex. The woman turned out to be an undercover policewoman. Howe was convicted.

5. *Representative Fred. W. Richmond* (D. N.Y.). Richmond was charged in 1978 with soliciting the sexual favors of a young man. He pleaded not guilty but later confessed that he had done what he was charged with. Nevertheless, he was re-elected to Congress.

6. *Representative John W. Jenrette, Jr.* (D. S.C.). He was convicted in the Abscam bribery scandal. Then his wife charged him with a dramatic list of extramarital peccadilloes and made a personal appearance tour to talk about it on national television. Later she posed for a *Playboy* magazine nude spread and wrote a book about her life with John. Shortly thereafter, she obtained a divorce.

27

*Here are some hints which may help you
to a healthier sex life.*

20 Birth-Control Methods

1. The pill
2. IUD (Intra-Uterine Device)
3. Diaphragm
4. Condom (rubber prophylactic)
5. Contraceptive foam
6. Fertility awareness (rhythm method)
7. Vasectomy (male)
8. Tubal ligation (female)
9. Coitus interruptus (withdrawing the penis before ejaculation)
10. Abstention
11. "Morning after" pill
12. Vitamin C solution (as spermicide)
13. Constriction of the shaft of the penis (manually or mechanically)
14. Thermally induced infertility (subjecting testes to extreme temperatures which temporarily render spermatozoa ineffective)

15. Fellatio
16. Anal intercourse
17. Masturbation
18. Cervical cap
19. Vaginal suppositories
20. Gossypol—made from cottonseed oil. It is presently being used experimentally in China and is taken by the male, a spoonful at a time. It has been found to inhibit the formation of sperm.

5 Centers for Sexual Rejuvenation

The following five centers are for the rejuvenation or revitalization of various parts of the body, including the sex organs. The centers do not confine themselves to improving the sexual function, but that is one of their purposes.

1. *Clinique Lemana*, Clarens, Switzerland. This clinic carries on the famous rejuvenation therapy of Professor Paul Niehans. Niehans discovered his method by accident in 1931. One day he was called in as a consultant when a young surgeon had damaged a gland of a young women patient.

   With no known procedure to turn to, Niehans took a gland from a steer, cut it into pieces, and injected it into the woman. She survived, and thus began the Niehans approach to helping the body help itself.

   Niehans's cellular therapy became internationally known when word got out that it was used on Pope Pius XII. The Pope, 77 years old, had become dangerously ill and the Vatican doctors had given up hope for his recovery. In desperation, members of the Pope's retinue called in Niehans. He administered cellular injections and the Pope recovered to praise and bless the treatment and make Niehans world-famous.

   The literature indicates that many prominent people have taken this treatment including Churchill, de Gaulle, Noël Coward, Marlene Dietrich, W. Somerset Maugham, and both the Duke and the Duchess of Windsor.

People from all over the world now go to the clinic for a general "youth recovery" treatment. Many are particularly concerned with retaining or recovering their sexual drive. The clinic claims to analyze those parts of the body which are weak or deficient. It then injects fresh cells taken from young sheep or their fetuses into the buttocks of the patient.

The treatment takes about a week and costs several thousand dollars, and many people throughout the world insist that their sex lives have been considerably improved by it.

2. *The Stephan Clinic*, Harley Place, London. This clinic was established by Dr. Ernest Stephan, who has since retired, and it is now being operated by Dr. Peter Stephan, his son.

His method is similar to that used by the Lemana clinic but is limited to cellular formulations which contain not the entire cell but only the DNA and RNA of the cell. Another difference is that in the Swiss clinic you have to stay in bed or at least remain in your room after the treatment, but at the Stephan Clinic, the injection treatment takes about ten minutes and then you are free to go your way.

The Stephan treatment can be completed in ten days but they prefer three weeks. Patients are also given suppositories to use for several weeks after the clinical treatment is over.

3. *Kent Private Clinic*, Sandwich, Kent, England. This clinic is directed by Dr. Brian Richards. Richards is one of the most thoroughly educated of all clinic operators. He has degrees in science, medicine and surgery and is a Fellow of the Royal Academy of Medicine and several other organizations, including the New York Academy of Science.

Dr. Richards' Clinic is operated along the lines of the Stephan Clinic, and, in fact, patients who prefer to have some of their treatment in the London area can do so, for Dr. Richards also uses the facilities of the Stephan Clinic.

Dr. Richards is a specialist in sex therapy and revitalization and people from all over the world come to him for that specialty.

4. *Renaissance Revitalization Center*, Cable Beach, Nassau, Bahamas. This center provides a number of therapies for body revitalization. The best-known therapy is embryo therapy, which includes the eating of fertile chicken eggs that (it is claimed) have been treated in ways that make them extremely potent.

This center also promotes an inhalation therapy which is of significance to smokers. The objective of the therapy is to clean out those parts of the body contaminated by the smoke.

5. *Rumanian Gerovital and Aslavital Therapies.* As a result of the research of the famous Dr. Ana Aslan of Bucharest, Rumania, there are several centers throughout Rumania which offer this form of therapy. It consists of a series of injections of a substance discovered by Dr. Aslan, given over a two week period.

The patients return home but take with them a two year supply of vials and pills. To continue the treatment the patient must be injected with the contents of the vials three times a week for four weeks and then go off treatment for a brief period. Then there is a return to a new cycle of pills and injections.

The centers in Rumania are located in particularly scenic places, in suburban Bucharest, in the mountains and on the Black Sea.

15 Sex Therapy Clinics

Since the success of Dr. William Masters and Mrs. Virginia Johnson and their sex therapy clinic such installations have proliferated. Accreditation is far from complete, and there are many problems with charlatans. The clinics change rapidly. Some (like Masters and Johnson) use surrogates for sex; others do not. The following list is just for starters:

1. Reproductive Biology Research Foundation
   4910 Forest Park Blvd.
   St. Louis, MO 63108
   (314) 361-2377

2. Human Sexuality Program
   University of California Medical Center
   San Francisco, CA 94143

3. Alexandra Fauntleroy, Psychiatric Nurse
   139 S. Washington Street
   Easton, MD 21601

4. Alexander N. Levay, M.D.
   161 Fort Washington Avenue
   New York, NY 10032

5. Virginia Lozzi, M.D.
   480 Park Avenue
   New York, NY 10022

6. Armando de Moya, M.D., and Dorothy de Moya, M.S.N.
   11016 Ticasso Lane
   Potomac, MD 20854
   (301) 365-0297 or 365-0299
   (The de Moyas are also on the Sex Therapy Certification Committee
   of the American Association of Sex Educators and Counselors. See
   list of associations on the subject.)

7. Loyola University Foster McGaw Hospital Sexual Dysfunction
   Clinic
   Domeena Renshaw, M.D., Director
   2160 South First Avenue
   Maywood, IL 60153 (312) 531-7350

8. Mount Sinai Medical School, Program in Human Sexuality
   Dr. Raul Schiavi, Director
   11 East 110th Street
   New York, NY 11029

9. Payne Whitney Clinic of New York Hospital
   Sex Therapy and Education Program
   Helen Singer Kaplan, M.D., Ph.D., Director
   525 East 68th Street
   New York, NY 10021
   (212) 472-5033

10. John B. Reckless, M.D., and Eileen Sullivan, B.S.N.
    John Reckless Clinic
    5504 Durham-Chapel Hill Blvd.
    Durham, NC 22707
    (919) 489-1161

11. Harvey L. Resnik, M.D., and Audrey R. Resnik, M.D.
    Chevy Chase Medical Center, Suite 201,
    4740 Chevy Chase Drive
    Chevy Chase, MD 20015
    (301) 656-4774

12. Philip M. Sarrel, M.D., and Lorna J. Sarrel, M.S.W., Directors, Sex
    Therapy Clinic, Yale Medical School
    333 Cedar Street
    New Haven, CT 06510
    (203) 436-3592

13. Marshall Shearer, M.D., and Marguerite Shearer, M.D.
    13A Tower Plaza
    555 East William Street
    Ann Arbor, MI 48108
    (313) 668-6341

14. Philip E. Veenhuis, M.D., and Joanne Veenhuis, M.A.
    1220 Dewey Avenue
    Wauwatosa, WI 53213
    (414) 258-2600

15. Dr. Harold Lief, Director
    Center for Sex Education and Medicine
    4025 Chestnut Street
    Philadelphia, PA 19104

14 Sexually Transmitted Diseases That You Should Know About

At one time, venereal disease meant five possibilities, the most important of which were syphilis and gonorrhea. The abbreviation used then was VD and "venereal" was named after Venus, the goddess of love.

Today, VD has become STD—meaning sexually transmitted diseases. Today medical science has identified some sixty different sexually transmitted diseases. Fourteen worthy of mention are:

1. *NGU*—non-gonococcal urethritis. Gonorrhea is an infectious inflammation of the mucous membrane of the urethra and adjacent areas. NGU was discovered when tests for what seemed to be gonorrhea turned out not to be gonorrhea, although the symptoms (an infection of the urethra) were similar.

   Unlike gonorrhea, which is treated with penicillin, NGU is treated with tetracycline or another antibiotic.

2. *Resistant gonorrhea*—a new strain that may cause the usual symptoms of the disease in the male (painful urination and a milky discharge) but does not respond to penicillin. Studies

on this strain of the disease have made medical science aware that a man can be a gonorrhea carrier for some time and not know he has it.

3. *Homosexual STD*—as the gay world comes out of the closet, physicians have become more aware that diseases once not identified with sexual activity do, in fact, originate from sex between males. These include bowel and throat infections.

4. *Herpes simplex*—an acute inflammation of the skin or mucous membrane, characterized by the development of a group of vesicles on an inflammatory base. This is caused by a virus. In the venereal version of herpes, blisters form on the genitalia and sometimes the buttocks and thighs. To date, medical science has not developed an effective cure. Condoms prevent transmission of this virus in most—but not all—instances where intercourse takes place between an infected person and one who is not infected.

   The genital herpes simplex virus causes sores that may last for days and then heal with or without treatment. In most people, the sores flare up again from time to time.

   An estimated ten million people suffer from this ailment and the National Centers for Disease Control say that an additional 400,000 people are contracting genital herpes each year.

5. *Chancroid*—a lesion produced by an infection involving the genitalia, usually multiple and painful.

6. *Climatic bubu*—inflammation of the lymph nodes.

7. *Crabs*—pubic lice; cause itching, rash and inflammation of the pubic area *(pediculosis pubis).*

8. *Granuloma inguinale*—a chronic and destructive ulceration of the external genitalia.

9. *Hepatitis B*—inflammation of the liver caused by a bacterial infection.

10. *Lymphogranuloma venereum*—a virus disease characterized by an initial lesion on the genitalia, followed by regional lymph-node enlargement. Sometimes called the Nicolas-Favor Disease.

11. *Syphilis*—a variety of lesions of which the chancre (primary lesion), the mucous patch, and the gumma are the most distinctive. Caused by a spirochete.

12. *Trichomoniasis*—Chronic infection of the vagina. Cause: *trichomor vaginalis.*

13. *Urethritis*—an inflammation of the urethra.
14. (Possibly) *Cancer of the cervix*—considered a sexual contact disease on the theory that nuns almost never get it.

11 Foods That Could Improve Your Sex Life

Many authorities believe there is a direct relationship between the quantity and quality of your sex life and the foods you eat. The following is a list of foods and vitamins, minerals, and additives that are suggested to improve your sex life:

1. *Wheat germ.* You can buy this in any supermarket or health food store. This is the most nutritious part of the wheat kernel, the germ. It is high in protein and contains several B vitamins, vitamin E, and a fair amount of iron, phosphorus, magnesium, zinc, copper, and even some folic acid and pantothenic acid. These are all important for health, and deficiencies of some of them cause sterility.
2. *Wheat germ oil.* Very high in vitamin E, which increases the sperm count and the volume of seminal fluid. Also aids females to prevent miscarriages and premature births.
3. *Sesame seeds* (or tahini.) High in vitamin E; helps ward off fatigue.
4. *Honey.* Contains much pollen, one of the best foods available. Also contains the gonadotropic hormone, which stimulates the sex glands.
5. *Raw nuts and seeds.* These convert sugar to glycogen, which is related to the sex drive.
6. *Milk.* A potent virility food. The casein in milk helps produce hypophyseal, a sex-stimulant hormone.
7. *Lecithin.* You can get this in capsule form or as a dry food additive in health food stores. It helps prevent the hardening of the arteries and improves circulation.
8. *Eggs.* Each one contains 1.1 milligrams of iron, of particular value to women.

9. Vitamin A. Of particular significance for the formation of healthy testicular tissue and linings of the mucous membranes (including those of the sex organs).
10. *Kelp.* Provides iodine to stimulate the endocrine glands which, when underactive, inhibit the sex drive.
11. *Oysters.* Yes, believe it or not, they are recommended as a sex food. They are high in protein, calcium, iron and vitamin A. All helpful, one way or another, in sex activity.

—Sources: *Sex and Nutrition,* by Paavo O. Airola, M.D.; *Harper's Bazaar,* April 1980; and *Vitamin Bible,* by Earl Mindell.

5 Steps to Calculate Weight Loss with Each Act of Sexual Intercourse

1. Substitute sex for the snack before going to bed.
2. Calculate the number of calories that would be in the snack you are giving up.
3. Add to the snack calories you omitted the calories you will lose in the average sex act, i.e., 200 calories.
4. Multiply this total (snack calories plus intercourse calories) by the additional sex acts during the month in which you wouldn't otherwise have engaged.
5. Divide the total by 3,500 (the caloric content of one pound of body weight).

Here is an example: You give up a piece of pie and a glass of milk or ham sandwich and a bottle of beer and either combination would total 700 calories. Add to this the 200 calories you will expend in sexual intercourse. Multiply this by 12 (the number of additional sex acts during the month). This gives you a total of 10,800. Divide this by 3,500 (the net amount of calories you need to lose a pound of weight) and you get 3 + pounds. So, if you substitute sex for a snack 12 times during the month you can lose 3 + pounds during that month.

Source: *How Sex Can Keep You Slim,* by Abraham I. Friedman

16 Pieces of Sexual Misinformation

1. It's harmful to the man or the woman to have sexual intercourse during menstruation.

    Wrong. It may be messy. The finicky may be turned off, but there's no harm to either the man or the woman. It's perfectly all right. Many couples are especially turned-on during this period.

2. The diaphragm by itself is a satisfactory means of birth control.

    Wrong. The best diaphragm in the world alone won't prevent conception. For a diaphragm to be truly effective it must be ringed by a spermicidal jelly or cream. This must be replenished if additional sex occurs more than six to eight hours after the first time. (Follow the directions on the package.)

3. Spanish Fly is an excellent aphrodisiac.

    Not so. Incidentally, Spanish Fly has nothing to do with flies, but is made from the wings of beetles. While it may sometimes cause an erection in a male, it will also usually bring on vomiting, diarrhea and other undesirable and painful side effects. Keep away.

4. Powdered rhinoceros horn is used as an aphrodisiac by wealthy Chinese in Taiwan and Hong Kong.

    Used, but the aphrodisiac effect is a state of mind. The powder is available, expensive and well on its way to causing the extinction of the rhinoceros. This powder produces no bad side effects. But then, again, it won't do a thing to heighten libido either.

5. When a girl starts menstruating she is fertile and may be impregnated.

    Wrong. Ovulation begins later. The menarche, or first menstruation, usually comes at age twelve or thirteen but in temperate climates ovulation doesn't normally begin until fourteen.

6. It takes a woman 28 days to manufacture an ovum (an egg).

    Wrong. At birth the two ovaries already hold a lifetime supply of eggs in sacs. There are as many as a million single cell tiny eggs. After puberty, each month an egg (ready for fertilization) leaves the ovary, enters the fallopian tube and if fertilized, pregnancy results. If not, menstruation occurs.

7. Sexuality begins at puberty.

   Wrong. Modern studies have demonstrated that male infants have erections and other sex manifestations at birth and possibly while still in the uterus. Female infants have manifested vaginal secretion, indicating sexual activity.

8. A boy who, at puberty, shows great attachment for his mother and hostility to his father is demonstrating the Oedipus complex.

   Wrong. It becomes a "complex" only if he carries it into adulthood.

9. When parents discover their young children are masturbating, they should discourage the continuation of the activity.

   Wrong. Children suffer acute sexual tension, and masturbation is a form of voluntary release.

10. When you discover your son is beginning to have wet dreams, you should ignore them so he won't feel self-conscious.

    Wrong. Ignoring would be better than criticizing, joking or poking fun at him. But what he needs is an explanation, reassurance and comforting so he'll understand the naturalness of what's happening so he won't feel guilty about sex.

11. A man who can't control his orgasm can get more practice only with intercourse.

    Not so. He can practice orgasm control during masturbation.

12. Transvestites (cross-sex dressing) are homosexuals.

    Not so. Fewer than one in four transvestites are gay. The rest simply get pleasure from dressing in the clothes of the opposite sex.

13. You can't have an ejaculation without an erection.

    Wrong. Older men frequently have ejaculations without achieving an erection. If intercourse is no longer possible, masturbation is a viable alternative.

14. If a man can produce an erection, a woman can always make it limp.

    Not so. There's a disease called "priapism" which produces a persistent erection, sometimes so bad that minor surgery is required. (They *don't* cut it off.)

15. A woman who does not bleed on the consummation of her marriage wasn't a virgin at the altar.

    Not true. Today many females engage in activities including horseback riding, masturbation, hand petting, use of tampons, and so forth which can obliterate the hymen or stretch it.

16. There's no way a man can tell if a woman has had an orgasm or not. If she wants to fake it, she can always get away with it.
    Not true. Watch her nipples. They almost invariably become erect during orgasm.

6 Sexual Fears and How to Overcome Them

Rigid attitudes with regard to sex can cause a person to feel enormous tension up to a point where they are unable to enjoy, or even participate in, sexual intercourse. Some fears can be dealt with and overcome more easily than others. (If you can identify a fear, you are on the way to removing it.)

1. *Fear of Pregnancy:* All women at some time in their lives encounter this fear. Denying it because you regard it as somehow "wrong" or unnatural only makes it worse. Your sex life will be greatly improved if you educate yourself in all available methods of birth control. Your gynecologist can be helpful.

2. *Fear of Birth-Control Pills:* Prescribed by your gynecologist and used exactly as ordered, they are relatively safe. However, some combination of other methods can be at least as effective and much less threatening. Rhythm, condoms, or diaphragms with spermicidal jelly can be used in a variety of combinations to make you both safe and comfortable.

3. *Fear of Internal Injury:* A frank discussion of this fear with your partner can result in a little extra care during active sex play and penetration until such time as the fear is gone.

4. *Fear of Failure:* When you worry about your own performance or that of your partner, the fear can become a self-fulfilling prophecy. Forget such myths as the need for simultaneous mutual climax. Forget the nonsense about the need to perform. Sex is not a contest or a test. It can be pleasurable if you relax and let it be so. Work to build your partner's confidence and your own will grow too.

5. *Guilt about sex:* Perhaps more than any other fear, feeling guilty or "dirty" about the sex act will cause you to tighten up and destroy your ability to enjoy sex. This is difficult to overcome alone, since the cause is generally buried deep in your childhood. However, an understanding partner can help. Or, try individual or a group therapy approach.

6. *Fear of being seen during the sex act:* If you are a person who feels an extreme need for privacy, a locked door and room darkening shades or curtains can help. Also consider participating in nude encounter groups or just nude recreation in a non sexual way. Such exposure can help you to desensitize yourself and eliminate this fear.

5 Sources of Sex Education for Children

Source	Male	Female
Parents	58.8%	73.3%
Teachers	21.5%	13.4%
Other young people	6.9%	3.1%
No one special	6.9%	1.0%
Miscellaneous	4.9%	9.2%

—Susan M. Bennett and W.B. Dickinson,
Journal of Sex Research

4 Sex Education Books for Children

Sex education for children remains one of the most controversial subjects in American culture. Because of their own limited training, most parents are unable to deal directly and candidly with their children on matters of sex.

Should children receive sex education at a young age, as they do in Sweden? Or should we limit teaching on the subject to a few high school biology lessons?

The questions remain open and feelings continue to heat up. Two books have made parent-child communication easier.

1. *Where Did I Come From?*, by Peter Mayle, was designed by Paul Walter. It presents the facts of life without any nonsense and with illustrations by Arthur Robins. It explains orgasm to a seven year old. Orson Bean talked about it on the Johnny Carson show and Dr. Spock said, "I give this book top grades for humanness and honesty. Some parents will find that its humorousness helps them over the embarrassment. Others may be offended."

   Where Did I Come From? is on its way to selling one million copies in the United States. It has been published in several languages including six separate dialect editions in West Germany. It was the first book to be published without prior approval of the censor in Franco's Spain, and before the censor could protest, more than 30,000 copies were sold in four days.

2. *What's Happening to Me?*, by the same trio that did the book described above. This one is a guide to puberty and has sold several hundred thousand copies. This one too has been published in several languages including German, Spanish, French, Swedish, Finnish, Japanese, Greek, Hebrew, and Dutch.

An amusing contrast is represented by books 3 and 4 on this list. For they were published seventy years ago (in 1911) and what they taught was trepidation, fear and guilt:

3. *What a Father Should Tell His Little Boy*, by Isabelle Thompson Smart.

4. *What a Mother Should Tell her Little Girl*, by Isabelle Thompson Smart.

28

*Much of our days and nights
are spent watching films and television.
Here is a guide to the X-rated land of porn.*

72 Widely Distributed X-Rated Video Cassettes

Twenty years ago, several booksellers served time in prison ranging from thirty days to one year. The crime? They sold books or magazines that contained a view of the female body in which the pubic hair had not been airbrushed out.

Today, your neighborhood video cassette shop most probably has a collection of X-rated films for sale or rent.

If your neighborhood doesn't have a video cassette shop with an "X-rated" department, write to Home Screen Theatre, 1580 Lemoine Avenue, Fort Lee, NJ 07024. They can supply you with any and all of the movies on this list.

1. *Aunt Peg*
2. *Aunt Peg's Fulfillment*, staring Juliet Anderson, John Leslie, and John Keys
3. *Autobiography of a Flea*
4. *Bad Company*, starring Mandy Lane, Tracey Butler, and Dorothy Le May

5. *Babylon Pink*
6. *Barbara Broadcast*
7. *The Best of Gail Palmers*
8. *Behind the Green Door*, starring Marilyn Chambers
9. *The Budding of Brie*
10. *The Blondes*, starring Annette Haven
11. *California Gigolo*, starring John Holmes
12. *Candy Goes to Hollywood*, starring Carol Conner
13. *China de Sade*, starring Linda Wong
14. *Debbie Does Dallas*, starring Bambi Woods
15. *Deep Throat*, starring Linda Lovelace
16. *The Devil in Miss Jones*, starring Georgina Spelvin
17. *Easy*, starring Jessie St. James and Georgina Spelvin
18. *The Ecstasy Girls*, starring Serena, Jamie Gillis, and Georgina Spelvin
19. *800 Fantasy Lane*, starring Chris Anderson, Candy Summer, and Jamie Gillis
20. *"11"*
21. *Eruption*, starring Leslie Bovee and John Holmes
22. *Expensive Taste*, starring Elaine Wells and Joseph Nassi
23. *Extremes*, starring Joey Civera, Serena, Eric Edwards and Jessie St. James
24. *Fantasy World*, starring Laurien Dominique and Jessie St. James
25. *Foxy Lady*, starring Valerie Driskell and John Leslie
26. *Frat House*
27. *French Teen*, starring Jacqueline Bardot and Sharon Mitchell
28. *Garage Girls*, starring Georgina Spelvin, John Leslie, and Lisa Deleeuw
29. *Getting Off*, starring Desiree Cousteau
30. *The Good Girls of Godiva High*
31. *High School Memories*, starring Annette Haven, Jamie Gillis, and John Leslie
32. *Hot Legs*, starring Jessie St. James
33. *Hot Rackets*, starring Candida Royalle and Desiree Clearbranch
34. *Hot Summer in the City*, starring Lisa Baer and Duke Johnson
35. *Insatiable*, starring Marilyn Chambers
36. *Inside Jennifer Welles*
37. *Inside Desiree Cousteau*, starring Desiree Cousteau, Serena, and Susan Nero
38. *Italian Stallion*, starring Sylvester Stallone and Henrietta Holme

39. *Little Girls Blue,* starring Tamara Morgan, Debby Damboise and Elaine Wells
40. *Love Syndrome,* starring Samatha Fox, Bobby Astyr, and Merle Michaels
41. *Night of the Spanish Fly,* starring Angel Barrett, Beerbohmtree, and Jeff Eagle
42. *On White Satin,* starring Seka
43. *The Other Side of Julie,* starring John Leslie and Gloria Roberts
44. *Pizza Girls,* starring John Holmes and Candida Royalle
45. *Pleasure Palace,* starring Serena and Eric Edwards
46. *Practice Makes Perfect,* starring Darby Lloyd Rains and Kim Pope
47. *Prisoner of Paradise,* starring John Holmes and Seka
48. *The Private Afternoon of Pamela Mann*
49. *Pussycat Ranch,* starring Samantha Fox, Coleen Anderson, and Eric Edwards
50. *Rocking with Seka,* starring Seka, John Holmes, and Jamie Gillis
51. *The Senator's Daughter,* starring John Holmes and Leslie Bovee
52. *Sex Boat,* starring Roxanne Potts and Kelly Nichols
53. *Sex Wish,* starring Harry Reems and C.J. Laing
54. *Sex World*
55. *Skin on Skin,* starring John Leslie, Eve Hausmann and Pat Manning
56. *Sodom and Gomorrah*
57. *Star Virgin,* starring Kari Klark
58. *Stormy,* starring John Holmes and Linda Wong
59. *Swedish Erotica* (24 volumes)
60. *Sweet Throat,* starring Beth Anna, Eric Edwards, and Al Lavinsky
61. *Taboo,* starring Kay Parker
62. *Talk Dirty to Me,* starring Jessie St. James and John Leslie
63. *Tangerine*
64. *That's Erotic,* starring John Holmes, Georgina Spelvin, and Serena
65. *That's Porno,* starring "32 of your favorite stars"
66. *Tramp,* starring Samantha Fox and Gloria Leonard
67. *Tropic of Desire,* starring Georgina Spelvin and Jessie St. James
68. *V—The Hot One,* starring Annette Haven and John Leslie
69. *Vista Valley P.T.A.,* starring Jamie Gillis, Jessie St. James and John Leslie

70. *Weekend Fantasy,* starring Jennifer West and William Margold
71. *Wet Dreams,* starring Lee Carroll
72. *Young, Wild and Wonderful*

The 10 Best-Hung Porno Movie Stars and Their Measurements

1. John Holmes (also known as Johnny Wadd) (14½ inches)
2. Marc Stevens (10½ inches)
3. Harry Reems (9 inches)
4. Bobby Astyr (9 inches)
5. Jamie Gillis (9 inches)
6. Ron Jeremy (9 inches)
7. Jack Wrangler (9 inches)
8. John Leslie (9 inches)
9. Ron Pacheko (9 inches)
10. Eric Edwards (9 inches)

—Prepared by Al Goldstein exclusively for *The Book of Sex Lists*

10 of the Best Porno Films of All Time

1. *Deep Throat*
2. *The Devil in Miss Jones*
3. *Behind the Green Door*
4. *The Opening of Misty Beethoven*
5. *Sex World*
6. *The Ecstasy Girls*
7. *Talk Dirty to Me*
8. *Insatiable*
9. *"11"*
10. *Amanda by Night*

—Prepared by the staff of *Screw* especially for *The Book of Sex Lists*

10 Types of People Who Attend
X-Rated Movies on a Regular Basis

1. The impotent male (married or unmarried) who hopes it will cure him of his sexual inadequacy.
2. The psychic or fantasy masturbator.
3. The sexually disappointed and frustrated husband whose wife is prudish and sexually unresponsive.
4. The "escapist" who uses X-rated movies to get his mind off the pressures of his job.
5. The unemployed male who doesn't know what else to do with his leisure time.
6. The widower who relives the sex experiences of his earlier years.
7. The curious male who is eager to learn "new tricks," new methods of sexual experimentation.
8. The woman who attends X-rated movies with other women for "kicks," excitement, and to learn more about "kinky" sex.
9. Homosexuals (male or female) who identify themselves with persons on the screen performing homosexual acts.
10. Scoptophiliacs (men who achieve greater sexual gratification looking at others performing sex acts) who overcompensate for their own sexual inadequacy.

28 Low-Class Hard-Core Porno Magazines

1. *Oral*
2. *Pleasure Chest*
3. *Comin'*
4. *Semen*
5. *The European Connection*
6. *Caresse*
7. *Swedish Erotica*
8. *Embrace*
9. *Knocked up Mamas*
10. *Breast Milk Feeders*

29

*Products that are said to help
and gadgets that are designed to turn you on,
even while they tap your till, are in the next
cluster....*

6 Products Sold to Men
to Help Them Maintain Erections

1. Pro-long
2. Stay Cream
3. Sta-Hard
4. Hard-on
5. Longtime Creme
6. Stud Delay Spray

14 Love Drugs and Sex Enhancers

1. NDA—a short acting psychedelic
2. Marijuana (research at the University of Texas shows that sex drive may be increased immediately after ingestion but that prolonged and heavy use will dissipate male sexual activity)

3. Alcohol
4. Inhalants (amyl nitrate & isobutal nitrites, sold over-the-counter as Rush, Bullet, etc.)
5. Cocaine
6. Quaaludes
7. PCP (Street-wise drug users say this substance has too much potential for violence and bodily harm.)
8. Ether
9. Nitrous oxide (A few devotees recommend inhaling, though timing is critical!)
10. Helium (ditto)
11. Psychedelics
12. Heroin—in titrated amounts
13. Downers—in general, used in small amounts
14. Uppers—sometimes in combination with downers to mellow the effect.

Good lovers avoid desensitizing themselves or their partners.

103 Alleged Aphrodisiacs

1. *Absinthe*—liquor
2. *Adenophora*—Chinese plant resembling ginseng
3. *Alcohol*
4. *Amanita*—hallucinogen
5. *Ambergris*—derivative of whale regurgitation
6. *Amyl Nitrate*—anti-angina drug
7. *Apple of Pero*—psychedelic plant of Peru
8. *Asarone*—related to mescaline
9. *Ash* (white)—seed used by American Indians
10. *Avocado* (seeds and skin)—brewed into tea
11. *Bamboo*—sap
12. *Bee Pollen*
13. *Beeswax*
14. *Betel Nut*—chewed
15. *Blister fly*—Chinese insect, powdered
16. *Cacti*—many contain mescaline

17. *California poppy*—gentle narcotic
18. *Cannabis*—marijuana
19. *Capsicum*—red pepper
20. *Chrysanthemum*—flowers soaked in wine
21. *Coca Leaves*—usually chewed
22. *Cock's Comb*—seeds powdered, mixed with milk
23. *Cotton Root*—bark is ingested
24. *Cuttle Fish*—taken as a tonic
25. *DMSO*—wood-pulp derivative
26. *DMT* (dimethyltryptamine)—a psychedelic
27. *Dulse* (and *Kelp*)—edible seaweed
28. *Eaglewood*—gum from Oriental tree
29. *Estradiol*—female sex hormone
30. *Fennel* (wild)—oil is hallucinogenic
31. *Garlic*—general health stimulant
32. *Ginseng*—grows wild in U.S. and Asia
33. *Granada*—pomegranate juice used as a sexual tonic
34. *Hawk-Moth Caterpillar*—powdered, for men
35. *Henbane*—seeds and leaves are powdered
36. *Henna*—leaves rubbed on head, fingertips, and soles of feet
37. *Hibiscus*—from San Francisco Valley, Brazil
38. *Hydrangea*—leaves are smoked
39. *Ipomoea*—alcoholic extracts from tubers
40. *Jimson Weed*—seeds and leaves used by Mariposa Indians

Juices:
41. Beet
42. Cabbage
43. Carrot
44. Cucumber
45. Dandelion Leaves
46. Green Pepper
47. Lemon
48. Lettuce
49. Lime
50. Onion
51. Orange
52. Potato
53. Radish
54. Strawberry
55. Tomato
56. Turnip Tops
57. Watercress

291

58. *Kava-Kava*—usually as a drink
59. *Kola*—stimulant
60. *L-Dopa*—anti-Parkinson disease drug
61. *Licorice*—native of Asia, Southern Europe
62. *"Magic Mushroom"*—psilocybin
63. *Mandrake*—a man-shaped root
64. *Methaqualone* (Quaalude)—sedative, hypnotic drug
65. *Morning Glory*—seeds contain LSD
66. *Myrrh*—tea made from resin
67. *Opium*—prolongs sexual acts
68. *Orchids*—roots are ingested
69. *Passion Flower*—sedative, narcotic
70. *Pumpkin Seeds*—reputed remedy for impotence
71. *Rhinoceros horn*—powdered, ingested
72. *Rhododendron*—leaves eaten raw
73. *Salamander*—boiled in oil, eaten
74. *Sarsaparilla*—root is powdered
75. *Sassafras*—oil used in tea
76. *Selinum*—seeds are eaten or brewed
77. *Shrimp*—rich in protein, vitamins, and minerals
78. *Silkworm*—pod is eaten
79. *Skullcap* (Chinese)—plant found in Mongolia, Siberia, and China
80. *Solomon's Seal*—root and shoots edible when boiled
81. *Southernwood*—European shrub
82. *Spanish Fly*—powdered beetle wing sheaths
83. *Spearmint*—oil used in tea
84. *Stag Phallus*—locally applied
85. *Stink Bug*—locally applied
86. *Su-Kung*—raw honey
87. *Sunflower Seeds*—eaten raw
88. *Testosterone*—male sex hormone
89. *Thinanthus*—bark from Brazilian climbing plant
90. *TMA*—trimethoxy amphetamine
91. *Toad venom*—drops are ingested
92. *Toe*—plant from Amazon River
93. *Tortoise Eggs*—mixed with water, applied locally
94. *Touch-Me-Not* (mimosa)—leaves attached to body
95. *Truffle*—used by ancient Romans
96. *Vanilla Pods*—fragrant climbing orchid
97. *Vervain*—sacred plant from ancient Britain

98. *Willow* (black—pussy willow)—bark and berries used
99. *Wood Louse*—powdered
100. *Wormwood*—salve applied locally
101. *Yage*—derived from vines, in Amazon Basin
102. *Zalov Root*—originated in Beirut
103. *Zygophyllum*—from western U.S.

The above list is included as an amusing curiosity. Actually we agree with the sages who have said that the only aphrodisiac worthy of the name is an attractive specimen of the opposite (or the same, depending on your preference) sex, usually (but not always) the younger the better (within limits, of course).

The 10 Most Popular Sex Gadgets

1. *The Orgasmatron.* An electric vibrator with a series of attachments. The various attachments are intended to provide "concentrated clitoral stimulation" with a guarantee of an orgasm. This vibrator is sold with a guarantee that if a woman doesn't have an orgasm, full payment will be refunded. Priced from $19.95 to $34.95, depending on the model.

2. *Motion Lotion.* Greaseless, stainless, and water-soluble, this lotion provides a pleasant, warm sensation when it touches the skin. It heats up when blown upon. Comes in lemon-lime, grape, orange, passion fruit, and strawberry. Price: $3.95 per bottle.

3. *Authentic Ben Wa Gold Balls.* Purportedly "authentic ancient Japanese auto-erotic balls, inserted in the vagina for additional stimulation." Price: $12.95.

4. *6-Inch Dildo with Harness.* Regular $10.95; with a leather harness, $19.95.

5. *Candy Pants.* Bikini pants made out of sweet edible material. Price: $5.49.

6. *Dildo Vibrator.* Operates on three "c" batteries and "squirms, rotates, stimulates, in uncontrollable throbbing vibrations." Various models from $14.95 to $19.95.

7. *The Magic Massager.* A rotating battery-operated tool on a plastic rod, intended to reach any part of the body. Price: $32.58.

8. *Wrist Restraints.* Price: $16.75.

9. *Ankle Restraints.* Price: $21.95

10. *The China Brush.* A liquid which is brushed on the penis at the proper time to prolong erection. It will not desensitize the penis. Price: $7.95.

> —Contributed by the personnel of the Pink Pussycat Boutique, 161 West 4th Street, New York, NY 10014 (catalog available upon request)

20 Places in the United States for the Purchase of Sex Gadgets and Aids

1. Uncle Sam's Umbrella Shop
   161 West 57th Street
   New York, NY 10019

2. The Underground
   390 West Street
   New York, NY 10014

3. At Home Magazine
   P.O. Box 2205
   New York, NY 10163

4. Lee's Mardi Gras
   2nd Floor
   565 Tenth Avenue
   New York, NY 10036

5. Pink Pussycat Boutique
   161 West 4th Street
   New York, NY 10012

6. Pink Pussycat Boutique
   3105 N.E. 9th Street
   Ft. Lauderdale, FL 33315

7. Pink Pussycat Boutique
   3419 Main Highway
   Coconut Grove, FL 33133

8. Pleasure Chest Stores
   152 Seventh Avenue South
   New York, NY 10014

9. Pleasure Chest Stores
   939 Second Avenue
   New York, NY 10022

10. Pleasure Chest Stores
    3143 North Broadway
    Chicago, IL 60647

11. Pleasure Chest Stores
    2039 Walnut Street
    Philadelphia, PA 19103

12. Pleasure Chest Stores
    208 Duval Street
    Key West, FL 33040

13. Pleasure Chest Stores
    7733 Santa Monica Blvd.
    Los Angeles, CA 90046

14. Pleasure Chest Stores
    1063 Wisconsin Avenue N.W.
    Washington, DC 20007

15. Pleasure Chest Stores
    1001 N.E. Second Avenue
    Miami, FL 33132

16. Mail order:
    Centurian
    P.O. Box AE
    Westminster, CA 92683

17. Mail order:
    Pleasure Chest Sales, Ltd.
    20 West 20th Street
    New York, NY 10011

18. Mail order:
    At Home
    P.O. Box 2205
    New York, NY 10163

19. Mail order:
    Valentine Products
    P.O. Box 214
    Mount Morris, IL 61054

20. Mail order:
    Adam & Eve
    Apple Court
    Box 800
    Carrboro, NC 27510

10 Gadgets for Swinging Couples

The Underground is a society of swinging couples. It schedules group sex encounters, publishes a newsletter, and sells sex gadgets and aids. For further information, write to P.O. Box 197, Village Station, New York, NY 10014.

The following ten products are reported by The Underground to be its best-selling items. Prices are approximate.

1. *Emotion Lotion.* A flavored body lubricant. Rub it on intimate areas and blow upon it. Available in fourteen flavors. ($3.95)
2. *Junior Double Dildo.* Double pleasure for either sex. ($14.00)
3. *Magic Massager.* Electric multispeed vibrator. ($34.95)
4. *Garter Belts and Black Seamed Stockings.* This irresistible outfit will often start an orgy all by itself. ($15.00)
5. *Kama Sutra Oil of Love.* This highly personal oil must be experienced to be fully understood. ($8.00)
6. *"At Her Command."* A unique double dildo which allows a female to experience the joy of giving and getting simultaneously. Comes with its own harness. ($12.95)
7. *Joni's Butterfly Massager.* May be worn at any time. This battery-operated clitoral massager can be worn all day or even during sex. ($12.00)
8. *The Pendant.* Sold throughout the country by recognized clubs as the symbol for swinging. (Sterling silver: $25.00; pewter: $3.50)

9. *Liquids.* Butyl nitrite with brand names such as Rush, Black Jack, Hardware, Quick Silver, Anti-Knock. ($4.00-$10.00)
10. *Fur-lined restraints.* Swingers are famous for a little very slight S & M, and these mink restraints are sensuous turn-on. ($20.00)

1 Sex Technique That Made a Best Selling Book

In 1960, an efficiency expert at the Prentice-Hall publishing house in Englewood Cliffs, New Jersey, noticed that the ladies in the mail order section were doing more giggling than mail opening. He investigated and found them agog over a circular offering a not-yet-written book.

He read the book's offering circular, blushed at what he read, and complained to the President's 80-year-old mother who told her son, the President, "You are not to publish this book."

The son was dutiful and obeyed his mother. The book went to another publisher. Quietly, so mother wouldn't be upset, Prentice-Hall arranged to share in the royalties.

Published in 1960, the book was titled *The Marriage Art.* It was written by John E. Eichenlaub, M.D., a physician turned writer. He had already written a best seller called *A Minnesota Doctor's Home Remedies for Common and Uncommon Ailments.*

The Marriage Art went on to sell more than three million copies in the United States. It launched a German publishing house. In Holland, at the equivalent of three dollars a copy, it outsold the next fastest-selling book of the year (which was selling for thirty-five cents) a thriller called *The Spy Who Came in from the Cold.*

"Cold" was the key theme responsible for the incredible success of *The Marriage Art.* For buried in its lively pages was something called "the ice-spurred special."

The ice-spurred special not only sold many copies of *The Marriage Art* but helped several other books as well. For example, a character in the novel *Naked Came the Stranger* used the technique. And that book, allegedly written by a demure Long Island housewife, was actually a hoax put together by twenty-four members of the staff of *Newsday* who wanted to write a novel with writing and plotting worse than that found in the fiction of Harold Robbins and Irving Wallace. It was difficult but they did it.

Here, by permission of the publisher, is the ice-spurred special in its entirety.

The Ice-spurred Special.

Freezing cold against your skin stimulates both pain and temperature nerves, which are exactly the types of fiber which trigger your sex climax. The ice-spurred special takes advantage of this fact. Before intercourse, the wife places at the bedside a bowl of crushed ice or a handful of cracked ice wrapped in a wet towel.

Both partners strip and enjoy sex in any face-to-face posture with the husband on top. As the husband starts his final surge to climax, the wife picks up a handful of crushed ice or the cold towel. Just as the paroxysms of orgasm start, she jams the ice-cold poultice against her husband's crotch and keeps it there throughout his conclusion.

The ice-spurred special works well in reverse also, with the wife astride and the husband performing the maneuver. In this position, however, the technique calls for a perfectly timed, mutual climax; the icy flood involves the husband as it cascades off the wife, and often upsets his erection-maintaining balance if it hits too early.

If you use ice on a preliminary female orgasm or if your timing sometimes is a bit off, use a method which avoids run-off. You can chill your hand in the ice bowl, then boost your wife's climax with the frigid hand instead of with the ice itself, for instance.

60 Brands of Condoms

It used to be a sure laugh-getter to have a teenager embarrassed in a pharmacy because he didn't have the nerve to ask for a package of condoms.

These were "under the counter" products. In many states their sale was unlawful because they were "birth control devices." It was also impossible for their manufacturers to advertise them. One New York City condom maker got around that by giving out books of matches at Madison Square Garden that said, "If you want a baby, that's your business. If you don't, that's our business!"

Today, to avoid problems, many companies cling to the pretense that the primary use of their product is to avoid venereal disease.

For decades two brand names dominated the field: Trojans and Sheiks. They are still quite popular. But condoms have come into their own. And, as in the old days, when cigarettes really meant a few top brands (Camel, Chesterfield, Old Gold, Lucky Strike and Pall Mall) and today there are hundreds of brands, so too there are hundreds of brands of condoms competing for customers. Prophylactics (the more delicate name for them) are advertised in magazines and catalogs, but in many localities they are also on the front counters of supermarkets and pharmacies.

Below is a random sampling of 60 brand names.

1. Stimula (Horizon) claims to be the first condom made for women. Ribbed surface latex with silicone lubricant.
2. Prime (Horizon)
3. Conture (Horizon). The maker of the Horizon brands is America's largest manufacturer of male contraceptives. The company offers free literature on the prevention of venereal disease. Write to Akwell Industries, Inc., Dothan, AL 36301.
4. SuperStud
5. Protex
6. Secure
7. Arouse
8. Touch
9. Sensuous Man
10. Sunrise
11. Man-Form Plus
12. Gold (Secura)*
13. Conture (Secura)
14. Super Moist (Secura)
15. Vital (Secura).

*For information on the Secura line of condoms, and other sex-related products, write to Valentine Products, Inc., P.O. Box 214, Mt. Morris, IL. 61054.

16. *Score* (with "pleasure probes"). This and all the condoms listed below are available from Adam & Eve, a shop-by-mail company that has been in business for ten years. Its catalog also lists other sex-related products. Write to Adam & Eve, Apple Court, Box 800, Carrboro, NC 27510. (If you are impatient, $19.95 will bring you their "Fabulous 55 Sampler," which consists of fourteen brands, fifty-five condoms in all.)
17. Stay-Tex
18. Slims
19. Cavalier Lubricated
20. Bareback (lubricated with SK-70)
21. Saxon
22. Trojan Guardian (with reservoir end)
23. Eros
24. Sheik (semi-transparent)
25. Trojan-Enz (the "old favorite")
26. Nuda

27. Jellia (imported from the Far East)
28. Tahiti Sunset Reds
29. Tahiti (morning blue)
30. Tahiti (dawn gold)
31. Tahiti (siesta green)
32. Jade (green). Jades are dry lubricated with a "love oil."
33. Jade (blue)
34. Jade (gold)
35. Jade (red)
36. Scentuals (with musk scent)
37. Scentuals (with banana scent)
38. Scentuals (with strawberry scent)
39. Scentuals (with lime scent)
40. Texture Plus
41. Bold 45
42. Conquer
43. Skin-Less Skin (Japanese)
44. Rough Rider
45. Wrinkle Zero-O
46. Stimula
47. Pleaser (advertised as "sure to be a crowd pleaser")
48. Geisha Thins (from Japan)
49. Fourex XXXX ("almost like wearing nothing at all")
50. Patrician (animal membrane)

.30

*Here is a guide to going in the nude
for those who want to let it all hang out.*

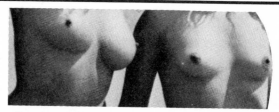

8 Items of Etiquette and Information
Regarding Visits to Nudist Parks

1. The most offensive individual at a nudist group is the voyeur, especially male. Nudists hate individuals who come to nudist parks or parties to stare and ogle. Don't go if that's your only purpose.

2. At all nudist parks the rule is that nudism is optional. When it rains members wear rain gear. When it's cold they wear sweat shirts. When women menstruate they generally wear shorts. In the cool of the night and at parties at night many nudists wear some covering. Comfort dictates the garb.

3. Rule 2 means that if you have never been to a nudist park or party, you can keep your clothes on until you're comfortable. Many people think there's a guard at the gate who makes everyone disrobe. Not so. No one cares—so long as you don't violate rule 1.

4. Until you are friendly with people at nudist organizations conversation is general and not personal. People use first

names only. Don't ask for last names or occupations until you are beyond acquaintanceship. (At nudist clubs and parks there are ministers, rabbis and priests, lawyers, doctors, etc. Respect their privacy.)

5. Nudists are health-oriented. Be careful where you smoke (if you must). Carry a towel to the restaurant or snack shop to sit on.

6. Know the situation before you make any effort to swing. Many nudist parks and groups are family oriented. Where swinging goes on, it is discreet, quiet and unobtrusive.

7. Unless you are a hopeless stick-in-the-mud, try a fling at a nudist park, club, or party. There's nothing like the feeling of nudism in the fresh air and bright sun. Whether you play volleyball (a favorite) or tennis (frequently available) or swim, boat, hike, or just sun-bathe, there's special enjoyment in doing it in a group enjoying freedom from clothing.

8. Primarily for men: A natural question is, Will I get an erection? I do at a burlesque striptease. Answer: You will not! Unless, of course, you want to spend your time imagining sex with this or that pretty girl. Without such psychological stimulation, no man gets an erection. Remember, clothes originated not for reasons of modesty but to call attention to sex. A low-cut dress or a mini-skirt is much more titillating than a completely nude woman.

8 Nudist Parks in the United States

Nudist parks are fixed installations with overnight facilities, restaurants (or snack shops), a great variety of recreational facilities, and enough land for participating nudists to have privacy.

1. Cypress Cove Nudist Resort
   4425 South Pleasant Hill Road
   Kissimmee, FL 32714

2. Jupiter Sunshine Gardens
   17801 North 130th Avenue
   Jupiter, FL 33458

3. Lake Como Club, Inc.
   P.O. Box 898
   Lutz, FL 33549

4. Mountain Air Ranch
   P.O. Box 808
   Littleton, CO 80160

5. Rawhide Ranch
   Rte. 1, Box 355
   Wilton, CA 95693

6. Samagatuma Nudist Resort
   Rte. 1, Box 405, Mussey Grade Road
   Ramona, CA 92056

7. Shangri-La Nudist Resort
   Box 4343 New River Rte.
   Phoenix, AR 85029

8. Condo resort under construction
   Paradise Lakes #764
   P.O. Box 750
   Land O'Lakes, FL 33539

For a complete list of resorts and parks in the United States and overseas, send $1.00 for an illustrated booklet and a complete directory to:

Sun West Information Service
P.O. Box 85204
Los Angeles, CA 90072

6 Nudist Travel Clubs

A nudist travel club is usually not a fixed installation but a group that does things together. Normally we suggest visiting a park before trying a club.

1. Chicago Sun Club
   P.O. Box 853
   Chicago Heights, IL 60411

2. The Sun Bunch
   P.O. Box 19924
   Columbus, OH 43219

3. The Northwest Mountain Bares
829 Leudinghaus Road
Chehalis, WA 98532

4. Diablos Del Sol
P.O. Box 3348
Walnut Creek, CA 94598

5. Pacificans Travel Club
P.O. Box 7842
Van Nuys, CA 91409

6. Sankobles
P.O. Box 4763
Hayward, CA 94540

5 Pieces of Advice About Nudist Camps

1. Do not drop in without an invitation.
2. Write or call in advance to learn the rules for admission. Every nudist organization has different rules and they change from time to time.
3. Be sure to check with the camp first if you intend to arrive alone. Many parks prohibit male singles; some frown on all singles.
4. Most parks will permit one or two trial visits so you can decide if you want to join.
5. Many parks (including those listed elsewhere in this book under "8 Nudist Parks in the United States") have overnight facilities. When you call, get information on this; you may prefer a weekend visit rather than just a few hours.

17 Things Other Than Sex That You Can Do in the Nude

1. Those who are willing to swim nude in the Arctic Ocean may contact Polar Bares, P.O. Box 245, Barrow, AK 99723.

2. For nude inner-tubing try the Salt and Verde rivers, where Route 87 (Beeline Road) crosses the river in the area of Phoenix, Arizona.

3. Hot springs for skinny dipping are waiting for you in the town of Indian Hot Springs, near Tucson, Arizona. You can stay at the 1890s-style hotel which serves vegetarian meals.

4. If rafting nude through the Grand Canyon turns you on, contact Club Nature, 1701 Clinton Street, Suite 207, Los Angeles, California 90026.

5. A wide variety of activities are available at Elysium Fields, 814 Robinson Road, Topanga, CA 90290. It's thirty miles from Los Angeles and has everything from new-life workshops to tennis.

6. Those looking for open sexuality can try Sandstone III, 22232 Plummer Street, Chatsworth, CA 91311. Be sure to bring with you a member of the opposite sex.

7. The ultimate in freedom may well be Treehouse Fun Ranch, 17809 Glen Helen Road, San Bernardino, CA 92497, where a major attraction is nude skydiving.

8. San Francisco Bay area offers an interesting variety of nude fun and games:

   —Grand Central Sauna & Hot Tub Co. has hourly spa rentals for a maximum of four persons. You get a Jacuzzi, sauna, shower, and double bed. The address is 15 Fell Street, San Francisco, CA 94102. They also have locations at 170 El Camino Real East, Mountain View, CA 94040 and 1915 University Avenue, Berkely, CA 94704.

   —San Francisco Plunge, 278 Eleventh Street, San Francisco, provides nude swimming and sun bathing for gay males only.

   —For sexual games where men outnumber women by ten to one, try Sutro Bath House, 1015 Folsom Street, San Francisco.

9. If you haven't yet been born again, but would like to explore the option, try the "rebirthing seminars" at Campbell Hot Springs, Box 38, Siennaville, CA 96121.

10. For Hatha Yoga and psychophysical integration, make tracks to Wilbur Hot Springs Health Sanctuary, Wilbur Springs, California. Advance arrangements are essential.

11. For those who enjoy nude hiking, a twenty dollar annual membership fee plus grounds fees admits you to Valley View Hot Springs, P.O. Box 175, Villa Grove, CO 81155.

12. Surprise! Surprise! The Hartford, Connecticut, YMCA has special "clothes optional" hours in the pool.
13. Do you like cruising with a congenial group? Try Wind Jammer Barefoot Cruiser, P.O. Box 112, Miami Beach, FL 33139.
14. Put a group together and go skinny rafting on the Salmon River in Central Idaho. Check in with the U.S. Forest Service, Middle Fork Ranger District. This trip is very popular with college groups.
15. Singles, both male and female, are welcome at Indian Hills, P.O. Box 52745 New Orleans, LA 70152.
16. Gays might enjoy a visit to Saugatuck Lodge, P.O. Box 406, Saugatuck, MI 49453. Only a two-hour drive from Chicago or Detroit, Oval Beach is nearby and nude.
17. A clothing-optional apartment complex may be to your liking. Try Manor Villa, 2401 Manor Road, East Austin, TX 78222.

The Bible and the bawdy

17 Sex Sections from the Bible with Comments by Dr. Arnold Boston

Dr. Arnold Boston is a student of the Bible. He is also a magician and humorist. Here he combines both interests in a list of sexy paraphrases and summaries from the Bible.

1. Any man who has a genital discharge is ceremonially defiled. When the discharge stops, he shall begin a seven day cleansing ceremony by washing his clothes and bathing in running water. On the eighth day he shall take two turtle doves or two young pigeons and come before the Lord and give them to the priest for sacrifice.
   Leviticus 15:13-15
   Dr. Boston says: "Forget the turtle doves and the pigeons. Have a physician give you some penicillin on the first day. It was probably a pigeon that got you into trouble in the first place."

2. One night as I was sleeping, I heard the voice of my beloved. He was knocking on my bedroom door.
   "Open to me, my darling, my lover."
   "But," I said, "I have disrobed."

My beloved tried to unlatch the door and my heart was moved by him. I jumped up to open it and my hands dripped with perfume, my fingers with myrrh. But he was gone.
Song of Songs 5:2-6
Dr. Boston says: "This will teach you to use expensive perfumes instead of those cheap essences."

3. O rarest of beautiful women, where has your loved one gone? He has gone down to his garden, to his spice beds and to gather the lilies.

Song of Songs 6:1-2
Dr. Boston says: "Your loved one is gay."

4. How beautiful your tripping feet, O queenly maiden. Your neck is stately as an ivory tower, your eyes as limpid pools in Heshbon, your waist is like a heap of wheat, your navel is lovely as a goblet filled with wine. Your rounded thighs are like jewels.
Song of Songs 7-9
Dr. Boston says: "Fool! You missed the best parts!"

5. We have a little sister too young for breasts. What shall we do if someone asks to marry her?
Song of Songs 8-8
Dr. Boston says: "Send the suitor to a psychiatrist!"

6. It was Herod's birthday and he gave a stag party for his high officials, army officers, and the leading men of Galilee. Herodias' daughter came and performed a dance and greatly pleased them all.
Mark 6:21-22
Dr. Boston says: "Stag parties haven't changed a bit."

7. My bed is spread with lovely colored sheets of finest linen. Come—let's take our fill of love until morning, for my husband is away on a long trip.
Proverbs 9:17
Dr. Boston says: "Then there's the story of the traveling salesman and the farmer's daughter. . . ."

8. But the man who commits adultery is an utter fool, for the woman's husband will be furious in his jealousy, and he will have no mercy on you in his day of vengeance.
Proverbs 6:32-35

Dr. Boston says: "Time to get out of town. Have you tried Minneapolis?"

9. If two men are fighting and the wife of one intervenes to help her husband by grabbing the testicles of the other man, her hand shall be cut off without pity.
Deuteronomy 25:11-12
Dr. Boston says: "Obviously, an eye for an eye and a tooth for a tooth can't apply here."

10. O feed me with your love,—for I am utterly love-sick. His left hand is under my head.
Song of Songs 2: #5-6
Dr. Boston says: "Watch that right hand. That's the one you'd better worry about!"

11. Solomon had seven hundred wives and three hundred concubines and sure enough they turned his heart away from the Lord.
I Kings 11:3
Dr. Boston says: "It seems to me that any man who has more than two hundred wives and one hundred concubines is downright greedy!"

12. It is illegal to bring the earnings of a prostitute (male or female) into the House of the Lord your God.
Deuteronomy 23:8-19
Dr. Boston says: "You can accuse the Lord of taking a lot of sacrificial offerings, but he ain't no pimp."

13. If a man's wife commits adultery but there is no proof, the man shall bring his wife to the priest with an offering of barley meal without frankincense as a suspicion offering to bring out the truth. The priest shall mix holy water and dust from the tabernacle. She shall drink the bitter water. If she is guilty her body will swell and her thighs will rot. But if she is pure and has not committed adultery, she shall be unharmed and will become pregnant.
Numbers 5:12-28
Dr. Boston says: "As Mary said to Joseph, 'Who needs you?'"

14. If a girl who is engaged is seduced within the walls of a city, both she and the man who seduced her shall be taken outside the gates and stoned to death. But if this deed takes place out

in the country only the man shall die; for it must be assumed that she screamed but there was no one to hear and rescue her out in the field.
Deuteronomy 22:23-27
Dr. Boston says: "I've heard that one before!"

15. If a man marries a girl, then after sleeping with her accuses her of having had premarital intercourse with another man, saying, "She was not a virgin when I married her," then the girl's father and mother shall bring proof of her virginity to the city judges.
Deuteronomy 22:13-15
Dr. Boston says: "What do we do then with all the bloody sheets?"

16. You shall not have sexual relations with your granddaughter—the daughter of either your son or your daughter. You may not have sex with a half-sister—your father's wife's daughter—nor your aunt—your father's sister, your mother's sister, or the wife of your father's brother. You may not have sex with your daughter-in-law—your son's wife nor your brother's wife. You may not have sex with both a woman and her daughter or granddaughter. You shall not have sex with your wife's sister.
Leviticus 18:6-18
Dr. Boston says: "How about maybe your aunt's doctor's wife?"

17. If a man doesn't like something about his wife, he may write a letter stating that he has divorced her, give her the letter and send her away.
Deuteronomy 24:1
Dr. Boston says: "Oh, for the good old days!"

9 Biblical Polygamists

1. Gideon
2. Jair
3. Ibzan
4. Abdon
5. David
6. Solomon

7. Rehoboam
8. Abraham*
9. Jacob*
*Concubines only

Bhagwan Shree Rajneesh's
Philosophy of Sex and Love

In seven years, Bhagwan Shree Bajneesh has uttered more than 33 million words in his daily discourses and evening darshans.

During that time, he has answered more than ten thousand questions.

His words have been transcribed into a total of 336 books published by the Rajneesh Foundation. A complete list of books, films, recordings, and video cassettes can be obtained by writing Chidivlas Rejneesh Meditation Center, 154 Valley Road, Montclair, NJ 07042.

Here are two of his pronouncements: one on sex and one on love.

Sex

Never repress it!
Never be against it
Rather, go deep into it
with great clarity,
with great love.
Go like an explorer.
Search all the
nooks and corners
of your sexuality,
and you will
be surprised and enriched and benefited.
Knowing your sexuality,
one day you will
stumble upon your
spirituality.
Then you will
become free.

The future will have
a totally different
vision of sex.
It will be
more fun, more joy,
more friendship,
more a play than
a serious affair,
as it has been
in the past.
Sex is just
the beginning,
not the end.
But if you
miss the beginning,
you will miss
the end also.

Love

has nothing
to do with somebody else,
it is your
state of being.
Love is not
a relationship.
A relationship
is possible
but love is not
confined to it,
it is beyond it,
it is more than that—
Man becomes mature
the moment he starts loving
rather than needing.
He starts overflowing,
he starts sharing,
he starts giving—
And when
two mature persons
are in love,
one of the
greatest paradoxes
of life happens,
one of the most
beautiful phenomena ...
they are together,
and yet
tremendously alone;

they are almost one.
But their oneness
does not destroy
their individuality.

Al Gerber's 25 Favorite Limericks

The limerick is one of the few literary forms peculiar to the English language, and it is particularly suitable to the sexual subject.

Clifton Fadiman wrote in *Any Number Can Play* that few poetical forms can meet the perfection of the limerick. He described it as follows: "It has progression, development, variety, speed, climax, and a high mnemonic value."

The origin of the limerick is cloudy. A good bet is that it originated as an Irish soldier's song and then became a party game. As the drinking (of the soldiers or the party goers) increased, the limericks got bawdier.

Although limericks are by no means always scatological, those that are best remembered usually deal with some humorous aspect of sex.

Here are 25 examples selected by Al Gerber.

1. There was a young sailor from Brighton
   Who remarked to his girl, "You're a tight one!"
   She replied, " 'Pon my soul,
   You're in the wrong hole;
   There's plenty of room in the right one."

2. A lady, while dining at Crewe,
   Found an elephant's whang in her stew.
   Said the waiter, "Don't shout,
   And don't wave it about,
   Or the others will all want one too."

3. A newlywed couple from Goshen
   Spent their honeymoon sailing the ocean.
   In twenty-eight days
   They got laid eighty ways.
   Imagine such fucking devotion!

4. There was a young monk from Siberia
Whose morals were very inferior.
He did to a nun
What he shouldn't have done,
And now she's a Mother Superior.

5. There was a young girl named Annheuser
Who said that no man could surprise her.
But Pabst took a chance,
Found Schlitz in her pants,
And now she is sadder Budweiser.

6. There was a young girl who begat
Three brats, by name Nat, Pat, and Tat.
It was fun in the breeding,
But hell in the feeding,
When she found there was no tit for Tat.

7. A notorious whore named Miss Hurst
In the weakness of men is well-versed.
Reads a sign o'er the head
of her well-rumpled bed,
"The customer always comes first."

8. Unique is a strumpet of Mazur
In the way that her clientele pays her:
A machine that she uses
Clamps onto her whosis
And clocks everybody that lays her.

9. Ethnologists up with the Sioux
Wired home for two punts, one canoe.
The answer next day
Said, "Girls on the way,
But what in the hell's a 'panoe'?"

10. I'd rather have fingers than toes,
I'd rather have ears than a nose,
And a happy erection
Brought just to perfection
Makes me terribly sad when it goes.

11. While Titian was mixing rose madder
His model reclined on a ladder.
Her position to Titian
Suggested coition,
So he leapt up the ladder and had 'er.

12. There was a young lady of Norway
Who hung by her toes in a doorway.
She said to her beau:
"Just look at me, Joe,
I think I've discovered one more way."

13. There was a young plumber of Lee
    Was plumbing a maid by the sea.
    Said the maid, "Cease your plumbing,
    I think someone's coming."
    Said the plumber, still plumbing, "It's me."

14. There was a young lady named Cager
    Who, as the result of a wager,
    Consented to fart
    The whole oboe part
    Of Mozart's Quartet in F Major.

15. There was a young girl of Cape Cod
    Who thought babies were fashioned by God.
    But 'twas not the Almighty
    Who hiked up her nightie,
    'Twas Roger the lodger, by God!

16. There was a young fellow named Cass
    Whose bollocks were made out of brass.
    When they tinkled together
    They played "Stormy Weather"
    And lightning shot out of his ass!

17. A very smart lady named Cookie
    Said, "I like to mix gambling with nookie.
    Before every race
    I go home to my place
    And curl up with a very good bookie."

18. Well buggered was a boy named Delpasse
    By all of the lads in his class.
    He said, with a yawn,
    "Now the novelty's gone,
    It's only a pain in the ass."

19. The new cinematic emporium
    Is not just a super-sensorium,
    But a highly effectual
    Heterosexual
    Mutual masturbatorium.

20. Nymphomaniacal Jill
    Tried a dynamite stick for a thrill;
    They found her vagina
    In North Carolina
    And bits of her tits in Brazil.

21. She wasn't what one would call pretty,
    And other girls offered her pity;
    So nobody guessed
    That her Wasserman test
    Involved half the men of the city.

22. This shortage of help has produced
    More kitchen-wise males than it used,
    Like that man of gallantry
    Who, leaving the pantry,
    Remarked, "Well, my cook is well goosed!"

23. There was a young man from Racine
    Who invented a fucking machine;
    Both concave and convex,
    It would fit either sex,
    With attachments for those in-between.

24. Every time Lady Bowbodice swoons,
    Her bubbies pop out like balloons;
    But her butler stands by
    With hauteur in his eye
    And lifts them back in with warm spoons.

25. If intercourse gives you thrombosis,
    While continence causes neurosis,
    I prefer to expire
    Fulfilling desire
    Than live on in a state of psychosis.

7 Censored Mother Goose Rhymes

This septet of nursery rhymes that many of us learned as little children is dedicated to the censors, who taught us how to read sexy meanings into harmless words!

1. Peter, Peter pumpkin eater,
   Had a wife and couldn't xxxxx her;
   He put her in a pumpkin shell
   And there he xxxxx her very well.

2. There was a little girl and she had a little curl
   Right in the middle of her xxxxx;
   And when she was good she was very, very good,
   But when she was bad she was horrid.

3. Jack and Jill went up the hill
   To xxxxxxxxxxxxxxxxxxxxx;

Jack fell down and broke his xxxxx
And Jill came tumbling after.

4. A dillar, a dollar,
A ten o'clock scholar,
What makes you xxxxx so soon?
You used to xxxxx at two o'clock,
And now you xxxxx at noon.

5. Solomon Grundy
xxxxx on Monday
xxxxx on Tuesday
xxxxx on Wednesday
xxxxx on Thursday
xxxxx on Friday
Died on Saturday
Buried on Sunday
This is the end
Of Solomon Grundy.

6. Cock-a-doodle-doo;
My dame has lost her shoe;
Gone to bed and scratched her xxxxx
And can't tell what to do.

7. See-saw Margery Daw,
Jenny shall have a new master;
She shall have but a penny a day
Because she can't xxxxx any faster.

11 Proverbs for Our Time

1. She was so involved with sex, she didn't see whether he wore a beard.
2. Love is blind, but most people do it in the dark anyway.
3. If the lady doesn't jiggle her things, the gent may not follow her.
4. Better to select a wife (husband) from a massage parlor than from a Sunday church picnic.
5. The bride may not be worth the expense of the wedding: try her first.

6. The University of Sex is also called "experience."
7. The second greatest sin is to turn away from your mate in bed when you know sex is desired. The greatest sin is to have sex when you don't desire it.
8. All lollipops don't have the same flavor.
9. The quietest clerk may have a sex life greater than anything you can imagine.
10. It ain't what you do; it's the way that you do it.
11. Get it while you can.